Diversity and Direction in Children's Literature Series

Child and Story: The Literary Connection

By Kay E. Vandergrift

Neal-Schuman Publishers, Inc.

Published by Neal–Schuman Publishers, Inc.
64 University Place
New York, New York 10003

Copyright © 1980 by Neal–Schuman Publishers, Inc.

Printed and bound in the United States of America.

Library of Congress Cataloging in Publication Data

Vandergrift, Kay E
  Child and story, the literary connection.

  (Diversity and direction in children's literature ; 1)
  Bibliography: p.
  Includes index.
  1. Children's literature—History and criticism.
2. Children—Books and reading.   I. Title.   II. Series.
PN1009.A1V29   809'.89282   80-21996
ISBN 0-918212-42-1

For Jake
For Jane
And For My Mother
Who
Each in a special way
Caused This Book to Be.

Contents

Figures

Acknowledgments

Grateful acknowledgment is made for permission to quote from the following:

Harcourt Brace Jovanovich, Inc. for *Rabbit Island*, text by Jörg Steiner, pictures by Jörg Müller, translated by Ann Conrad Lammers;

Verlag Sauerländer, Switzerland for *Rabbit Island*, text by Jörg Steiner, pictures by Jörg Müller, translated by Ann Conrad Lammers;

Wesleyan University Press for permission to reprint from *Centering*; Copyright © 1964 by Mary Caroline Richards;

Harper & Row, Publishers, Inc. for text excerpts from *na-ni: A Story and Pictures by Alexis Deveaux*. Copyright © 1973 by Alexis Deveaux;

Thomas Y. Crowell, Publishers for text excerpts from *A Taste of Blackberries* by Doris Buchanan Smith. Copyright © 1973 by Doris Buchanan Smith;

Philomel Books for *The Stone Book* by Alan Garner. Copyright © 1976 by Alan Garner;

David Higham Associates, London for *The Stone Book* by Alan Garner. Copyright © 1976 by Alan Garner.

Philomel Books for *The Secret Hiding Place* by Rainey Bennett. Copyright © 1960 by Rainey Bennett;

Blackie & Son Ltd., Glasgow, Scotland for *The Secret Hiding Place* by Rainey Bennett. Copyright © 1960 by Rainey Bennett.

Editor's Preface

Diversity and Direction in Children's Literature is a new series that will encompass precisely what its title suggests; it will serve as a forum for diverse approaches and different directions that scholarship in children's literature may take. Books in the series will examine this field using a range of ideas drawn from theories of literary criticism, popular culture, American studies, and other disciplines, allowing readers to see children's literature from the various perspectives of scholarly study.

All the books in this series, however, will have the literature itself as the focus. They will also demonstrate that children's literature must be judged in relationship to its audience. These works will recognize that any study of children's literature must value the child reader and keep the concerns of that reader central to its considerations of the literature. Neither maudlin approaches to the child that diminish that child's standing in the world nor works that so lose sight of the child that they border on pretentiousness or obscurity will be included. In addition, simple overviews of the field of children's literature, topical bibliographies, and unfounded opinionation, many examples of which already exist, will not be a part of this series.

What the books in this series will have in common is a valuing of both children and the literature created for them, a commitment to and a joy in children's literature, and approaches to that literature grounded in research and scholarship.

Child and Story: The Literary Connection, the first book in the series, exemplifies these qualities in its approach to children and literature. Those reading this book cannot help but be aware of the author's love of children's literature and her respect for the child. She uses various theories of literary criticism to look at story for children, exploring complex issues and expressing them in language that draws readers into a process of sharing ideas. Using her skill as a teacher of children's literature, the author helps readers to recognize what it is they already know about this literature and opens up new possibilities for the extension of that knowledge. She refuses to let readers be passive, requiring them to interact with her matrices as systematic ways of looking at the body of this literature. Dr. Vandergrift encourages us to challenge her opinions and takes joy in the critical dialogue that comes from such informed disagreements. This book conveys a sense of the totality of the role of story in a child's life. It includes experiences with popular as well as with more literary forms of story and discusses the child's personal composition of story as a way of ordering his or her own world. Vandergrift's connection with the child and story is evident in the many instances in which she uses children's own responses or stories about her own experiences with children to illustrate literary ideas.

It is a great pleasure to introduce this new series, and it is an even greater privilege to begin the series with the work of a friend and a colleague with whom I have been able to share concerns from my own years of teaching children's literature. As the editor of this book, I have grown in my understanding of children's story through an exciting and argumentative dialogue with its author. I hope that readers will be able to share some of my experience through their interaction with these printed pages.

I want to express my gratitude to all of those who care about children's literature, who believed in the possibilities of this work, and had faith that the time was right to begin such a series. My appreciation is extended to Patricia Glass Schuman, who expressed her faith in the idea during our first discussion of it and who has continued her caring during the production of this manuscript. Special thanks are due to Leland B. Jacobs, who responded to this idea with a sparkling enthusiasm that said "Let it be done!"

Jane Anne Hannigan,
School of Library Service
Columbia University
New York, New York

September 1980

Foreword

Frequently one hears about making children's time with literature a happy interlude in the day, or a strong motivation to read and to learn to read, or a kind of therapy, or a springboard to one's own creative endeavors. All of these can, of course, be used as justifications for children's experiences with literature.

However, they are not the central, the pivotal reason, which is—simply stated—that literature, like all art forms, is a way to know. Through story, biography, poem a child can, with aesthetic feeling, enter into questings, copings, circumstances, longings, happenings that are possible for the individual in no other way. The child can come to know persons, places, times that exist only in the imagination, that *are* but only because a writer has given them their existence. As a way to know, literature becomes for the reader or listener an exploration and illumination of life and living. Humans' abiding quests for love, acceptance, belonging, achieving, and being are brought to the person enjoying the writing in metaphorical, symbolic terms.

Dr. Kay Vandergrift knows this about literature and the experiencing of it by girls and boys. She knows, too, that all literature is one domain in which what is written for children exists within the same boundaries as that written for adults. Peter Rabbit, the Peterkin and Moffat families, Mary Poppins, Pecos Bill, the Highwayman, and Huck Finn inhabit the same realm of the imagination as do the characters made possible by masters of literature for adults. To be sure, there are differences, just as there are differences between any of us as adult and child. But literature's living space is one world.

Dr. Vandergrift makes it quite clear that children's literature deserves the same definitive consideration and critical study as does adult literature. She delineates what can be done to make children's experiences with literature as realism, romance, and fancy authentically critical. Such criticism, she asserts, "leads not to final answers but to more insightful questions and to a more appreciative sense of wonder" that is the literary connection between children and what has been written for them. In the development of this thesis she uses well-chosen practical examples of children's abilities in responding to their reading and listening.

One of Dr. Vandergrift's closing statements is this: "If we are to be accountable to children, we must provide them with a variety of literary experiences that are both aesthetically sound and personally meaningful." Her book does, in many ways, provide the bearings and the practices for helping children develop "educated imaginations."

Leland B. Jacobs
Professor Emeritus of Education
Teachers College, Columbia University
New York, New York

September 1980

Preface

This book is about the child and about story. It is about the connection between the two, which is, first of all, a rich, imaginative, intensely personal experience that paradoxically awakens the child to a sense of a community of human meaning. At its second stage, when the child emerges from this highly personal experience to share story meanings with others in the human community, this connection becomes a recognition of children's story as a part of a literary world—a world in which Peter Rabbit and Hamlet are powerful partners in that persistent human process of discovering ourselves both as we are and as we might become. The connection between child and story is thus threefold: it is personal, it is communal, and it is critical.

Any consideration of child and story must begin with respect for the child as an intelligent, sensitive, self-determining maker-of-meaning in the world, and with respect for children's stories as literary works that are as worthy of critical attention as works for adults. It includes a recognition of the importance of story in the development of what Northrop Frye has called "the educated imagination," which helps persons to cope with and to compose aesthetic as well as scientific forms of human meaning. A child comes naturally to literary criticism, and adults who work with children and story must have a solid knowledge of such criticism so that, without imposing "literary language," they may help that child to engage in a process of continually matching her own knowing about story to the established knowledge of the literary community. For children's literature is not to be set apart from all other literature or judged by criteria distinct from those used to evaluate adult literature. Within children's stories are found some of the most powerful and certainly some of the most memorable of all fictional characters and events. The child who has escaped Mr. McGregor's garden with Peter Rabbit or risen on a balloon with Winnie the Pooh does, in some sense, take these experiences with him as he goes down the rabbit hole with Alice, whitewashes the fence with Tom Sawyer, fights the white whale with Ahab, and suffers the tragic fate of Hamlet. Both the understanding and the appreciation of story are cumulative and developmental, with each authentic encounter building upon previous encounters and preparing the way for those that follow. One never really leaves loved literature behind; part of the beauty and the magic of story is that it becomes lived experience that one can go back to and dwell in again and again. All literary experiences spiral around each other, coming back to but enlarging those that have gone before.

The content of this book is organized in an attempt to replicate that spiraling movement so that ideas and materials dealt with in one chapter are enlarged or seen from a different perspective in another. Knowledge of and respect for the child, for literature itself, and for literary criticism are the bases upon which this spiral evolves and the end to which this work aspires. From the days of primitive tribes gathered around campfires, story has always been a vehicle for carrying both informational and aesthetic content. As knowledge developed and specialization increased, logical factual or scientific content was separated out from story in most disciplines. Some areas of endeavor, notably teaching, continue to contain and pass on much of the feeling as well as the factual content of the field through stories. This book also uses that technique, conveying its content in stories and in reports of children's literary encounters as well as in more scholarly approaches to ideas and information. Most of this work can be read easily by anyone with an interest in the topic, but those who have had limited experiences with children's literature or with literary criticism may need to spiral around and return to certain segments or chapters to fully comprehend the relationships among the various parts of the work.

No attempt was made to include all of the "best" books for children. For the most part, only story is included, although a few examples of other types of works are compared with story forms. The examples used were selected for their value in communicating ideas about the field or because of experiences I have shared with children that imprinted these works indelibly on my mind and made me want to recommend them to others. Hundreds of titles that I enjoy are not found within these pages because I do not believe that there are any "magic lists" of books that all children should know. In fact, I doubt that there is a single title that should be read by everyone. The suggestion that all children should read a particular book denies the uniqueness both of human beings and of literary works. Most of us as adults, even the most literate and literary adults, have not read every "classic," and we have no right to ask this of children. One should read what is of value in his or her own life, not just that to which others attribute value. A primary aim of this work is to introduce adults who work with children and story to some of the means of helping children develop their critical abilities so that they will increasingly be able to discriminate and seek out the best among all that they read. This is not to say that they will no longer read easy, popular literature, but that they will also read more demanding works and be increasingly able to distinguish between the two.

The first three chapters of this book are the basis upon which the rest of the work rests. "Child and Story" sets the stage by exploring the importance of story in a child's life as a means of sorting out her own identity, gaining control over her world, and making connections with others in that world. The second and third chapters present syntheses of information about story as a literary form and about the practice of literary criticism. The third chapter particularly is one to which those with little experience in the field may wish to return after seeing the total pattern of all that is contained in this work.

"Illustration and Book Design" follows because it is through picture story books that most young children come to know story most profoundly, and their critical abilities are practiced in respect to illustration before they can decode the words of the text. Chapter Five takes readers back again to story to examine character, point of view, mood, tone, language, symbol, and other elements of the composition of story. The matrix of the following chapter ties these compositional elements to various genres and subgenres of children's literature, exploring the relationships between the two. It is perhaps this chapter that best demonstrates a basic premise of this work, that its value is only realized when readers enter into an interaction with it, considering and challenging what is contained in these pages.

Chapter Seven, "Planning Encounters with Story," synthesizes all that has gone before in a recounting of various ways in which adults have helped children to develop and demonstrate their critical abilities in respect to story. Children are producers as well as consumers, composers as well as critics, and it is in composition that their literary knowledge is very naturally and very fully brought to life. The chapter on composition suggests a process of "modeling" in which children use what they know about the stories they read to create their own original works. Composition is seen as a means of both deepening and demonstrating an understanding of literature while increasing the child's presence in the world through the creation of original forms.

Chapter Nine, on nonprint media, is essential in an age in which many children come to know television stories before those on the printed page. It contains suggestions for comparing and contrasting stories in different media and for means of developing critical abilities in relation to film and television stories. The final chapter represents a return on the spiral to summarize factors that either strengthen or weaken the connection between child and story and introduces the concept of "centering," which metaphorically holds together all the ideas that spiral around each other in the exciting process of working with children and story.

For the benefit of the reader, expository footnotes (marked with asterisks) are placed at the bottom of the page while simple references (numbered footnotes) appear at the conclusions of the chapters. Full bibliographic information on all of the children's books referred to is also given after each chapter. The Bibliography at the end of the book is a selective one, including representative works about children's literature as well as sources from other subject areas that have been influential in my thinking about the contents of this book.

The ideas contained in this work have evolved over the past fifteen years, during which I have worked with children and with parents, teachers, and librarians concerned with children and books. As a classroom teacher, a librarian, and a school administrator, I have shared a variety of literary activities with children and have increased my own awareness of and respect for their critical and compositional powers. To all of the children who have shared their thoughts and their stories with me over these years, I owe a great debt; and those now old enough to read this book will find much of themselves within. Many graduate students from my classes at Teachers

College and the School of Library Service, Columbia University, have helped to expand or to refine ideas first experienced with children. Leland B. Jacobs, Professor Emeritus, Teachers College, Columbia University, was my teacher during the early years of my career; his friendship, his respect for and delight in children, and his understanding of literature continue to refresh and renew me both intellectually and spiritually. Those who have been privileged to know him will recognize his work as the foundation upon which my own is built. Jane Anne Hannigan, the editor of this series, is a colleague who shares my joy in children and their literature and is always eager to discuss ideas with me. It was she who convinced me that the writing of this book was a meaningful way of focusing my concerns as an educator, and it was her support and encouragement that led to the completion of the manuscript. She too will find reflections of her work and her ideas on many pages of this book. Ellen Kronowitz, a dear friend with whom I shared several years of working with children, was kind enough to read parts of this manuscript in its early stages and made useful suggestions that have been incorporated into this final version. Patricia Glass Schuman, president of Neal-Schuman Publishers, and Maureen Crowley, editor, acted with great care and concern in the final production of the manuscript. I am grateful to these people and to the constellation of friends, family, and colleagues, particularly those in the Columbia University community, who are a part of my personal and professional support system.

Kay E. Vandergrift
School of Library Service
Columbia University
New York, New York

September 1980

Chapter One
Child and Story

Childhood is a time of wonder. It is a time of intense feelings, a time of testing life out and trying it on for size, a time of imaginative encounters with the world. It is a time when children come naturally to story, for much of the essence of story is the essence also of the child's own life. The inward experience of story, perhaps even more than most outward activities, helps a child to gain what we all strive for as human beings—a sense of personal identity, a sense of control over one's own existence, and a sense of connection with others in the world. An acquaintance with and an understanding of literary characters is one of the first ways a young child has of making sense of what it is to be human. We all come to know more clearly who and what we are while reaching out, imaginatively, for what we might become. As the child dwells in and wonders at the lives lived in story, she comes to know both herself and the world and begins to see that world as something over which she, as a character in life, might exercise some control. The events of story are a means of exploration of the world, helping her to confirm, to illuminate, and to extend her own life experiences, in ways that give her power over them. Story gives public form to private meanings and thus helps those who receive its messages to reach out to other human beings in the world, knowing that they share some of the same concerns and feelings. This is what might be called the "Ah, Ha" response to literature, in which the reader or listener experiences the shock of recognition, realizing that what was thought to be unique in the deep and dark and private places of one's own life is shared by others.

If literature is to help children toward identity, control, and connection in the world, the stories written for them must deal honestly with a broad range of life experiences. Obviously, not all experiences are appropriate for or interesting to children, but to deny children in their literature what they experience in life is to deny them their dignity as human beings. The lives of children, like the contents of story, contain tragedy as well as triumph, pain as well as pleasure, and disturbance as well as delight. Most adults would like to believe that childhood is a time of almost continual bliss, of freedom and openness and joy; many of us can even blot out enough of our own childhoods to convince ourselves that this is so. Nonetheless, there are contradictory views. Lloyd de Mause begins *The History of Childhood* by saying "The history of childhood is a nightmare from which we have only recently begun to awaken."[1] He and many others see childhood as a time of fear, uncertainty, and powerlessness. Albert Cullum's controversial book *You Think Just Because You're Big You're Right* records some of the horrors of childhood experiences for children themselves and horrifies many adults in the process. Childhood may indeed be so difficult that no adult could or would tolerate it. Perhaps children suspect this and try to rush into growing up because they sense adulthood is easier. This is not a new or an unusual image of childhood. Think back to the Puritan concept of original sin and recall *The New England Primer*, which introduced children to the written word with "In Adam's fall, we sinned all. Thy life to mend, this book attend." Or as Eugene O'Neill has put it more recently, "Man is born broken. He lives by mending. The grace of God is glue."

As a means of exploring our perceptions of childhood, it may be useful to look at some of the metaphors with which adults have referred to young people. What did it mean, for instance, to describe a child as a tabula rasa, a lump of clay, an empty vessel, or the growing plant from which our word kindergarten comes? No one seriously uses these metaphors anymore, but there is a kind of residue in the minds of many adults who still talk of children as if they were not yet human beings and will become so only when filled with or shaped by preconceived notions of the world.

On the one hand, adults seem to value and enjoy, even envy, the freshness of vision characteristic of childhood. On the other, we insist on destroying this vision and replacing it with conventional or authorized ways of seeing the world. My favorite story illustrating this practice is that of the young city child who had gone for his first picnic in the woods. He was fascinated by the birds and the bugs and the bushes, and he alternated between pressing his face to the grass and stretching as high as he could to reach the trees. He frequently jumped up on the picnic bench for this stretching ritual and was as frequently warned by his mother that he would fall off. Of course warnings did not deter him, and he climbed back onto the bench in pursuit of a butterfly circling the table. As the butterfly flew toward him, he leaned back and toppled off the bench. His mother rushed to him and, after making certain that he had not cracked his skull, said, "See, I told you you'd fall off that bench." The child looked up with innocent surprise and replied, "I didn't fall; the butterfly pushed me."

We must all (as parents, teachers, librarians, or other

concerned adults) ask ourselves how we would have received that child's explanation. I am afraid that most of us would have gently (hopefully, at least this) led this child to see the error in his reasoning. We might have failed to see that the child was not really misrepresenting the truth; he was quite simply going beyond the facts of scientific observation to the truth of human understanding. He was demonstrating through language that aesthetic ways of knowing the world are just as important as scientific ones, that knowing what it feels like to have something happen to you is just as important as knowing how it happens. He was, in fact, composing the events of his own world in much the same manner as a poet or story-teller might.

Children must come to know the world discursively and scientifically, of course, but such knowledge need not be a total displacement of or a replacement for nondiscursive or metaphoric ways of understanding their lives.[2] An "educated imagination" is as essential to the fully-lived life as a trained intellect.[3] Northrop Frye, from whom I have borrowed this phrase, points to literature as a primary means of developing an educated imagination. He reminds us that literature is just as important in the lives of future scientists and politicians as it is for tomorrow's artists and philosophers. Without an educated imagination one cannot envision new relationships and stimulate new developments in any field of endeavor. Literature helps to sharpen our observations and perceptions of the world, develop our emotional sensitivity, and extend our acquaintance with life. When the adults in their lives try too hard to convince children that life is a puzzle to be solved—with all the pieces precut to fit their proper places— story reminds them that after all the puzzles are solved, life is still a mystery with its own sense of order that may dissolve when the bright light of explanation is focused on it. Perhaps the greatest legacy that adults can pass on to children is the respect for and preservation of that mystery—that sense of possibility—that enables each new generation to, as Robert

Frost has said of poetry, make their own shapes out of the chaos of their world.

Almost from the first moments of consciousness, the child's attempts to shape the world she experiences take many of the same forms as those used in literature. Even from the crib, her responses to the simple plot of "rock-a-bye-baby" or to parent-child games such as "peek-a-boo" begin to implant patterns and impose associations on the child's mind. In such simple forms are the beginnings of dramatic entrances and exits as the child notes what is "in my life" and "out of my life." Other games that parents commonly play with very young children serve similar purposes in developing both language and a sense of story form. Through story— her own compositions in imaginative play or the world of picture story books—the child reaches out to the world and to other human beings and attempts to make sense of the chaotic experiences that bombard her from all sides. Perhaps most important of all, story helps a child to attribute value to and take joy from the world, for appreciation and enjoyment are the bases upon which the literary experience exists and brings meaning into our lives.

Scholars from many fields and from very different perspectives have discussed the primacy of symbolic representation in the language development of the young child.* The child selects his own world and sorts himself out from the larger world of which he is a part with the help of active games and language-learning events initiated by adults or older siblings. Even before he can put words to it, the child

---

*Among the most helpful writers in this area are the following: Susanne K. Langer, *Philosophy in a New Key* (New York: Mentor Books, 1958); Kornei Chakovsky, *From Two to Five* (Berkeley, Calif.: University of California Pr., 1966); L.S. Vygotsky, *Language and Thought* (New York: John Wiley, 1962); Jean Piaget, *The Language and Thought of Children*, trans. M. Gabain (London: Routledge and Kegan Paul, 1926); Iona Opie and Peter Opie, *The Lore and Language of Schoolchildren* (London: Oxford University Pr., 1959) and Arthur T. Jersild, *Child Development and the Curriculum* (New York: Teachers College Pr., 1946).

projects the world-of-his-own-making in dramatic play. Then as he develops his ability to speak, his first words are ordinarily operative in nature, that is, they are not just denotive but are used as action-objects in which each word connotes a whole sequence or symbolizes a complete event. Thus, the word "milk" in a young child's vocabulary may come to mean not only the substance itself but the parent's bringing it in the bottle, holding and rocking him, perhaps singing to him, and eventually putting him in the crib to sleep, a complete scenario in a single word.

As the child grows in his ability to represent the world symbolically in language, he exhibits a playfulness with that language that few but the best poets manage to retain into their adult lives. This playfulness may be, in part, because the child's life expresses itself in movement and his language is often a corollary to that movement. He enjoys the recurrences of sounds and phrases, often in conjunction with repeated physical movements. To some extent bodily rhythms regulate rhythms in language development, while the physical mechanisms of the throat impose accent and the lungs impose pause. The child's language development is thus inexorably bound with his physical development, and both are stimulated by imaginative play. Of course, much of the child's expressive language is unrelated to any desire to communicate. He may derive a great deal of pleasure from the activity of talking, regardless of its content, as he experiments with his speech mechanisms.

Jean Piaget's studies of the language of children reveal that the structure of adult language is often used with no purpose beyond the talking itself. Those who have listened in on the language of the young child at play will recognize a kind of rhythmic talking-to-oneself accompanying this activity and the child's responses to immediate events as he gives voice to unique perceptions in often very concrete sensory or motor terms. Such expressions of one's unique perceptions of the world in concrete terms are the very beginning of story.

Like all storytellers, children are questioners. They seek a sense of order in the world and are continually asking "Why?" As they make associations and sort out relationships among things, they often fill in the unexplained with their own hypotheses or personal myths. For example, television newscasts that have large gaps in their explanations of world events, or the evasion of adults in regard to human reproduction, may stimulate children to invent their own symbolic answers to explain all that adults have not told them. In the same way, children fill in their own answers to the "why" questions that arise from bits of gossip overheard, television serials incompletely understood, and mysterious adult behaviors observed. Thus, children create their own mythical explanations of the world and exhibit a natural affinity with myth — which many believe is the origin of all literature.[4]

It might even be said that each child, in his own life, recreates much of the history of the human development of language. From single operative and denotive utterances to metaphoric and mythic interpretations of the world to scientific explanations, the child's language, like that of primitive humans, is continually "de-centered" until the primary reference points to help one make sense of the world exist outside the self rather than within. Just as humankind has moved from a primitive to a technological society, the child moves from a personal to a scientific understanding of the world. The worlds of poetry and story are, unfortunately, too often lost along the way. In our adult eagerness to have children understand "the way the world really works," we sometimes forget that literature is itself an authentic and essential way of knowing through feeling, which is just as critical to today's life as scientific knowledge. As Meindert de Jong has said, the adult who has grown up properly still retains the essence of childhood within.[5] In spite of the protective distancing of science and technology, the truly whole human being must still protect that childlike freshness of vision, appreciation, and enjoyment that enables us to respond fully to the world in our uniqueness as human beings.

Children's enthusiasm for Superman, Wonder Woman, the Hulk, and other television superheroes may reflect their affinity with mythic interpretations of the world. In an age when too many children are denied the heroes of the ancient mythologies, they seek heroic images and models wherever they can find them. For most children, this is in television where old myths are reborn each season in more modern dress. Jane Yolan writes of children's needs for folklore and identifies some of the mythological ancestors of television's Spiderman, Flash Gordon, Fonzie, and the Bionic Woman.[6] Every age has its own mythology, but basic human concerns recur in all mythologies; it is to these, and to the continued affirmation of the power of good over evil that permeates the stories of all these superheroes, that critics of the spectacular gimmickery employed might direct their attention.

Play is, of course, the natural setting in which much of the child's most significant growth takes place, and it is here that she develops her first real understanding of the conventions of story. The young child is both author and actor of imaginative stories in dramatic play. She begins to learn about character as she separates herself out from the world to assume a role. At first she really *is* the character she plays; but later, along about age seven or eight, play takes another form as the child is able to *pretend* to be a certain character. Through dramatic play, the younger child seeks merely to put life's experiences into some perspective through the processes of language and movement, but later she selects and orders elements of her play to the ends of style, that is, for effect. It is at this point that the child seeks a wider audience than herself and attempts to communicate her own unique sense of the world to others.

As a child participates in dramatic play, she increases her ability to organize facts and events with some sense of beginning, middle, and end by deciding "first this . . ., then this . . ., then this . . . ." Even many of the street games played by somewhat older children have a kind of lingering plot, such as that often found in games of cops and robbers or the like. In addition, a child's growing knowledge and concern for detail may require her to develop more complex and elaborate fantasies in order to make her own story convincing to herself as well as to others. The young child may be content to imagine arriving on the moon as if by magic; as she grows older, she will most likely want to include her understanding of missile guidance, weightlessness, and the atmosphere of the moon in the composition of her world of play. In all of these ways, as Carolyn Horovitz points out, "the imaginative flights and sustained fantasy that are a part of play are not only closely related to fiction, but are part of the receptive background that children bring to their reading of fiction."[7]

It is hoped that the child, at the same time she is developing a readiness for literary stories through her own language development and her participation in dramatic play, will be hearing good literature read and told to her by the adults in her life. The first riddles, nursery rhymes, and sometimes even television commercials introduce her to simile, metaphor, and other forms of figurative language, which she incorporates so naturally in her own talk. The young child's attempts to impose order upon the events of her world are reinforced by her association with the literary form of story compositions. By the time she is able to verbalize her responses to literature, the child's sense of narration and story form are usually already well developed. Very early she senses the recurring patterns and the need for resolution in story, that somehow the form of the story will pull together all the ideas, characters, and events into some aesthetically satisfying conclusion.*

---

*This idea is discussed in the following: Peter F. Neumeyer, "The Child as Storyteller: Teaching Literary Concepts through Tacit Knowledge," *College English* XXX (April 1969): 515–17; "A Structural Approach to the Study of Literature for Children," *Elementary English* XXXXIV (December 1967): 883–87; and Northrop Frye, *Anatomy of Criticism: Four Essays* (Princeton, N.J.: Princeton University Pr., 1957).

Children are often more able than most adults to perceive and participate in the aesthetic experience of story. They have not yet lost the ability to believe firmly both in the "here and now" of actual experience and the "there and then" of the world of story and to move with ease back and forth between the two. They, like the skilled author, know what it is to hold life still with the aid of imagination and to exercise personal creative power over their existence. They are ordinarily more willing than adults to enter into an engagement with story and participate with it on its own terms. Such engagement with story requires belief in the author's created world, as well as the re-creative powers of the reader's or listener's imaginative response.

Even without the aid or intervention of adults, the child exercises her imaginative and re-creative responses to experience a variety of story forms. In fact, the experiencing of story is not something that can be directed or taught. Each human being must make her own connections between the content and form of the stories she encounters and her own understanding of the world. The development of literary taste is similar to the development of taste for food. It is, in part, dependent upon what is made available and what is valued by others, but we can no more be certain that someone else experiences a particular story as we do than that she tastes precisely what we do when we both eat peas. And if she does not enjoy Pooh, neither our arguments nor our own enjoyment will change that anymore than we can convince one who thinks peas distasteful that they are delicious.

Because our experiences with story are individual does not mean that we make no attempts to develop a child's tastes for story. We cannot be satisfied with a child's association with story extending only from television cartoons and comic books to Nancy Drew and the Hardy Boys anymore than we would allow her to subsist on a diet of hot dogs, cookies, and soda pop. On the other hand, adults frequently have unrealistic expectations of a child's associations with story.

Parents, teachers, and librarians who get upset because a child watches too much television and reads mostly series books rather than good children's literature might be asked to examine their own reading and viewing habits and the various roles that story plays in all our lives. The prime purpose of all literature is entertainment and enjoyment, but we entertain stories at different levels and enjoy them in different ways. Leland B. Jacobs, in his classes at Teachers College, Columbia University, and in his many speeches, has pointed to the fact that children aproach their reading with various levels of interest in the topics—from curiosity, to concern, to real commitment. He also speaks of the many purposes of reading—from putting in time, to escape, to entertainment, to real enlightenment. When we entertain a story in order to escape or to put in time, we ordinarily do not expect as much either of ourselves as readers or of the work as we do when reading for insight or exultation. At the end of a busy and tiring day, most adults are more likely to watch television or read the adult equivalent of the Hardy Boys and Nancy Drew than to turn to Shakespeare or Dostoevski, because the former activities are less demanding.

If this behavior is true of us as adults, how much more true must it be for the child who has to exert so much more effort than we in the simple decoding of written language. The truth is that almost all real readers spend more time reading trivial popular literature than they do "the classics." The important thing is that they know the difference! It is this knowledge that is important for the child reader as well. Concerned adults need not attempt to take anything away from the child; they need only to add to her literary diet, helping her become more discriminating about all the things that she reads and views. After all, one could no more exist on a diet of caviar than one could on candy. In helping a child make distinctions about the value of various story compositions in her world, we help her to develop her critical abilities. The adult who forces his or her judgment on a child denies that child her own critical abilities, her sense of self, and thus her opportunity for growth.

The child is quite naturally a critic of story. Long before she can decode words on paper, she is making choices among various television programs, games, and the stories read to her. From the time of her first "Tell me a story," she is exercising a kind of personal judgment that is the first step toward criticism. She is making a choice of literature out of all the other options that may be open to her at that time. Once she has made this original, albeit nonliterary, judgment, she can, with a little guidance, move to the kind of choices that are a form of literary criticism appropriate to her stage of development.

Too often literary criticism is thought of as an activity of only the most experienced and sophisticated readers, and the critic as one who hands down judgments from a position above other readers. However, if one accepts the premise that literary criticism is a cumulative developmental process that grows with an individual's continual search for that which is most meaningful and most valuable and most enjoyable to him, then all those who read or hear stories must be critics.★ Even before a child begins to read independently, he learns to listen attentively and to respond appreciatively to works of literature. In so doing, he demonstrates the ability to apprehend literary form and to recreate for himself the impact and the import of the story world. At this stage also, a child will frequently respond physically to the reading of a story, indicating with his whole body his receptivity to and involvement with the rhythms and movement of the story. The anticipation of events and prediction of the outcome of story, often shouted aloud, is another indication of the child's feel for form, his tacit knowing of the need for unity, coher-

---

★See Kay E. Vandergrift, "Children as Critics," in *Literature with Children*, ed. Monroe D. Cohen (Washington, D.C.: Association for Childhood Education International, 1972), pp. 24–27; and Glenna Davis Sloan, *The Child as Critic* (New York: Teachers College Pr., 1975).

ence, and resolution in story.

Adults often first notice a child exercising his critical abilities in regard to the illustrations of picture story books as he demands absolute accuracy in relation to the text. Frye has noted that probably the most complex form of criticism that pre-readers exhibit in their responses to story is the ability to group like stories together.[8] The child who asks, at the beginning of a story hour, "Is this believe or make-believe?" may be indicating not only that he can distinguish between these two basic approaches to story but that he understands that he, as a listener, needs to participate in the re-creative experience differently for each. The pre-reader who asks for a "Once upon a time" story, expecting it to end with "and they lived happily ever after" or requests "another story like..." is again exhibiting a fairly sophisticated form of literary criticism for his age and stage of development.

These immediate forms of apprehension and re-creation of story are necessary for the full enjoyment of literature—the primary aim of all literary activities with children. Without this enjoyment, the child will have no reason to develop his critical abilities further. Although children are normally eager to share their responses to story, it is only after they have had many genuine and enjoyable encounters with literature that adults may want to provide more structured channels for these responses. Involvement and personal reaction always come before reasoned judgment in the development of critical abilities, and every child should be given ample time to dwell in and wonder at that involvement. Only through his own enthusiastic reaction will the child reader reach toward reasoned critical opinions.

Those who work with children would be wise to remember that reading is basically a very private affair; nothing we can teach will have the impact of the reader's personal intuition and apprehension. This is not to say, however, that a child should be allowed to stop at that point. A sympathetic adult can help him to enter intuitively into a work of art, to celebrate that work, to sharpen his intuition, and finally to expand his awareness, refine his discriminations, and widen and deepen his perceptions. In this way, the child moves toward genuine literary criticism.

The aim of such criticism is to enable the child to expand her understanding, her appreciation, and her enjoyment of story so that, through story, she may perceive the world in new ways. She may learn to comprehend both herself and others as she begins to think about what it feels like to be in another time, place, or situation, to be for a time someone "not me" but in many ways "like me." Such felt knowledge can give a child insight into human experience and help her understand the complexities of human possibilities. Young children are natural explorers in the world, and story allows them to explore many worlds far beyond their immediate range of actuality. It helps them to remain fully alive to language and life and, at the same time, to sharpen that sense of identity, control, and connection that we all seek.

Footnotes

1. Lloyd de Mause, ed., *The History of Childhood* (New York: Psychohistory Pr., 1974), p. 1.

2. Susanne K. Langer, *Philosophy in a New Key* (New York: Mentor Books, 1958).

3. Northrop Frye, *The Educated Imagination* (Bloomington, Ind.: Indiana University Pr., 1964).

4. Northrop Frye, *Fables of Identity: Studies in Poetic Mythology* (New York: Harcourt, Brace & World, 1963), p. 1.

5. Meindert de Jong, "Acceptance Paper for Newbery Award: The Wheel on the School, 1955," in *Newbery Medal Books: 1922–1955*, ed. Bertha Mahoney Miller and Elinor Whitney Field (Boston: Horn Book, 1955), p. 434.

6. Jane Yolan, "How Basic Is SHAZAM?," *Childhood Education* 53, 4 (February 1977): 186-91.

7. Carolyn Horovitz, "Fiction and the Paradox of Play," *Wilson Library Bulletin* 44 (December 1969): 397-401.

8. Northrop Frye, *On Teaching Literature* (New York: Harcourt, Brace, Jovanovich, 1973).

Children's Books Cited in Chapter One

Cullum, Albert. *You Think Just Because You're Big You're Right*. New York: Harlin Quist, Inc., 1976.

Milne, A.A. *Winnie the Pooh*. New York: E.P. Dutton, 1926.

Chapter Two
Story as Literary Form

We all know story. We know it as that world of make-believe we wondered in as children and return to from time to time in our adult lives. We know it as a beloved story book from the past or as the hottest best seller on the market today. Or perhaps we know it as what we told our friends when what really happened was just not good enough. Although there is a great deal of difference between our own untutored imaginings and the finely crafted work of a skilled literary composer, there are some elements in common that cause us to call all of the above "story." In order to work with children and story, we must begin to sort out those ideas and elements of story as a literary form that distinguish it from less precise uses of the word "story" and identify those that are accessible to children.

Story is distinguished by its fictionality, invented fact in permanent aesthetic form. All story deals with some aspect of the human condition. It is a metaphorical composition of some components of a particular author's subjectively experienced world aesthetically ordered and narrated as an imagined series of events. Story creates a significant unity of action and meaning in which a problem is posed and then resolved in the action of character to the end of an impactful and believable fictionality. At each point in the narrative, the relations between retrospect and anticipation continually and cumulatively reinforce the total structure and meaning of the work. The parts of the story thus have meaning only in relation to the whole composition and together create "a world that is but never was."* As Erskine Caldwell has noted, "Such creation is the making of something which did not previously exist and which thereafter becomes a lasting landmark in the eyes of all who behold it."[1]

The world of story exists in all its fullness only in words and in the minds of those who encounter it; it exists in time but not in space. We may know the Land of Oz as well as our own backyard, but we can never go there except through the words of its creator and our own re-creation of the imaginative whole of the author's world. Within such a created world, the totality of story comes symbolically or metaphorically to some revelation or testament of life presented by a particular author and experienced uniquely by each reader.

There is no way to talk about any form of literature without raising as many questions as are answered. The experience of literature is a very private experience that cannot be fully communicated to another. When a reader moves back from that experience to talk about it, the literature itself becomes more and more distanced as shared meanings in language replace personal experience as the focal point of the response to literature. At this point the reader is involved in criticism or in studying about literature rather than engaging

---

*Leland B. Jacobs used this phrase in his graduate classes in children's literature to characterize the fictional world created in story.

in an experience with literature.

The experience of story is always a unique and personal encounter and an immediate one. The unity of story form allows a reader to apprehend the totality of meaning at once through inward consciousness or insight rather than through comprehension of individual elements of story. This is what Langer has called the "presentational immediacy" of literature.[2] Each reader explores the created world of story and uses his own personal knowing to re-create, with the symbols posited by the author, the literary world he experiences. Although all readers share the particular images created by the author, the deliberate ambiguity of literature allows, even encourages, individual readers to make their own personal meanings from the same story. Literature is its own voice and speaks for itself, but each reader is alone with that voice and hears it in a personal, private way. Thus, a story created by an author is re-created with each new reading in the fresh meeting of reader and work. This experience cannot be taught; it just is. Nevertheless, through repeated encounters with symbolic form, a reader can increase the capacity to experience story and to see more clearly in his own re-creation that which the author imagined. Only through these encounters does a reader learn to submit to an author's guidance and to participate fully in the imaginative experiencing of story. Such submission does not preclude criticism but is the necessary first step if one is to sympathetically evaluate a particular story form.

The essence of story can never be studied because it is not available to an outside observer. The printed page can contain the basic elements of story, but its compositional whole exists only in the interaction between a reader and those printed symbols. Just as one can talk about his sensation of color and never be certain that anyone else perceives it as he does, no reader can be sure that another has read precisely the same story even though they read from the same page. In fact, if we are to respect the uniqueness of each person and consider reading as anything other than a basically passive activity, it is impossible for identical readings to occur.

Yet most inquiries about story are attempts to be independent of the experience of particular persons and to communicate or compile literary knowledge within a given system. One can never completely divorce himself from his personal experience, but in critical discussions of story, one illuminates those areas of concern that can be identified by and shared with other readers. Although a reader's original experience with story may seem to be unordered and perhaps even chaotic, the inquiry into it must be an entrance into and an extension of a disciplined order. The study of story leads to an explication and interpretation both of the reader's experience of it and of the author's aesthetic composition and craftsmanship. In a serious investigation of story, one must, to a greater or lesser degree, move away from the particular story as experienced, to place that story in a larger context of systematized knowledge about story in general. In short, it is impossible to teach or learn literature *per se*; what one teaches or learns in this process of inquiry is criticism.

René Wellek and Austin Warren make a distinction between extrinsic and intrinsic studies about story.[3] External methods are those concerned with the setting, environment, and external causes of literature while intrinsic studies examine the nature, function, form, and contents of the work of literature itself. In looking at intrinsic studies of story, Wellek and Warren refer to literature in terms of "matter" and then of "form," that which aesthetically organizes its matter. "The 'materials' of a literary work of art are, on one level, words, on another level, human behavior and experience, and on another, human ideas and attitudes. All of these, including language, exist outside the work of art, in other modes; but in a successful poem or novel they are pulled into polyphonic relations by the dynamics of aesthetic purpose."[4]

Although story is composed of language with cognitive meanings, these meanings are made aesthetically meaningful through the imaginative integration of matter and form. Story identifies objects but points to them as symbols; or, as Santayana has said, literature turns events into ideas.[5] Literature does not denote; it connotes. Nevertheless, the world of denotation, the actual world, limits what can be connoted. Literary form also imposes its own limits on the world of story, but these limits are themselves of value. They force the author to avoid too precise a presentation of the real or too definite a realization of the ideal. Thus, through its limitations and literal incompleteness, story becomes complete in literary form and addresses itself not to recognition or to reason, but to aesthetic sensibility. It is judged not by any external criteria but by its integrity and the inner consistency of its verbal structure, the truth of fiction.

All of these intrinsic values exist only potentially in the literary structures of story and must finally be realized by a perceptive reader. Story is both totally complete and continually in process. Intrinsic studies about story are both implicit and overt. They start with sensed particularities and then move to rational judgments and abstraction, combining both subjective and objective responses to total story form. In the final analysis, we must say of story as Elizabeth Sewell has said of poetry: "To demand an interpretation of a poem is evidence of misunderstanding of the nature of poetry. All one can ask is admission to the world of the poem, and permission to explore . . . ."[6]

Before exploring further some of the means of providing insight into the world of story, it may be useful to clarify some of the misconceptions we unwittingly convey to children because of the popular uses of the word "story" in our language. The classroom assignment that requires students to "write a story about what you did on your vacation" is not only an uninspired assignment, it is also a misuse of the word "story." Normally what teachers want in response to this assignment is not a story at all, but a report. The child who actually writes a story, perhaps about her trip to Mars in a homemade space capsule, is likely to be taken aside and asked: "That's all very nice, but what really happened?" The most unfortunate aspect of such incidents is that the teacher does not seem to value the imaginative product of the child's mind and often fails to realize that the imaginary trip may have been much more exciting and meaningful in the child's life than the family's actual trip to the Grand Canyon.

Langer makes a distinction between discursive and non-discursive means of ordering ideas that may be useful here.[7] She describes discourse as factually, logically, linearly ordered material to the end of verifiability. Nondiscourse is relationally or metaphorically ordered to the end of believability. Discourse is literal; nondiscourse is literary. Discourse is thought about thought; nondiscourse is thought about feeling. Discourse deals with the actual, apparently logical, world and is concerned with precision in the pieces, while nondiscourse deals with an imagined or "felt" world and is concerned with sensitivity to the whole. As a third grader once explained it to me, "It's the difference between *what happened* and *what happened to me.*"

This comment was made in a discussion with a group of youngsters about their field trip to the Museum of Natural History in New York City. The trip had been planned for what unfortunately turned out to be one of those cold, rainy city days. Knowing that public transportation is often somewhat erratic on such days, two adults and twenty-three children stood on a Broadway corner waiting for a city bus when an elderly lady in a black raincoat, black hat and scarf and carrying a black umbrella joined us. She was obviously not pleased to be in such company and, with fierce looks and body language, let us all know it. When the bus finally arrived, she entered first and found a seat near the rear. As the twenty-three dripping young bodies vied for standing room near her, the woman very slowly and carefully marked off with her umbrella a semicircle in front of her seat in which no one dared stand. Nothing else happened—actually. However, when we returned from the museum and the children were discussing the day's events, one child, in the midst of talk of dinosaur bones and the many varieties of cockroaches, told of the witch on the bus who drew a magic circle around herself. He had almost been jostled into that circle but, knowing that dire consequences would await him there, had just managed to save himself! All the children knew what he was talking about, but many of them laughed. When others pointed out that she was not really a witch, the young man replied: "Well, she was to me! I don't care what you think happened; that's what happened to me!"

This child's response was, it seems to me, the very essence of the distinction between report and story—in fact, the very essence of story itself. Story, even the most fanciful forms, begins with human experiences; then, with the aid of the imagination, an author heightens and shapes those experiences to compose a story world that is aesthetically believable. And, as strange as it may seem, fiction is almost always more believable than fact. The actual events of the world are so chaotic that it is often difficult to make any sense of them. A fictional account of those events, on the other hand, shapes and orders them in such a way that we are convinced and taken into that fictional world and believe in it, at least for the time of our encounter with it. The child who describes story as "make-believe" is very knowing in the ways of literature. The author of story is always trying to make readers believe in the world that has been created. *Hamlet* and *Peter Rabbit* are read today because both William Shakespeare and Beatrix Potter were masters at composing story worlds that successive generations could respond to and believe in.

A distinction that also needs to be made is that between narration and plot. Narration is an ordering of events in their time sequence so that "this happened . . . then this . . . then this . . . ." Narration is "conversational" in tone; it conveys the sense and the sound of the spoken word. Plot is a particular kind of narration in which events are chosen and arranged in such a way that all parts work toward a final outcome or resolution. Here I am defining narration basically as E.M. Forster has defined story. His much quoted statement, " 'The king died and then the queen died' is a story. 'The king died and then the queen died of grief' is a plot,"[8] reduces "story" to its very lowest form of popular usage rather than emphasizing its use as a literary term. As the terms are used in this book, "The king died and then the queen died" is *narration*; "The king died and then the queen died of grief" is a simple *plot*.

One could say that newspaper reports and "how-to-do-it" manuals may have narration and frequently even causality, but they are not literary in nature because their prime purpose is to communicate events rather than aesthetic feelings. Most of the mood and concept books for young children are excellent examples of aesthetic works that have narration but no plot. In these books, many events are linked together to create a particular mood or to convey a specific concept, but one does not necessarily follow another in any order other than that selected by the author for literary ends. The emphasis is often on the total movement of sounds and images rather than on a series of events or scenes. Concept books are included here because they, unlike information books, are nondiscursive in nature; and, although they convey specific concepts to young children, they are designed more to inspire an investigative spirit than to be absolutely accurate or verifiable. The notion that kisses and umbrellas and ice-cream cones are round while a walk around the block is square is not only mind-stretching for the young child; it is highly entertaining as well.[9]

Narration without plot is also seen in many forms of traditional literature and their modern counterparts. Cumulative and circle tales are often referred to as "loosely plotted" stories. In fact, they are not plotted at all. These works use such strong patterns of narration that plots are implicit; however, they are not made explicit. It is left to the reader or listener to provide the final connections that make plot, and such involvement adds to the enjoyment of the tale. Cumulative tales such as *The House That Jack Built* and *There Was an Old Woman Who Swallowed a Fly* use progressions in size as well as in time to order events.* A young child's early attempts to compose story may also result in the narration of a series of events rather than fully developed plot because she has not yet learned to imaginatively select, order, and shape the report of "what happened" so that it may truly "happen to" the reader.

The author who has learned to transform events into ideas and feelings may approach the creation of a believable story world as realism, romance, or fancy. "Fancy" and "fanciful" are used here rather than "fantasy" and "fantastic" because psychology has so influenced our language that the latter pair of terms are tied to psychological meanings rather than literary ones. Fancy implies a compositional ordering not ordinarily present in psychological fantasy. Realistic fiction is composed of characters, settings, and events that might possibly exist in the actual world. This does not mean, however, that realistic literature seeks to represent the actual world or portray a "happy medium" in the presentation of such images. Those who reject a story because they "don't know anyone who would behave that way" are misunderstanding the nature of literature. Story deals with common human feelings and experiences but, even in realism, these may be revealed through very unique characters and situations. If all literature encourages wonder, realism may be said to discover and develop interesting aspects of the knowable and order those experiences so that others may wonder at

---

*See *The House That Jack Built*, illus. by Paul Galdone (New York: McGraw-Hill, 1961); early versions often included political satire as a major component. *There Was an Old Woman Who Swallowed a Fly*, illus. by Michael Kohn (Dandelion Pr., 1979) is one of several versions of this work, including a film production by the National Film Board of Canada.

them. For the young child who has not yet experienced much of the world, the real is every bit as "wonder-full" as the highly imaginative. This is why some of the realistic narratives or very simple stories for pre-school children remain in print and retain their appeal to youngsters even though many adults find them painfully dull to read aloud. Lois Lenski's "Little" books are excellent examples of this. As physical objects they are child-sized, and although nothing much happens in them, they do order and confirm for a young child much that he has experienced or observed in his own life.

Fanciful literature, on the other hand, invents occasions for wonder that, although believable within the limits of its own created worlds, are not restricted by the dictates of the natural world. While realism suggests the familiar, fancy stretches the imagination so that one may experience the unlikely and the unfamiliar in a world in which the ordinary expectations of life are suspended.

There are two basic types of fanciful stories for children with very fundamental differences between the two. Many of the picture story books for young children are talking animal stories in which rabbits or mice or badgers think, talk, dress, and behave as very realistic human characters.* The fanciful element in such works is most often used not so much to the ends of fancy but as a literary device to tell a story with a very realistic appeal. The Hobans' books about Frances, in which the main character is a youngster who does not want to go to

---

*Margaret Blount in *Animal Land: The Creatures of Children's Fiction* (New York: William Morrow & Co., 1974) speaks to this question of personification. Blount writes: "Human is what the child wants his toy or pet to be, the substitute friend or brother, like himself but exempt from all the dreary rules attached to childhood and growing up, the eternal confidant or companion, steadfast and unchangeable. . . . How many little girls have always spoken to their dolls and answered for them? But it is not until Hans Andersen in 1846 that you get a story like *The Little Tin Soldier;* and in nurseries, the gradual additions of strange characters to the more conventional 'human' families — toy animals, the Golliwog and that indispensable piece of nursery furniture, the enduring Teddy Bear. Adults made the toys talk, and they became a child's companions on magic adventures" (p. 170).

bed or does not want to eat anything except bread and jam or does not want her life interfered with by a younger sibling, are excellent examples of this type of fanciful literature. The fact that Frances is a badger is almost incidental; it is appealing and mildly humorous, but it does not alter the child's ability to understand and relate these stories to his or her own realistic life experiences. When we think of fanciful literature, however, we most often call to mind works of the second type, such as *The Phantom Tollbooth, The Borrowers*, or *Alice in Wonderland*, in which the overall handling of the relationship between the familiar and unfamiliar and the reader's awareness that these stories take place in worlds that could not actually exist are major ingredients in their appeal.

For most children in our society, the first associations with fanciful literature come through the folktales, fairy tales, and myths originally passed down in the oral tradition. The supernatural or preternatural characters in these stories were most likely created in an attempt to explain the complex realities of human beings and their world. (All fictional characters who are beyond the range of what is "normal" are sometimes called supernatural. Supernatural heroes, however, are actually those mythical larger-than-life characters. Preternatural is a more generic term meaning the smaller-than-life "little people" of story as well as fictional superheroes.) The origins of almost all modern fancy can be traced back to the various forms of traditional literature. Frye, for instance, states that virtually all the literary archetypes of Western society are based on the Christian mythology contained in the Bible.[10] Most fancy also makes extensive use of such literary patterns as the quest, the journey, the struggle between good and evil, and the triumph of the underdog. The fanciful works of Susan Cooper and Lloyd Alexander are deeply rooted in traditional Welsh mythology, while *Millions of Cats* is a modern folktale and many talking animal stories are obviously related to fables.

Hans Christian Andersen is often referred to as the father

of modern fanciful literature for children and his influence is certainly evident in many realms of children's literature today (see Figure 1). Often there is a movement from realism to fancy within story, and a number of literary devices have been used to make the transition from one imagined world to another. A dream (*Alice in Wonderland*); an opening such as a door, a cave, or a closet (*The Lion, The Witch and the Wardrobe*); some form of transportation (*The Phantom Tollbooth*); or a natural phenomenon such as water, fog, or wind (*The Wizard of Oz*) have been used very successfully as forms of conveyance from a realistic to a fanciful world.

Science fiction is a form of modern fanciful literature that, through speculation and extrapolation, moves from the world as we know it to explore the extensions of scientific, technical, political, and philosophical ideas in an imagined world or time. Its connections with the actual world of today are more concrete and its creations often fairly realistic possibilities or sometimes even predictions of the future. Although science fiction primarily has been thought of as a twentieth-century literature portraying rocket ships, space travel, and alien planets, some have traced its origin to Plato's *Republic*, which used a fictional mode to raise questions about the existence of and the value of alternative worlds. Janice Antczak's recent study of science fiction for children examines this body of literature and calls attention to its role in modern myth-making and its origins in the romantic tradition.[11]

Romance as one of the three regulative or basic approaches to story is grounded in realism but expanded and exaggerated to create a world somewhat beyond the realistic but not totally into the realm of fancy. The characters of romantic literature are often somewhat larger than or beyond the limits of ordinary life, either better or worse than those found in a realistically believable story; they are frequently secondary to the events of a highly adventurous plot. Romantic heroes and heroines are noted for their ability to triumph over almost impossible odds. Settings, often pastoral ones, may be major

Figure 1: Hans Christian Andersen: Influence on Fanciful
Literature

contributors to the establishment of an idyllic or nostalgic, romantic mood in which coincidence and sentimentality can play a major part. (Sentimentality refers to the use of sentiment for its effect on readers rather than as a genuine expression of feeling.) *Treasure Island*, one of the best-known of all romantic novels for children, clearly exhibits most of these characteristics. In romance there generally are no characters, settings, or events that could not be present in the actual world, but the continual exaggeration of their characteristics makes it impossible for one to believe in the story in a realistic manner. Mysteries and most historical fiction are forms of the romantic novel having widespread appeal for both adults and children. The majority of the literature for children, over the years, seems to fall within the romantic tradition.

One of the causes of confusion in discussing "romance" in children's literature is that it refers both to one of the three basic *approaches* to story and to one of the four basic *modes* of story (see Figure 2). As an *approach*, it indicates the relationship between the elements of the story world and the facts of the actual world, while as a *mode* it points to the overall patterning of events or the basic plots of story.

Northrop Frye has said that there is one basic story originating in myth that can be told in only four structural modes or generic plots: (1) romance, (2) comedy, (3) irony/satire, and (4) tragedy. These four modes are not rigid categories but general plot structures classified according to the hero's power of action. In romance the hero is somewhat idealized so that his powers are perceived as greater than those of ordinary men and often greater than those of his environment. This mode is distinguished by its exaggerated characters and the marvelous adventures of its hero through a perilous journey and a crucial struggle to a wish-fulfilling resolution. In comedy the hero has powers equal to those of ordinary humans, although he often finds himself in an incongruous relationship to a situation, to society, or to himself. Typically this hero has a very realistic desire that is thwarted by those in authority, often parental figures. Nevertheless, he overcomes almost insurmountable obstacles to arrive at a happy and satisfying resolution. In irony or satire, the hero's powers seem less than those of ordinary mortals, causing him to become the victim of his environment and of often chaotic circumstances. In tragedy, the hero's powers may be somewhat greater than those of most humans, but he has no real superhuman capabilities. He is a character overcome by his environment, but overcome with his heroic qualities intact. The tragic hero recognizes his fate, makes a choice in spite of the consequences, and demonstrates courage in the face of the inevitable. Frye suggests that romance and comedy are the modes of almost all story for children and should be stressed in our literary activities with them.[12] In recent years the emphasis on psychological novels or problem stories for children, even very young children, has introduced some books of the ironic mode for this audience. This was to be expected, since major trends in publishing for adults usually filter down to the children's field, and adult literature seems to have been in an age of irony for at least a decade or two.

Figure 2 (which follows) may help to distinguish between romance as an approach and as a literary mode and to demonstrate how the three approaches may be imposed upon the four modes.

Story, whether realistic, romantic, or fanciful and in whatever mode, is made manifest at and may be comprehended at three different levels (at least). Helen Huus calls these literal, interpretation, and assimilation or psychological integration levels, and Leland Jacobs refers to the verbal, behavioral, and transcendent levels.[13] For our purposes, we shall refer to these as the *narrative level*, at which a verbal imitation of action can be recognized and followed by readers; the *interpretive level*, at which an aesthetic reality is created that is believable and convincing; and the *transcendent or residual level*, at which one becomes aware of some special symbolic significance. These levels may be used both in looking critically at an author's composition of a literary work and at a reader's response.★

Although these three levels progress in complexity from the perspective of both composition and response, it is not true that only older or more skillful readers can reach the higher levels. It may be useful here to make a distinction between reading skills, those that permit one to decode the printed symbols of the page, and literary abilities, which enable one to interpret and appreciate aesthetic meaning.[14] Prereaders are often able to respond to story at more complex levels than beginning readers because they are not tied to the drudgery of the decoding process and are free to engage in more imaginative re-creative experiences with the literary work. Older children able to read on their own are also quite likely to have literary abilities far in advance of their reading skills. It is therefore important for adults to continue to read and discuss literature with youngsters long after the child has mastered the decoding process.

A story that is successful at the narrative level is one that engages a reader's attention based on plot, language, and physical conflict. In such works, the characters are believable enough for a reader to identify with them on a somewhat simplistic, often romantic, level; but they are not complex or interesting enough to draw attention from a rather straightforward, if often very lively, series of events. The series books such as Nancy Drew and the Hardy Boys are extremely successful on this level and are excellent practice material for those developing mastery in the reading process because they require little more of their readers than simple decoding skills. Some of the "I-Can-Read" or "Beginning Reader" books for younger children are successful at this

---

★*Children's Literature in Education* publishes a variety of articles both from the author's and the reader's point of view that, without using these terms, are excellent examples of these various levels of meaning.

Figure 2: Relationship of Approaches to and Modes of Story

		ROMANCE	TRAGEDY	SATIRE IRONY	COMEDY
APPROACHES TO STORY	**REALISM**	Call It Courage Julie of the Wolves	The Jazz Man Sounder	The Pigman The Chocolate War The House of Stairs	Blue Willow North to Freedom Summer of the Swans Crow Boy
	ROMANCE	Charlie and the Chocolate Factory Little Tim and the Brave Sea Captain Treasure Island	White Mane	The Pushcart War	Dorp Dead
	FANCY	The Tale of Peter Rabbit Black Beauty Where the Wild Things Are	The Steadfast Tin Soldier	The Gingerbread Boy The Emperor's New Clothes	Cinderella Snow White The 500 Hats of Bartholomew Cubbins Charlotte's Web

MODES OF STORY

level also, but too many controlled vocabulary books are not fully developed stories at all but merely more pleasant practice material for the mastery of the decoding process than the Dick and Jane readers of previous generations.

At the interpretive level, story involves the reader with some sort of physical-psychological conflict in which character development is often critical to the appreciation of the work. Here characters must "ring true;" they must convince the reader that people would really behave as they have in this story. In fact, the totality of the composed story world must convince readers that the work has both validity and integrity. The validity of story is established by its consistency in its own values and beliefs and its adherence to the posited limits of the world of that story. Realistic literature must establish a validity in comparison with the actual world, while fancy must propose and sustain its own knowledge and beliefs. A story has literary integrity or authenticity when it does not manipulate life but attempts to present honest human sentiment rather than sentimentality. The majority of good popular reading, either for children or adults, is strong at the interpretive level.

At the transcendent or residual level, story evokes symbolic meaning over and above the literal; it goes beyond the facts within the work to leave the reader with some residue of truth, often as the result of a psychological-spiritual conflict. Those works that reach the transcendent or residual level may do so for an individual in a very personal and private way. While the first two levels may be identified in the composition by a skilled critic, the third exists in the reader, in what the work means to that reader. Although a particular story's attainment of this level may be unique to one reader, there are also works that, if read and enjoyed at all, are probably responded to at the transcendent or residual level. At the narrative and interpretive levels, *The Little Prince* might be considered silly and unconvincing, but the many fans of this story read and love it for its special transcendent or residual meanings. Allegorical works and those of mystical fancy require comprehension at this level if they are to succeed at all.*

Too often stories for children have been thought of as something set apart from, and perhaps less significant than, the larger field of imaginative literature for adults. However, the qualities of excellence in literature remain the same regardless of the age of the audience for whom the work is intended. Nobel Prize winning novelist Isaac Bashevis Singer has said that while adult literature, particularly fiction, is waning in quality, literature for children has made great strides. He points out that the child

> . . . has become a consumer of a great growing literature — a reader who cannot be deluded by literary ends and barren experiments. No writer can bribe his way to the child's attention with false originality, literary puns and puzzles, arbitrary distortions of the order of things, or muddy streams of consciousness which often reveal nothing but a writer's boring and selfish personality. I came to the child because I see in him a last refuge from a literature gone berserk and ready for suicide.[15]

One must keep in mind that the development of a separate body of literature written especially for children is a relatively recent phenomenon. Originally children and adults shared the stories of the rich oral tradition of the culture. The first printed books claimed by children were not written with them in mind but were adult books that in some way aroused

---

*James E. Higgins, in *Beyond Words: Mystical Fancy in Children's Literature* (New York: Teachers College Pr., 1970), writes: "The writer of mystical fancy is dealing with an art form. Like any artist, through the power of imagination he takes his communicant 'beyond' his material surroundings in order to lay bare those realities which are imperceptible to the physical senses. His work is expressed—and best understood—through intuition and emotion, rather than through logic. He concerns himself with a spiritual universe" (p. 5).

the interest and imagination of young readers. It was later, when society evolved so that the concerns and activities of childhood were distinctly different, sometimes even remote, from the ways of adults, that a separate body of children's literature grew up. There are, nonetheless, some important characteristics of children's story that distinguish it from story for adults. As C.S. Lewis has noted, children's stories have more often remained close to the great oral tradition in their use of repetitive, rhythmic language and a lean, symmetrical plot.[16] Although story for children may have a somewhat lesser range of language, there is a great deal of ingenuity and flexibility within that range. Children's stories depend more on action than on subtleties to convey ideas and thus have a less complex combination of language, character, plot and theme. They may be less concerned with probability than with consistency within a posited set of circumstances and may provide more detail in some of the connecting ideas than adult works. Quite often children's story concentrates more on characterization, encouraging stronger identification with the protagonist. Of course, there is a greater integration of visual and verbal patterns, especially in books for young children. More important, children's story uses images from the child's world and preserves some of the freshness and clarity that children bring to that world. At its best, story for children gets back to the childlike essences of things often buried beneath our adult lives and appeals to readers of all ages.

The range of content in stories for children, particularly those for older children, has expanded greatly in the past two decades. Topics and treatments of topics that were taboo in children's books twenty years ago have become commonplace today. Children's literature has moved beyond the moralizing tales, the patriotic stories, and the high adventures of the nineteenth and early twentieth century to deal more realistically with personal and societal problems of the contemporary world. Parents or other adult authority figures in children's books are no longer the wise and benevolent role models helping young people to solve their problems. In fact, in many instances, the adults are themselves the problems with which child characters must cope. The following are a sample of the many titles of this type: John Donovan's *I'll Get There, It Better Be Worth the Trip* (New York: Harper & Row, 1969); Betsy Byars's *The Pinballs* (New York: Harper & Row, 1977); M.E. Kerr's *Gentlehands* (New York: Harper & Row, 1978); Kim Platt's *The Boy Who Could Make Himself Disappear* (Radnor, Pa.: Chilton, 1968); Irene Hunt's *Lottery Rose* (New York: Charles Scribner's Sons, 1976); Willo Davis Roberts's *Don't Hurt Laurie* (New York: Atheneum Publishers, 1977); Paula Danziger's *Can You Sue Your Parents for Malpractice?* (New York: Delacorte, 1979); and Charlotte Culin's *Cages of Glass, Flowers of Time* (Scarsdale, N.Y.: Bradbury Pr., 1979).

This might be thought of as a move away from romance toward the ironic mode in which characters no longer control their own fate but are controlled by others or by circumstances. Even modern fanciful literature, which seems to be more widely accepted and appreciated in post-World War II years, often focuses much more on problem situations than on the liberation of the imagination. Science fiction, for instance, has moved quite dramatically from high adventure in other worlds to social and philosophical considerations of science and technology's potential impact on our world.

Such trends to a certain extent have been very welcome in the field of children's literature. Adults must acknowledge that children live in the same world we do and are as susceptible to its pain as they are to its joy. Consistently unrealistic and romantic views of that world may lead children to believe that they are alone with their problems rather than to see how others, albeit fictional others, cope with similar concerns. In addition to getting some perspective on their own experiences, children may, through identification with characters unlike themselves, extend their capacity to understand other situations and other people. All children, even those who do not live in the kind of idealized, romanticized, and protected environments in which most adults would like to imagine them, have a right to find themselves and their world in the stories they read. They also have the right, just as we do, to a literature that can move them powerfully to tears and return them to the world renewed and refreshed because of those tears. At the same time, we do not want to rob young people of their idealism and strip of their heroic qualities all those in whom they might believe. If, as a society, we have any faith in the future, we must encourage the development of a literature that will assist children in imagining a world better than the one we now know. This does not take us back solely to romantic literature but neither does it preclude romance. The truly educated imagination feeds on alternative views of the world from which it may fashion its own world; it requires the kind of diversity from which one may choose direction and act with dignity in that world.

It is unfortunate, however, as John Rowe Townsend notes, that just as children's literature is beginning to be taken seriously by the literary community, our emphasis on contemporary problems in children's story seems to be leading us toward another era of moralizing tales and didactic messages.[17] Of course, most literature does convey a kind of pervasive morality inexorably interwoven into the whole fabric of the work, but such a world view is very different from the narrow utilitarianism of the modern moral tract in story form that warns of the evils and dire consequences of drug abuse or mistreatment of minority groups or the contamination of the environment. Concerns with racism, sexism, ageism, and the portrayal of the handicapped seemingly are taking precedence over literary quality in much recent criticism of children's books. These are unquestionably important issues of our time and as such will naturally show up in contemporary literature for children as well as for adults. However, heavy-handed treatments that throw the artistry of the literary composition out of balance or attempt to substitute social consciousness for imaginative creation are likely to have little positive impact on readers, either socially or literarily. In fact, they may have a negative effect. Critics who concentrate on such concerns with inadequate consideration of literary qualities are doing neither readers nor children's literature a service, nor are they improving in society the conditions they seek out in story.

Literature is a means of reaching out to others, of sharing ideas and life experiences; as such, it can influence the ways one perceives and responds to people and situations in "real life." Nonetheless, the basic value of story is the aesthetic value of "imaginative life-likeness," and those who work with children and literature must accept this as their primary concern in the evaluation and selection of children's books. All other considerations, no matter how important in life, must remain secondary in the evaluation of literature. Only through aesthetic enjoyment will children increase their capacity to become involved with and appreciate story form and thus their capacity to think about issues in the world. Too often adults ask what a story is *good for* before inquiring if it is in itself a *good* story, with the potentiality of engaging children in its created world. We at times place more emphasis on a story's usefulness than on its believability and its feelingfulness, on its literal importance rather than on its metaphorical import or literary significance.

Story for children may indeed serve many social, educational, and practical needs, and the intention here is not to set it off as some precious commodity to be approached only reverently as "art for art's sake." Literature is made from the stuff of life, and like life itself, can be approached joyously, searchingly, matter-of-factly, gravely, or hesitantly as well as practically or reverently. The enemy of literature in the lives of children is none of these. The real enemy of story is indifference, indifference to the primacy of the aesthetic experiencing of a work of art and its importance as a potentially unique way of knowing about the world.

Footnotes

1. Erskine Caldwell, *Writing in America* (New York: Phaedra Publishers, 1967), p. 76.

2. Susanne K. Langer, *Feeling and Form* (New York: Charles Scribner's Sons, 1953).

3. Rene Wellek and Austin Warren, *Theory of Literature* (New York: Harcourt, Brace, Jovanovich, Rene/3rd ed. 1977).

4. Ibid., p. 241.

5. George Santayana, *Essays in Literary Criticism*, repr. of 1956 ed., ed. Irving Singer (Philadelphia: Richard West Pr., 1973).

6. Elizabeth Sewell, *The Structure of Poetry* (New York: Charles Scribner's Sons, 1952), p. 93.

7. Susanne K. Langer, *Philosophy in a New Key* (New York: Mentor Books, 1958).

8. E.M. Forster, *Aspects of the Novel* (New York: Harcourt, Brace, Jovanovich, 1955), p. 86.

9. Blossom Budney, *A Kiss Is Round* (New York: Lothrop, Lee & Shepard, 1954).

10. Northrop Frye, *Anatomy of Criticism: Four Essays* (Princeton, N.J.: Princeton University Pr., 1957).

11. Janice Antczak, *The Mythos of a New Romance: A Critical Analysis of Science Fiction for Children as Informed by the Literary Theory of Northrop Frye*, D.L.S. dissertation, Columbia University, 1979. (New York: Neal-Schuman, in prep.)

12. Northrop Frye, *The Educated Imagination* (Bloomington, Ind.: Indiana University Pr., 1964).

13. Helen Huus, "Critical Aspects of Comprehension," *Elementary English* 48 (May 1971): 489–94; Leland B. Jacobs in his writing and speeches and classes over a twenty-five-year period used variations of these levels.

14. Elizabeth Ann Parker, *Teaching the Reading of Fiction* (New York: Teachers College Pr., 1969), pp. 46–89.

15. Isaac Bashevis Singer, "I See the Child as a Last Refuge," *The New York Times*, November 9, 1969.

16. C.S. Lewis, "On Three Ways of Writing for Children," in *Of Other Worlds: Essays & Stories* (New York: Harcourt, Brace, Jovanovich, 1966), pp. 22–34; also appears in *Horn Book Magazine*, October 1963.

17. John Rowe Townsend, "Didacticism in Modern Dress," *Horn Book Magazine* (April 1967): 159–64.

Children's Books Cited in Chapter Two

Alexander, Lloyd. *The Book of Three*. New York: Holt, Rinehart & Winston, 1964.

———. *Taran Wanderer*. New York: Holt, Rinehart & Winston, 1967.

———. *The High King*. New York: Holt, Rinehart & Winston, 1968.

Andersen, Hans Christian. *His Classic Fairy Tales*, trans. Erik Haugaard and illus. Michael Foreman. New York: Doubleday, 1978.

———. *The Little Fir Tree*, illus. Nancy E. Burkert. New York: Harper & Row, 1970.

———. *The Emperor's New Clothes*, illus. Virginia Lee Burton. Boston: Houghton Mifflin, 1949.

———. *Thumbelina*. Mahwah, N.J.: Troll Associates, 1978.

———. *The Snow Queen*, illus. June A. Corwin. New York: Atheneum Publishers, 1968.

———. *The Steadfast Tin Soldier*. New York: Atheneum Publishers, 1971.

Ardizzone, Edward. *Little Tim and the Brave Sea Captain*. New York: Oxford University Pr., 1936.

Armstrong, William H. *Sounder*. New York: Harper & Row, 1969.

Atwater, Richard, and Atwater, Florence. *Mr. Popper's Penguins*. Boston: Little, Brown, 1938.

Bailey, Carolyn Sherwin. *Miss Hickory*. New York: Viking Pr., 1946.

Baum, L. Frank. *The Wizard of Oz*, illus. W.W. Denslow. New York: Macmillan, 1970. (First published as *The Wonderful Wizard of Oz* in 1900 by George Hill Co., it was reissued as *The New Wizard of Oz* by Bobbs-Merrill Co, in 1903; very quickly the "New" was dropped from the title, as is noticeable in a title cover published in 1920.)

Brown, Marcia. *Cinderella*, illus. Marcia Brown. New York: Charles Scribner's Sons, 1954.

Budney, Blossom. *A Kiss Is Round*. New York: Lothrop, Lee & Shepard, 1954.

Burkert, Nancy Ekholm. *Snow White & the Seven Dwarfs: A Tale from the Brothers Grimm*. New York: Farrar, Straus & Giroux, 1972.

Burton, Virginia Lee. *Mike Mulligan and His Steam Shovel*. Boston: Houghton Mifflin, 1939.

Byers, Betsy. *The Summer of the Swans*. New York: Viking Pr., 1970.

Carroll, Lewis. *Alice in Wonderland*. New York: Norton, 1971. (First published in 1865; *Through the Looking Glass* in 1871.)

Caudill, Rebecca, and Ayars, James. *Contrary Jenkins*. New York: Holt, Rinehart & Winston, 1969.

Christopher, John. *The White Mountains*. New York: Macmillan, 1967.

———. *The City of Gold and Lead*. New York: Macmillan, 1967.

———. *The Pool of Fire*. New York: Macmillan, 1968.

Clark, Pauline. *The Return of the Twelves*. New York: Coward, 1963.

Collodi, Carlo. *The Adventures of Pinocchio*. New York: Macmillan, 1978.

Cooper, Susan. *Over Sea, Under Stone*. New York: Harcourt, Brace, Jovanovich, 1966.

———. *The Dark is Rising*. New York: Atheneum Publishers, 1973.

———. *Greenwitch*. New York: Atheneum Publishers, 1974.

———. *The Grey King*. New York: Atheneum Publishers, 1975.

———. *Silver on the Tree*. New York: Atheneum Publishers, 1977.

Cormier, Robert. *The Chocolate War*. New York: Pantheon Books, 1974.

Cunningham, Julia. *Dorp Dead*. New York: Pantheon Books, 1965.

Dahl, Roald. *Charlie and the Chocolate Factory*. New York: Knopf, 1964.

Engdahl, Sylvia L. *The Far Side of Evil*. New York: Atheneum Publishers, 1971.

Field, Rachel. *Hitty, Her First Hundred Years*. New York: Macmillan, 1937.

Fleming, Ian. *Chitty-Chitty-Bang-Bang*. New York: Random House, 1964.

Gag, Wanda. *Millions of Cats*. New York: Coward, 1928.

Galdone, Paul. *The Gingerbread Boy*, retold and illus. Paul Galdone. New York: Seabury Pr., 1975.

Gates, Doris. *Blue Willow*. New York: Viking Pr., 1940.

George, Jean. *Julie of the Wolves*. New York: Harper & Row, 1972.

Geisel, Theodore Seuss. *The 500 Hats of Bartholomew Cubbins*. Chippewa Falls, Wisc.: E.M. Hale & Co., 1938.

Grahame, Kenneth. *The Reluctant Dragon*. New York: Holiday House, 1953.

———. *The Wind in the Willows*. Cleveland, Ohio: World Publishing Co., 1966. (First published in 1908.)

Gramatky, Hardie. *Little Toot*. New York: G.P. Putnam's Sons, 1939.

Hale, Lucretia P. *The Complete Peterkin Papers*. Boston: Houghton Mifflin, 1960.

Hoban, Russell. *Bedtime for Frances*. New York: Harper & Row, 1960.

———. *Bread and Jam for Frances*. New York: Harper & Row, 1964.

———. *A Baby Sister for Frances*. New York: Harper & Row, 1964.

Holm, Ann. *North to Freedom*, trans. L.W. Kingsland. New York: Harcourt, Brace, Jovanovich, 1965.

The House That Jack Built, illus. Paul Galdone. New York: McGraw-Hill Co., 1961. (A reprint of an 1854 copy of the tale that H.G. Hine illustrated is available from Scolar Press in London or through The Green Tiger Press in La Jolla, California. In several versions political satire is obvious with reference to William Pitt as Jack.)

Juster, Norton. *The Phantom Tollbooth*. New York: Random House, 1961.

Kastner, Erich. *The Little Man*. New York: Alfred A. Knopf, 1966.

Kendall, Carol. *The Gammage Cup*. New York: Harcourt, Brace, Jovanovich, 1966.

Lamorisse, Albert, and Daunant, Denys. *White Mane*, taken from the film by Albert Lamorisse. New York: E.P. Dutton, 1954.

Lawson, Robert. *Rabbit Hill*. New York: Viking Pr., 1944.

Lenski, Lois. *Little Auto*. New York: Henry Z. Walck, Inc., 1934.

———. *Little Train*. New York: Henry Z. Walck, Inc., 1940.

———. *Cowboy Small*. New York: Henry Z. Walck, Inc., 1949.

Lewis, C.S. *The Lion, The Witch and the Wardrobe*. New York: Macmillan, 1950.

Lindgren, Astrid. *Pippi Longstocking*. New York: Viking Pr., 1950.

MacDonald, George. *At the Back of the North Wind*. New York: Macmillan, 1964. (First published in 1871.)

Memoirs of a London Doll, Written by Herself, ed. Mrs. Fairstar. Boston: Ticknor, Reed, and Fields, 1852.

Merrill, Jean. *High, Wide and Handsome*, illus. Ronni Solbert. New York: William R. Scott, Inc., 1964.

———. *The Pushcart War*, illus. Ronni Solbert. Reading, Mass.: Addison-Wesley, 1964.

Milne, A.A. *Winnie the Pooh*. New York: E.P. Dutton, 1926.

Norton, Mary. *The Borrowers*. New York: Harcourt, Brace, Jovanovich, 1953.

O'Brien, Robert C. *Mrs. Frisby and the Rats of NIMH*. New York: Atheneum Publishers, 1971.

Ormondroyd, Edward. *Time at the Top*. Emeryville, Calif.: Parnassus Pr., 1963.

Potter, Beatrix. *The Tale of Peter Rabbit*. New York: Frederick Warne, 1902.

Saint-Exupery, Antoine de. *The Little Prince*. New York: Harcourt, Brace, Jovanovich, 1943.

Sendak, Maurice. *Where the Wild Things Are*. New York: Harper & Row, 1963.

Sewell, Anna. *Black Beauty*. New York: Charles Scribner's Sons, 1952. (First published in 1877.)

Singer, Isaac B. *The Fearsome Inn*, illus. Nonny Hogrogian. New York: Charles Scribner's Sons, 1967.

Sleator, William. *The House of Stairs*. New York: E.P. Dutton, 1970.

Snyder, Zilpha K. *Below the Root*. New York: Atheneum Publishers, 1975.

Sperry, Armstrong. *Call It Courage*. New York: Macmillan, 1940.

Steele, William O. *The No-Name Man of the Mountain*. New York: Harcourt, Brace, Jovanovich, 1964.

Stevenson, Robert Louis. *Treasure Island*. New York: Charles Scribner's Sons, 1894. (First published in *Young Folks* from October 1, 1881 to January 28, 1882, where James Henderson, Editor, changed the title from *The Sea Cook* to *Treasure Island*; first published in book form in 1884.)

There Was an Old Woman Who Swallowed a Fly, illus. Michael Kohn. Dandelion Pr., 1979.

Tolkien, J.R.R. *The Hobbit*. Boston: Houghton Mifflin, 1938.

Travers, Pamela. *Mary Poppins*. New York: Harcourt, Brace, Jovanovich, 1964.

Weik, Mary Hays. *The Jazz Man*. New York: Atheneum Publishers, 1966.

White, E.B. *Charlotte's Web*. New York: Harper & Row, 1952.

Williams, Margery. *The Velveteen Rabbit*. New York: Doubleday, 1958.

Yashima, Taro. *Crow Boy*. New York: Viking Pr., 1955.

Zindel, Paul. *The Pigman*. New York: Harper & Row, 1968.

Chapter Three
Critical Theory
and Story

All human beings are critics. We make critical judgments constantly, whether we are buying a tube of toothpaste, entering a voting booth, or reading a novel. In each of these instances, we are seeking out and demonstrating our appreciation of what we consider to be among the best of its kind. This is the essence of criticism. Of course, all criticism is not equally developed or equally sound, but it is the necessary "other side" of all human creation. It is only when we have more sensitive critics that the quality of our lives will be improved, whether this is reflected in our toothpaste, our government, or our literature.

There are several theories and types of literary criticism that have had varying degrees of influence over time. Each of them views a work of literature in a particular light, for as Henry James has described it, the house of fiction is one of many dissimilar windows through which many pairs of eyes watch the same show but see many different things.[1] A critic may move from window to window, but he cannot approach a work of literature without relating it either implicitly or explicitly to some framework of ideas or facts, and his choice of this framework will of necessity determine the nature of the results he can achieve. The important thing, however, is not the particular framework used but that the critic maintains a focus on the literary object as a work of art and does not lose sight of that fact in using it as evidence for some other kind of study. The practice of criticism, for the young child as well as the professional critic, is the cultivation of one's ability to seek out and to appreciate more fully a work of art.

It is unfortunate that the word "criticism" carries with it a negative connotation for many people when, at its best, it is a very positive process. Real criticism is a discriminating search after excellence. It directs attention to and illuminates the finest qualities of a work of art. It is, as John Dewey explains, not fault-finding but "judgment engaged in discriminating among values."[2] The aim of criticism is to increase a reader's capacity to receive and respond to works of literature, to sharpen perceptions by pointing to literary elements and implications that might not otherwise be seen, and, through these means, to enhance enjoyment. James states it beautifully when he writes "To criticize is to appreciate, to take intellectual possession, to establish a fine relation with the criticized thing and to make it one's own."[3] Criticism might be thought of as the intelligent approach to a work of art with its first duty to enjoyment rather than evaluation. It is precisely because criticism enhances both understanding and enjoyment that the development of critical abilities is essential for child readers and that adults who wish to assist them in this development must be knowledgeable enough to do so.

Criticism provides both a means of thinking about particular works and a probative tool to inquire into that which is not completely knowable. Many modern approaches to criticism take an eclectic view. They assume that there is no one way of looking at or bringing meaning to one's encounter with literature, but that the greater number of authentic perspectives we can bring to bear on a work, the more we will see in it and be able to communicate about it. Criticism is not a body of substantive knowledge but a mode of activity distinguished by the asking of appropriate questions. These questions are unanswerable in factual, scientific terms, but the asking of them encourages a particular means of ordering and creates new perspectives through which one may view a work of art.

Of course, all criticism is empirical in that it begins and ends in an appeal to the facts of the work itself. However, its statements are not to be judged by empirical verifiability out of context but by their function in the process of illuminating the qualities and forms of diverse encounters with a work of art. As R.S. Crane noted, a number of significant critical approaches may be used in understanding any work, "each of which exhibits the literary object in a different light, and each of which has its characteristic powers and limitations."[4] Each is a critical tool to serve as a basic premise or as a starting point for the development of a coherent set of categories and terms to be used in classifying, describing, and appraising particular works. Such criticism is intended to alter a reader's experience in the literary encounter by revealing more about the work and expanding the awareness of it rather than attempting to tell the reader what it "means." One does not approach the criticism of story with checklists of criteria but with informed ways of thinking about that story as literary form. In this sense, children are often better critics than adults because they are less likely to be concerned about how they "should" react to a work of art and therefore are more able to respond authentically.

Those who engage in literary criticism act to explain, to explicate, to interpret, or to evaluate works of art. The varieties of ways in which critics work have been systematized to reduce complexity and increase competence, but they cannot be reduced to a body of absolute propositions. A system cannot make judgments but rather provides a form in which judgments may be made. All critical systems remain provisional and subject to modification both over time and in the practice of creative individual critics. Nevertheless, there are, as there must be, some elements common to all criticism.

Kwant identifies the three basic elements of all critique as (1) the person exercising the critique, (2) the object criticized, and (3) the light in which that object is viewed.[5] The critic must have the freedom to respond to the object openly and authentically and the knowledge to compare the work as it is with an image of what it might be. The light in which the work is viewed is always in the form of comparison with some posited norm. This norm is not a social fact in the sociological sense, but an informed and sensitive image that transcends facts to impose critical standards on what is relative to what might be. Herbert Read refers to this as "positing dogmas." He says that "The positing of dogmas—that is to say, *a priori* principles, whether concerning life or literature— is the only considerable business of criticism."[6] Of course, it is the task of the critic to evaluate the norms posited to be sure they are appropriate ones, "for the final object of criticism is the criticism of dogma, and only those dogmas that express universal values will survive the assaults of the critical spirit."[7]

In order to deal meaningfully with all the diverse and highly individualistic forms of literary criticism, one must impose some theoretical framework upon the whole field of criticism that will artificially "hold still" what is a dynamic, relative, and ever-changing human concern. M.H. Abrams did this as clearly as any when he suggested that all critical theories could be discussed in terms of the various emphases and alignments that can occur between four coordinates of art criticism: the artist, the audience, the outside universe, and the work itself.[8] W.K. Wimsatt's theory is more concerned with relationships between subject and object in a work of art and treats the four coordinates or main types of literary theory in terms of the tensions between opposing pairs. He calls these the genetic, the affective, the contentual, and the formal. He places a fifth type of criticism, the tensional, in the center of the four coordinates and focuses his attention on the axis between contentual and formal types of literary analysis.[9]

Although historically differences among literary theories most often have been identified according to which of Abrams's four variables assumes primary signficance, most theories of criticism touch on all those variables and, to some degree, consider the relationships among them. All criticism must begin with an encounter with a literary object and then that object is related, either implicitly or explicitly, to some framework that focuses attention on certain aspects of its being and determines the kinds of results that can be achieved. The person of the critic as reader or audience is the one critical context that cannot totally be eliminated and is used, to some extent, by all critics.

Figure 3 represents the various aspects of the life of a literary work that may be taken into account in criticism. The work itself must be at the center of any critical activity; it is the starting point for the study and the basic referent to which it must return. The total circle of meaning in which the work exists contains many possible meanings from each of the four coordinates. Mimetic approaches to criticism are those that emphasize relationships to the world outside the work; pragmatic approaches emphasize the audience; expressive approaches emphasize the author; and objective or formal approaches emphasize literary knowledge. The lines connecting the four coordinates represent the tensions between and among the various sources of meaning that exist in any critical activity. Existentialist aesthetics is one approach to works of art that insists upon including references to author, audience, and literary knowledge. According to existential critics, an author creates oneself as the work is created but that work then exists independently as a presentation to, not a representation of, the world. That presentation comes to life only when it is read and an intersubjectivity comes into existence between author and audience. This shared meaning cannot be fully realized without an understanding of the structure of the work, that is, literary knowledge. Most forms of literary criticism throughout history have been more closely aligned with a particular one of the four coordinates. Attention to any of these variables may shed some light on the literary work, but just as often critics lose sight of the literary work and engage in a totally different study only tangentially related to the story as an aesthetic composition.

Although the following discussion will attempt to contain all literary criticism within one of the four basic approaches to a work of art, it must be pointed out that there are many other ways of categorizing critical activity. One might classify all critical studies as being either theoretical, practical, formal, or judicial. The same studies might also be divided into such categories as psychological, sociological, impressionistic, historical, ethical, moral, archetypal, mythic, biographical, existential, phenomenological, Marxist, Freudian, structuralist, textual, comparative, or genre criticism. These are variously called the types or schools of criticism and obviously are not always mutually exclusive. Many useful references about criticism★ will help the reader to sort these out, and those seriously concerned with literature ought

---

★For a useful introduction, see "Criticism" in Alex Preminger, ed., *Encyclopedia of Poetry and Poetics* (Princeton, N.J.: Princeton University Pr., 1965), pp. 158–174. A good beginning book on the topic is that of Sheldon Norman Grebstein, ed., *Perspectives in Contemporary Criticism: A Collection of Recent Essays by American, English, and European Literary Critics* (New York: Harper & Row, 1968). For one of the classic works on literary theory see René Wellek and Austin Warren, *Theory of Literature*, 3rd edition (New York: Harcourt, Brace, Jovanovich, 1977).

Figure 3: Aspects of a Literary Work

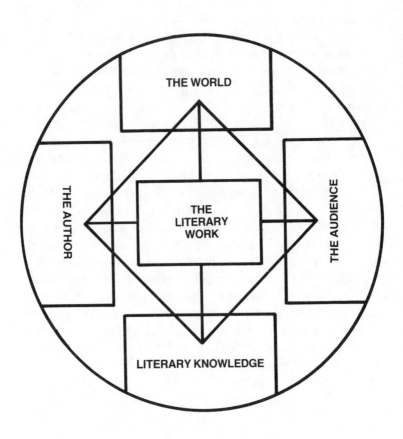

to understand some of the distinctions among them. However, for beginning critics and for translation to children, the four basic approaches outlined in this work seem to be an appropriate starting point. The reader is reminded, however, that those using other categories, types, or schools of criticism might well include a particular work cited here within a quite different classification and apply a very different label to the identical work.

Some of the earliest forms of literary criticism were based on mimetic theories, those that emphasized the relationship of the literary object to an outside universe. Although Plato was more concerned with man in society than with the unique qualities of works of art, his understanding of art as an imitation of an imitation was influential in the history of mimesis. Plato believed that an artist attempted to copy aspects of a world of sensations or appearances that was itself an imitation of an ideal world of pure and eternal form. It is interesting to note that poets were unwelcome in Plato's *Republic* because they would lead people to turn away from the "just society" and become attached to the world of sensation.[10] Aristotle's *Poetics* did not separate reality into Plato's two worlds but conceived of a ladder of being on which man stood between unformed matter and pure form. Aristotle saw the artist as an efficient cause, making it possible for readers to see through the world to the ultimate and art as the imitation not of things but of the forms of things, that which is the essential or preexistent form within each being or action.[11]

Variations of the mimetic theory of literary criticism have persisted from the time of Plato to the present day. Most often mimesis has been thought of as a mirror held up to objects of the sensible world. This view was very influential with the neo-classicists in eighteenth century England who were primarily concerned with art as an imitation of nature. In the following century, the romantic poet Shelley took a monistic view of reality in *A Defense of Poetry* and stated that all literature imitates the same basic forms in which value resides and thus provides models for all human activities and products.[12] The impressionists or post-romantics returned to the more common mimetic view of art as the imitation of objects of the sensible world. In this case, however, that imitation was not so much of a sensible reality "held still" but of a world in flux. The neo-humanists of the twentieth century referred back to the work of Plato and used that as the basis for a moral approach to literature in which the work of literature is itself a very direct criticism of life.

Both historical and sociological types of literary criticism are based, to some degree, on mimetic theories of literature. Historical critics maintain that the full meaning of literature is yielded only in the original context of that work. This form of criticism tries to re-create the time and place of a work's composition, the larger social setting in which it came to be, and its reception by the people of its own time. It deals more with historical significance than with intrinsic worth. Beyond that, historical criticism attempts to generalize from all such information an account of the literary past and to sort out meaningful patterns and relationships over time.

Sociological criticism begins with the premise that literature is a social phenomenon, an expression of the times formed and conditioned by social, economic, and political views. The French historian Hippolyte Taine is credited with the beginnings of a fully developed sociological criticism in his *History of English Literature*.[13] Here he identified the three factors that come together to create a work of art: (1) the race, (2) the milieu or the totality of social attitudes and conditions at a given time, and (3) the moment. Primary attention has been given in sociological criticism to the milieu, with interest in the other two moving toward anthropology on the one hand and psychology or biography on the other hand. Often sociological criticism moves from the strictly descriptive or interpretive to a kind of moral judgment of the society reflected rather than remaining with the intrinsic merit of the work of literature in itself.

Pragmatic theories of literary criticism shift the emphasis from the nature of the world to the nature of man and treat literature as if it were, at least in part, a means to some instructional end. Horace, who in his *Ars Poetica* stated that pleasure is the ultimate end of literature but that serious readers will not be pleased by works without some moral matter,[14] was one of the most influential of Western pragmatic critics. Philip Sidney said that the aim of literature was "to teach and to delight,"[15] and Dr. Johnson referred to the end of poetry as "to instruct by pleasing."[16] As in any school of criticism, there are many and wide divergences, but pragmatists are similar in their acknowledgement of a work of art as a made object deliberately designed to achieve predetermined ends. The craftsmanship of the aesthetic form is very important in this theory, and some literary pragmatists have attempted to reduce the creative act to a set of prescriptions or rules of craftsmanship. Divergences from actuality or fact, which in mimetic theories were explained as imitations of ideal forms, in pragmatic theories are based on moral requirements made visible through a selected and heightened reality.

Too much emphasis on a pragmatic view of literature often leads to what Wimsatt and Beardsley have called the "affective fallacy" of literary criticism in which a critic is more concerned with the psychological effects on the reader than with the work itself.[17] Often ideas of moral discipline intervene, and there is little distinction made between the literature itself and its results. Another type of criticism related to this theory is impressionistic criticism, which concentrates on the direct insights or impressions of the individual reader. This type of criticism is not held in high esteem in literary circles today because it has often resulted more in autobiography of the reader rather than insight into a work of art.

If mimetic theorists see literature as a mirror held up to

life and pragmatic theorists see it as the artistic shaping of inherent powers to achieve complex ends, expressive theorists see a literary work primarily as a reflection of its author. The mirror that was held up to the world or to the moral nature of man is now held up to a particular author, and that author's personal sincerity becomes a cardinal virtue. In his *Preface*, Wordsworth speaks of literature as the "spontaneous overflow of powerful feelings" but goes on to explain that the success of such spontaneous composition depends upon prior thought and practice.[18] The source of literature is no longer something in the outside world but in the person of the author, and the subject matter becomes the author's own feelings. From the pragmatic value of affecting an audience, literature moves to John Stuart Mill's definition of poetry as "feeling confessing itself in moments of solitude."[19] Although Mill thought that any attempt to make an impression on a reader in a sense invalidates literature, most expressive theorists would agree that art as a "dynamic form of feeling"[20] must also communicate.

Two well-known writers who stressed the emotional rather than the rational use of language and felt that literature must emphasize such language over form, character, or plot were Tolstoy and I.A. Richards. The primary principle of Tolstoy's "infection theory" of art is that literature is basically emotional communication.[21] I.A. Richards in his *Principles of Literary Criticism* and in his work with C.K. Ogden[22] proposed an emotive theory of literature in which the work has no "meaning" or proposition, only expression.

Several particular types of criticism refer back to expressive theories, all of which might be included under what Wimsatt and Beardsley have called the "intentional fallacy" of literary criticism.[23] Psychological and biographical criticism are forms of this and frequently tend to confuse the work itself with its origins. The most common use of these forms traces the psychological or biographical sources of a work of literature in an attempt to determine what the author meant rather than looking for meaning in the work itself.

If one considers story to be primarily the personal expression of a particular author, then the work itself would be revealing of that author's biography, or, conversely, that biography would be of definite value in interpreting the story. The psychological study of literature may, in one form, be an extension of literary biography as it attempts a psychological analysis of the author. A similar but more encompassing study attempts to analyze the creative process itself and the various ways in which authors compose. (On the other hand, psychology has been used to study the effects of literature on its audience— which falls within the realm of pragmatic studies.) A psychological approach focusing more on the literature but still not of purely literary value is that of the behavioral analysis of characters and relationships within story to determine their psychological soundness. A knowledge of or a grounding in psychology in studying these aspects of story may make the fiction more readily believable, but in the final anaylsis the tests of story must be literary, not psychological, soundness and authenticity.

Objective or formal theories of literature emphasize the belief that art does not imitate the sensible world but creates its own world, an entity subject to its own internal requirements of unity, variety, and originality. Objective theories of literature have dominated criticism during much of this century, although specific types of criticism or ways of conceiving the identity and the composition of literary objects have varied greatly. The most commonly accepted view, however, is that literature is itself a presented universe of discourse rather than a representation of any object, person, or event in the empirical universe. The objective theory of the New Critics (among them J.C. Ransom, Allen Tate, Cleanth

Brooks, R.P. Warren, R.P. Blackmur, Kenneth Burke, Yvor Winters) concentrates on a complex apparatus for the explication of isolated literary works. Within the organic unity of a work, these critics studied such elements as semantics, imagery, meter, and symbol in dealing with the tone, texture, and tensions of literature. The particular type of criticism most closely allied with the objective theory is textual criticism. This theory treats the work of literature almost as documentary evidence, clarifying and recording all the information about the internal composition needed to detect patterns, decipher semantic illusions, or comprehend symbols.

René Wellek and Austin Warren, in their discussion of intrinsic studies of literature, assert that the only sensible starting point for work in literary scholarship is the interpretation and analysis of the work of literature itself. The work itself, however, is often a very elusive item. It is much easier to pinpoint and study the life of an author, the social environment, or the process of literary creation than it is to focus on the compositional work itself.

> It is neither real (physical, like a statue) nor mental (psychological, like the experience of light or pain) nor ideal (like a triangle). It is a system of norms of ideal concepts which are intersubjective. They must be assumed to exist in collective ideology, changing with it, accessible only through individual mental experiences, based on the sound–structure of its sentences.[24]

The term "norms" is used here for implicit norms extracted from many experiences of story that together make up the story as a whole. Each story, as a structure of norms, is realized only partially in an individual's reading of it. Just as we know no object in our world completely because we always look on it from our own peculiar perspective but nonetheless identify it through the recognition of some normative structures, so we identify story. It is possible to proceed from there to recognizing and classifying stories according to the types of norms they embody and thus to identify certain genres, archetypes, or even whole theories of literature.[25]

Frye is one critic who has attempted to delineate the structural principles of literature in what he assumes to be the total coherence of an "anatomy" or unity of criticism. His archetypal criticism, in which he sees recurring literary images as means of suggesting an identity between human beings and the world outside, points to the mythical tale of the loss and recovery of human identity as the "one story" of literature.[26] Frye believes that there are two basic patterns or structures of literary images, the cyclical and the dialectic. In other words, all the traditional or archetypal images of story can be categorized according to a cyclical pattern corresponding to the seasons of the year, the stages of human life, or what Frye calls the four generic plots or basic structure of story: romance, tragedy, irony/satire, and comedy. These images can also be categorized according to a dialectical structure that demonstrates the struggle between opposites, between innocence and experience or between what people desire and what they fear. Although he is known as a leader of the archetypal school of literary criticism, Frye insists that no critical system is either correct or incorrect but that all are complementary. Context, rather than meaning, is the organizing principle of his critical theory, with each work of literature viewed in light of three basic contexts: (1) mythos (narrative or verbal imitation of action), (2) ethos (characterization), and (3) dianoia (meaning or verbal imitation of thought). Frye is particularly concerned with the tension between archetypal and ethical criticism, which he equates, to some extent, with the tension between the freedom of the individual imagination and the concern for society.

Frye's work is of special interest to those who work with children and literature for several reasons. First, he is concerned with the unity of all literature and sees children's literature as a part of that whole. Second, as an educator, he is concerned with the imagination as the constructive power of the mind and with literature as the center and source of all verbal knowledge. Third, he has offered his own suggestions regarding the literary education of children and has encouraged others to relate his theories to the study and teaching of children's literature.[27] In short, he has exhibited a respect for both children and their literature. Frye's theory of literature, for example, is clearly an archetypal one, but it might justifiably be called theoretical criticism as well because Frye refers to general principles that hold true for all literature. In attempting to fit the work of Frye and other archetypal critics into one of the four basic approaches to criticism used here, I have chosen to include it under objective criticism because these critics do take an intrinsic approach, that is, they consider the world of literature to have a life and structure of its own separate from the other three, or extrinsic, approaches. On the other hand, it has been thought that Frye's work may, in some way, be closer to the mimetic because the archetypes that he insists deal only with literary ideas seem to correspond with the anthropological and psychological studies of scholars such as Campbell[28] and Jung[29] and therefore reflect that which already exists in the world of human beings. I believe this to be a mute question. If we truly value the work of any critic or critical theory, we ought to spend less time and effort fitting that person or work into a particular classification and applying an appropriate label and more on using the work as a means of insight and illumination into the literary objects that should be the basic focus of our attention. Critical categories are of value only as long as they assist us in rendering a particular work more useful in that process of insight and illumination.

Much of what passes for literary criticism in the popular press is not criticism at all but some other kind of judgment. The primary data of criticism are the immediate felt responses to a work of art, but judgments of aesthetic value based only on a personal encounter are reflections of an individual's intuitive reaction to known works, not the knowledgeable act of criticism itself. Such responses are at what the phenomenologists such as Remy C. Kwant would call the stage of pre-predictive critique or a kind of nonspoken, tacit knowledge of the work.[30] Beyond that, one moves to a predictive or spoken level of judgment in which verbal expression helps the critic focus on the causes of his immediate, nonspoken response. At this stage, he attempts to communicate his insights and, in some instances, to make value judgments regarding the particular work of literature. Although many critics do acknowledge that making value judgments is an important aspect of their work, Frye is one who has said that value judgments have no place in the work of criticism.

Both synthesis and analysis are fundamental activities of the mind that are present in all critical discourse. The character of the critic's synthesis determines, to some extent, the nature of his analysis; and that analysis, because it is systematic, implies a corresponding impulse toward synthesis. Frye has said that the first act of criticism is one of identification, that is, to see a work of literature in its literary context but as a unique individual of a class.[31] In order to identify a work, it is necessary to begin with a concept of unity both within the work itself and in the total structure of literature. The critic does not look for external values but for integrity and consistency within the verbal structure of literature. He asks, "Is it significantly formed as a compositional whole so that it is both believable and feelingful for the reader?"

Criticism is often thought of in terms of the resolution of various literary tensions. A critic looks for both simplicity and complexity within aesthetic unity, for universality and novelty in expressive originality, and for control of and denial of the medium of language in the execution of craftsmanship. These terms cannot be defined absolutely nor these tensions really resolved, for they do not represent ideas or states of affairs that are replicable or verifiable. Rather they express an attitude and make assertions that, while not necessarily verifiable, do affect people in certain ways. Criticism always exists in its own time and is subject to the interpretations of that time in its resolution of literary tensions. It cannot, therefore, achieve the perfect balance of a man standing on a tightrope with time suspended but rather the living balance of a man who is right now moving across that tightrope. Only as he moves in hazard on that line between his personal judgment and abstract literary knowledge can the critic achieve the balance that passes for safety in the act of criticism.

Aesthetic unity, the compositional development of the work as a whole, is achieved through the balance and harmony of a variety of contrasts and complexities in content and form so arranged that the continuity of the whole appears to be simple, lean, and effortless. The originality of literature results from the merger in form of unique and peculiar ideas and events that, at the same time, give the reader a sense of universality, of being in and of humankind.

Fine craftsmanship, or control over the medium of language and finesse in the execution of literary design, allows a writer to actualize in the product the promise of the ideas and form. Once all these are achieved, the critic seeks authenticity, validity, and beauty in the work of literature. Authenticity is characterized by an internal, believable world view, one that does not manipulate life but exists honestly in succeeding levels of depth of meaning. Validity is the agreement between what a work appears to be and what it is, an entity that proposes and sustains its own logic and is true to its own beliefs and values. The final criteria of literary excellence is beauty, not external beauty or "prettiness," but the containment of feeling in appropriate form, the compositional complementation of spirit, idea, and language.

In summary, criticism looks sensitively to the aesthetic whole without slighting the parts and their relationships. It is a judgment of the rational imagination that seeks to understand a work by responding to literary devices that reinforce each other and direct attention in appropriate channels to a search for excellence. Each reader becomes a critic, developing sensitivity to the perception of literary form. The reader/critic looks to specifics not for themselves but as a way of understanding how that work as a whole shapes experience. Literary criticism requires both the personal shock of recognition and more disciplined means of looking at ways literary conventions and associations are used to create that unique and unified aesthetic whole. As Frye says, "The attempt of genuine criticism is to bring literature to 'life' by annihilating stock responses, which, of course, are always value judgments and regularly confuse literature with life."[32] The child who takes joy from reading will gradually but continually grow in that sensitivity to and perception of literary forms that is the basis of criticism. At the same time, adults who have a knowledge of critical theories can help children increase both their appreciation and understanding by the appropriate introduction of critical ideas in their shared discussions of story. This is not an imposition of adult theories or language on children, but a recognition of the developing critical abilities of those who value the unique and authentic responses to story forms as a means of making sense of both literature and their own lives.

Footnotes

1. Henry James, *The Art of the Novel: Critical Prefaces* (New York: Charles Scribner's Sons, 1934), p. 46.

2. John Dewey, *Construction and Criticism* (New York: Columbia University Pr., 1930), p. 12.

3. Henry James, *The Art of the Novel: Critical Prefaces*, p. 155.

4. R.S. Crane, *Critics and Criticism: Essays in Method*, abridged edition (Chicago: University of Chicago Pr., 1957), p. iv.

5. Remy C. Kwant, *Critique: Its Nature and Function* (Pittsburgh, Penn.: Duquesne University Pr., 1967).

6. Herbert Read, *Poetry and Experience* (London: Vision Press Limited, 1967), pp. 24–25.

7. Ibid., p. 22.

8. M.H. Abrams, *The Mirror and the Lamp: Romantic Theory and Critical Tradition* (New York: W.W. Norton, 1953).

9. W.K. Wimsatt, *Hateful Contraries: Studies in Literature and Criticism* (Lexington, Ky.: University of Kentucky Pr., 1965), pp. 35–40.

10. Plato, *The Republic*, repr. of 1894 edition, ed. B. Jowett and Lewis Campell, The Philosophy of Plato and Aristotle Series (New York: Arno Pr., 1972).

11. Aristotle, *Poetics*, trans. by S.H. Butcher and intro. by Francis Fergusson (New York: Hill and Wang, 1961).

12. Percy Bysshe Shelley, *A Defense of Poetry & A Letter to Lord Ellenborough*, repr. of 1948 edition (Folcroft, Penn.: Folcroft Library Editions, 1973).

13. Hippolyte A. Taine, *History of English Literature*, 2 vols., repr. of 1871 edition, trans. H. Van Laun (Philadelphia: Richard West Pr., 1973).

14. Horace, *The Poetic Art: A Translation of Horace's Ars Poetica*, trans. C.H. Sisson (England: Carcanet New Pr., 1979).

15. Philip Sidney, *The Defense of Poesie*, repr. of 1890 edition, ed. Albert S. Cook (Philadelphia: Richard West Pr.).

16. Samuel Johnson, *Mr. Johnson's Preface to His Edition of Shakespeare's Plays*, repr. of 1765 edition (Elmsford, N.Y.: British Book Center, 1974).

17. William K. Wimsatt, Jr. and Monroe C. Beardsley, "The Intentional Fallacy," *Sewanee Review* 54 (Summer 1946): 468–88, repr. *The Verbal Icon* (Lexington, Ky.: University of Kentucky Pr., 1954).

18. William Wordsworth, *Preface to Lyrical Ballads*, ed. W.J. Owen (Westport, Conn.: Greenwood Pr., 1957).

19. John Stuart Mill, "Thoughts on Poetry and Its Varieties," in Emmanuel Davis Jones, ed., *English Critical Essays—Nineteenth Century* (London: Oxford University Pr., 1916), pp. 398–429.

20. Susanne K. Langer, *Problems of Art* (New York: Charles Scribner's Sons, 1957).

21. Leo N. Tolstoy, *What Is Art?*, trans. Aylmer Maude (New York: Bobbs-Merrill, 1953).

22. C.K. Ogden and I.A. Richards, *The Meaning of Meaning* (New York: Harcourt, Brace, 1923).

23. W.K. Wimsatt, "The Affective Fallacy," *Sewanee Review* 54 (Winter 1949), reprinted in *The Verbal Icon: Studies in the Meaning of Poetry*, pp. 3–18.

24. René Welleck and Austin Warren, *Theory of Literature*, 3rd edition (New York: Harcourt, Brace, Jovanovich, 1977), p. 156.

25. Ibid., p. 156.

26. This theme runs through all of Frye's work. For the fullest treatment, see Northrop Frye, *Anatomy of Criticism* (Princeton, N.J.: Princeton University Pr., 1957).

27. Northrop Frye, *On Teaching Literature* (New York: Harcourt, Brace, Jovanovich, 1972).

28. Joseph Campbell, *The Hero with a Thousand Faces*, 2nd edition, Bollingen Series XVII (Princeton, N.J.: Princeton University Pr., 1968).

29. Carl Jung, *Man and His Symbols* (New York: Doubleday, 1964).

30. Remy C. Kwant, *Critique: Its Nature and Function*, pp. 40–67.

31. Northrop Frye, "Literary Criticism," in *The Aims and Methods of Scholarship in Modern Language and Literature*, 2nd edition, ed. James Thorpe (New York: Modern Language Association of America, 1970), p. 78.

32. Northrop Frye, *The Stubborn Structure: Essays on Criticism and Society* (Ithaca, N.Y.: Cornell University Pr., 1970), p. 72.

Chapter Four
Illustration and Book Design

Children live in a highly visual world. They are often unable to symbolize from what they hear because even simple words are still abstract to the very young. Children use objects or their visual representations to explore the physical environment and make sense of the world. One of the best ways to extend a young child's visual experience beyond her immediate environment and the flickering images of the small screen is to provide a variety of picture story books for her enjoyment. Such books not only offer multiple perspectives on the world but they also give the child the advantages of exercising some selectivity among them and of holding the image still long enough to absorb, enjoy, or just wonder over it.

Such provision is especially important when one considers the speed of television images or of the world from the child's perspective as she is carried, wheeled, or driven through it. As a child engages herself with a book and moves through and with it at her own pace, she can recognize something of herself in those pages, be in a position of power over this activity in her world and, at the same time, reach out to consider another's interpretation or world view. In these ways, she moves toward identity, control, and connection in her own world and with the world of others.

Most adults, when they think of children's books, think first of the elaborately and very beautifully illustrated picture story books for young children. A large number of books for children do fit into this category, but it is necessary to distinguish between these works and other types of illustrated books for children. This chapter includes discussions of the art work in picture books, illustrated books, mood books, and concept books as well as that in the picture story book.

Picture books are those in which illustrations stand alone, without words, or are at least the primary means of conveying content in the work. William Anderson and Patrick Groff refer to such works as "nonliterary" extensions of television that act to limit a child's interest in linguistic forms.[1] It is equally possible, however, that these books may introduce a child to the world of print and the idea of a sequential ordering of images and ideas within the context of the printed page. Through picture books, also, a child may learn to value the intimacy of the personal experience with books that allows him to return to them at any time he chooses and enjoy them at his own pace.[2]

Some of the reading series developed for classroom instruction now begin with visual stories in book format so that the beginning reader can know the success of "reading" and enjoying and understanding a whole story on his own before he learns to decode the written word. Many of these picture book texts, such as Mercer Mayer's *Walk, Robot, Walk,* are created by well-known and respected children's illustrators and might well be successful trade books if they were published for that market. In most of these books, the visual presentation of the story is accomplished with fairly clear and simple illustrations that do not require a major effort on the part of the child to follow and/or to interpret. On the other hand, there are picture books in these series that seem to build on the sophisticated viewing skills of children who grow up with comic books and television; these books rely on rather complex images that are more demanding to follow and less obvious to interpret. *In a Sofa*, a wordless fanciful story in comic strip frames of various sizes and degrees of complexity, is intended for the pre-literate child. The advantage of such books in a basic reading program is that they provide practice in left-to-right, top-to-bottom orientation in following a story line while, unlike many worded texts, respecting children's intellectual curiosity and re-creative abilities. In this way, these wordless reading texts demonstrate that there is something of interest and value to be found in books; they encourage children to put in the effort for that very difficult process of learning to decode those strange symbols on the page that represent the words they hear and use in the business of living.

Some of the most interesting of recent picture books for the trade market are informational books that, for example, portray the life cycle of a particular species of plant or animal through pictures. One must examine these books very carefully to be certain that the illustrations are clear and precise enough to convey the information accurately. It appears that, with at least some of these books, the "reader" must already have a certain amount of information before understanding the visual explanations. For instance, *The Tadpole and the Frog*, which the publisher recommends for nursery school through second grade, may not be very informative to the youngster who interprets the eggs and tadpole embryo as "bubbles" in the water. Many of these informational books are beautifully done and contribute to a child's understanding, but we cannot assume that the translation from the representation (often of something that cannot be seen by the human eye) to conceptual knowledge is either complete or accurate.

Although most picture books obviously are intended, in size, format, and content, for young children, there are a few full-length wordless picture books for older children. *The Wonder Ring: A Fantasy in Silhouettes* relies on the familiarity and the appeal of elements of the traditional folk and fairy tales as well as very delicate and detailed silhouettes to entice young readers to enter this story world. Lynd Ward's *The Silver Pony* is a modern fanciful work that requires a more mature "reader" to follow its story line and to comprehend its meaning. Although this book was well noted by adults in the children's book field, it never caught on with children, perhaps because older children find it as difficult to follow a sustained story line only in pictures as young children do to follow one only in words.

Illustrated books are those in which the pictures are not really an integral and necessary portion of the basic meaning of the work but rather serve as an extension or an illumination of certain aspects or details of the text. Books for older children often have such illustrations at the beginning of each chapter as much to break up the visual monotony of the printed page as to highlight certain characters, ideas, or events in the language of the work. Other books have illustrations that stand as paintings to set a mood. One may occasionally even find children's books that are decorated rather than illustrated, that is, those in which whatever pictorial work is included does not necessarily either illustrate or illuminate the text but rather serves a purely decorative purpose. Maurice Sendak's art for Randall Jarrall's *The Animal Family* is decorative rather than illustrative because, as the artist has said, the words convey the images so well that illustration is unnecessary and might even be distracting.[3] Book illustration or decoration may at times encourage the reader to slow down or pause to savor the language or the experience of the work and to reflect on its meaning. As Walter Crane said in his classic work on this topic:

> In a journey through a book it is pleasant to reach the oasis of a picture or an ornament, to sit awhile under the palms, to let our thoughts unburdened stray, to drink of other intellectual waters, and to see the ideas we have been pursuing, perchance, reflected in them.[4]

Picture story books may be thought of as "twice-told tales" in that the stories they contain are communicated through both words and pictures and can be comprehended in either their visual or their verbal forms. The young child can "read" the illustrations and understand the story either on her own or as an adult reads the words aloud. The illustrations in picture story books are an integral part of the action of the story, a form of pictorial literature that complements, but is not totally limited by, the narrative elements of the language of story. In these books, illustrations are intended not to stand alone as single works of art but to contribute to the sequence and the mood that pushes the story ahead and keeps the reader moving with it. There are, however, some picture story books in which the story is not told separately in language and in picture but in the interaction between the two on the page. *Nothing Ever Happens on My Block* makes sense as story only in the contrast between the words and the illustrations. *Conrad's Castle* might be understood pictorially, but the words, almost nonsensical on their own, add to the understanding and the interpretation of the pictorial narrative.

With picture story books, the child reader ordinarily identifies with the main character, and the illustrations help her to enter into the story and feel what it must be like for that character to be coping with the situation there. However, there are additional, non-story books for young children in which text and illustration contribute almost equally to conveying the message. Mood books are plotless narratives in which the primary purpose is the creation of a mood rather than the telling of a story. In such books, the child reader does not identify with character but rather "becomes" a main character, reflecting upon how it might feel if she were herself experiencing the events of the text. Alvin Tresselt's *Hide and Seek Fog* is much more concerned with the effect of fog on various people (mood) than with either an individual character (story) or with the fog itself (information). Through narration so smoothly written that it has the feel of being told, and through strong appeals to sensory perceptions, one knows what it is to be "blue-lipped and shivering" on the sand that was "suddenly cold and sticky," to be listening to "the mournful lost voices of the foghorns calling across the empty grayness of the bay."[5] However, it is Roger Duvoisin's shadowy shapes almost hidden on the blue-grey pages that really convey to the reader the sensation of being in the fog. Sendak's illustrations for *The Moon Jumpers* also convey what it must feel like to be in a particular situation or setting, in this case, the mysterious enchantment of children dancing and playing in the moonlight of a summer night. *Rain Makes Applesauce* creates quite a different mood with its intricate and fanciful details in illustrations that perfectly complement the playfulness and just plain "silly talk" of the text.

Concept books for young children, even more than mood books, are dependent on illustration as well as text. Many of these books introduce basic concepts such as sizes, shapes, or colors by simply labelling a series of visual representations of that concept. Others employ narration, often rhymed, or even simple plot, to reinforce the concept. What ties all of these together as concept books is the emphasis on specific facts or events as elements of an abstract idea. Since one cannot experience abstract concepts, these books select phenomena from the child's world and point to a specific series of concrete events from which young children are expected to extract the abstract quality that these items have in common. These concrete events must be interesting to a child, but they should not be so dramatic that they distract attention from the abstraction, and they should encourage the child reader to go on beyond the book in identifying other examples that keep the concept growing in her mind.

Let us consider three books that, each in its own way, are intended to help children identify the various colors (concepts) or understand the idea of color itself (a generalization). *Colors* by Jan Piénkowski uses simple but very boldly colored illustrations to demonstrate to the young child what is meant by "red," "yellow," "blue," etc. The word "red" is lettered in black on a totally red page opposite a large red flower on a clear yellow background. The problem with this particular illustration is that there is a great deal of orange in the red, and it is difficult to distinguish between the two colors—which may be misleading to young viewers. *The Strawberry Book of Colors* features Jack, Max, and Axle, housepainters who represent the primary colors, and who, through their misadventures, demonstrate how these colors are combined to make other colors. *Color Seems* deals with much more complex abstractions on the nature of color, the way human beings perceive color and are influenced by it. The abstract presentation of color theory in the illustrations of this book encourages readers to think about their own understanding of and responses to color.

In all of these books for young children, the placement of illustrations in relation to the text is critical. If pictures are to help move the story along, create a mood, or convey an abstract concept, they must neither get ahead of nor fall behind what is conveyed in language. Illustrations placed on any page other than that containing the corresponding details of the text are disruptive of the literary experience, causing children to turn pages forward or backward in an attempt to match the visual and the verbal content of the composition. The illustrations of all these picture story, mood, or concept books must also be appealing enough not only to attract and hold the attention of young readers and the adults who select their books but also interesting enough to satisfy and reentertain those youngsters who return to them again and again.

In some instances this lasting appeal can be ascribed to the amount of detail in an illustration, which allows one to go back and find something new in each of many subsequent viewings. There are also those books with very simple line drawings, such as *Curious George*, that adults are likely to dismiss with a glance but that young readers pore over to discover the subtle changes in the line of George's mouth or an item in the background that they had not noticed before. Such specific detail in children's book illustration must be matched precisely to the details of the text because young listeners frequently check such precision while listening to stories read aloud. This practice is logical when one remembers that children see the world close-up and in detail. They are eager to explore, and they demand explanations of all that they see, whether in life or in literature.

Children do not see the world, however, from the same perspective as we adults. This difference has to do with their physical stature as well as with their freshness of vision. A favorite story illustrating this point is that of the nursery school class who visited a city fire station. The teacher had carefully prepared these four- and five-year-olds for their visit by telling them about firefighting and by describing in detail the work of the firefighters and the various tools of the trade. When they left for their trip, the children were given simple cameras to record what they saw. As the teacher pointed out the broad view of things, the boys and girls took pictures of tire treads, hub caps, running boards, and hose nozzles. What the teacher had not accounted for was the fact that fire stations are not the most spacious buildings, and those visitors less than four feet high could not get far enough away from the engines to see them whole and entire. Their size was giving them a very fragmented view of what the teacher and the firefighters were explaining to them.

It is interesting to note that, although children often do have such a fragmented view of the world, most studies of their preferences in illustration have concluded that they are distressed by pictures that portray only partial images of objects or people. Perhaps children want to be able to rely on the pictures in their books to put the pieces together and to reveal the larger picture in a way that is sometimes denied to them in life. At the same time they are pleased to recognize the details that they ordinarily focus on and find so fascinating. A recent article detailing the experiences of a particular child and her parents reinforces the notion that children do indeed use book illustrations to make sense of how the partial images of the child-sized world come together to reveal whole objects.[6] In this instance, the parents were available to explain to their daughter that the rest of the object was still attached but "just off the page," but the child's need for continual confirmation of this idea seems to support the conclusions of the previous studies.

Detail in children's book illustration may be of many kinds and serve many purposes. It may be primarily decorative, as in *Rain Makes Applesauce* or in Beni Montresor's *May I Bring a Friend?* However, *Rain Makes Applesauce* also has a realistic subplot in small pictures on the lower right-hand corner of the pages that show the whole process from the planting of the apple seeds to the making of applesauce. Some of the most intriguing uses of subplots are seen in Joseph Wright's illustrations for Frank Muir's *What-a-Mess* books, in which all sorts of fanciful creatures have their own adventures in and around the main action of the stories. Mercer Mayer's *Little Monster's Mother Goose* employs a similar technique to reveal an ongoing search for someone named Alice among the numerous dialogue balloons that contain side comments on the particular rhyme on the page. At the end of the book, Alice appears from Wonderland to share in a final tea party.

Illustrative detail may also be used to reinforce a concept, as in *Ed Emberley's ABC*, which has a key at the back to identify all the items pictured on the page representing each letter of the alphabet. In addition, there are characters on each double-page spread who humorously and very effectively demonstrate the proper formation of the letters for those just learning to print.

Marguerite de Angeli's illustrations for her stories of Quaker and Pennsylvania Dutch children add dimension both to the settings and to the life styles of her characters. In some illustrations, elaborate details do not confirm or add to what already exists in words but rather extend our perceptions of a work by placing it in an altogether new context. Nancy Ekholm Burkert's *Snow White* is one of the best examples of this kind, with its attention to costumes and decorative arts reflective of the Flemish painters of the fifteenth and sixteenth centuries.

Realism and attention to detail may not always be key considerations for young readers in their enjoyment of picture story books, but even those who were not obviously aware of the costumes in *The Tailor of Gloucester* will probably delight in the Victoria & Albert Museum's exhibit of the costumes and the sketches Beatrix Potter made of them in preparation for the telling of this story. It is such attention to detail in illustration, whether viewers are consciously aware of it or not, that makes pictures come alive on the page and satisfies successive generations of children.

The saturation of detail as seen in the books of Peter Spier or Steven Kellogg adds depth to their work and provides ample fare for visual enjoyment as youngsters return to their pages again and again. The minute and often humorous detail of the settings in their work may be realistically informative, as in Spier's *The Erie Canal*, or fancifully engaging, as with Kellogg's use of signs and labels in *The Island of the Skog*.

The comic-strip format in children's books also is frequently filled with detail, both visually and verbally. Raymond Briggs, whose comic-strip illustrations for the Father Christmas books are well-known to readers, has apparently almost reached the limits of saturation in his *Fungus the Boogeyman*, a picture story book so filled with visual and verbal puns that it took this adult over an hour to decipher them. Very young readers may experience difficulty coping with all the details of this work, but slightly older children are delighted by its playfully irreverent treatment of some of the conventions imposed upon them by adults. At the same time, Briggs provides ample fare to satisfy an adult's sense of humor with visual and verbal references not necessarily obvious to children.

The inclusion of material for adults is not an uncommon practice in books for children; their adult creators add elements unknown to most children, either for their own satisfaction or to catch the eye of the adults who select these books and share them with children. The Laurel and Hardy caricatures in Sendak's *In the Night Kitchen* are an example of such use of detail; although not necessarily recognized by children, they give an added dimension to this book for adults.

An interesting balance between very simplified cartoon-like drawings and those with very intricate detail is found in Isobel Harris's *Little Boy Brown*, a somewhat dated but still very appealing picture story book. In this story, told in the first person by a four-year-old, François combines simple, childlike drawings of people and events with the elaborate detail of a cross section of a city apartment house and its occupants. Even these very complex illustrations, which could not possibly be executed by a young child, retain many aspects of a child's vision of the world.

Ordinarily children seem to resent adult attempts to imitate the simplicity and the rather crude perspectives of their drawings, perhaps because they are often dissatisfied with their own attempts to capture on paper what they perceive of the world. On the other hand, children are at least as dismissive of adult versions of the world of childhood that might be called "sweet" or "cute," probably the two most damning descriptors from the point of view of most children.

What is critical in the evaluation of children's book illustration is neither style nor medium nor is it even the inherent excellence of the work as art. Rather it is the way in which illustration supports and enhances the totality of *the book* as a work of art. A beautiful painting that distracts from the text in a book may be good art but it is poor illustration. On the other hand, rather simple, even rough, pictures may so match and complement both the sense and the spirit of the written word that they can only be described as excellent illustrations, even if they would not be accepted as fine art in and of themselves.

A problem may arise in the evaluation of illustration, just as it does in the evaluation of the written word, when one mixes sociological concerns with literary or aesthetic concerns. Those who would do away with *The Five Chinese Brothers* because both its text and illustrations perpetuate the stereotype supposedly held by many Americans that "all Chinese look alike" seem to me to be denying the very essence of all of folk literature and its modern counterparts. The stylized cartoonlike drawings used to illustrate this and many other folk tales are intended to reflect the commonality of human foibles as seen in the activities or the quest of particular characters in a specific setting.* The folklore of a nation or group of people points to its foolish as well as its heroic nature, and reminds us that all men and women are both foolish and heroic in turn.

It is true that if there is only a single book, or a very few, available about a culture or group of people, that work may exert undue influence on children's perceptions of those people. Nonetheless, the remedy is not to remove a book such as *The Five Chinese Brothers* but to increase the availability of other

---

* A version of this tale is found in the recently published book by Cheng Hou-tien, *Six Chinese Brothers: An Ancient Tale* (New York: Holt, 1979). Although this book is technically delightful, with scissor cut illustrations, the tale seems diminished because its believability depends upon the "look-alike" qualities of the characters, which are no longer represented in these illustrations.

types of stories dealing with the Chinese people. It may also be true that few people other than those in a particular social or cultural group can fully appreciate stories indigenous to that group, but to deny this literature to others denies the power of literature to help readers extend their own life experiences and become aware of the very real connections between themselves and all those who may never be known to them in any other way.

In order to appreciate the importance of illustration in a children's book and its relationship to the text, one might profitably examine several different sets of illustrations for the same written work. Folk and fairy tales, along with some of the more modern classics, provide ample fare for such examination. Traditional works in the public domain have been illustrated so often and so variously that it would be virtually impossible to identify "the one" most recognized or most loved visual representation or interpretation of *Cinderella, The Seven Ravens*, or *The Three Billy Goats Gruff*. Notable, if somewhat controversial,[7] exceptions to this statement are Walt Disney's characterizations of such stories as *Snow White and the Seven Dwarfs*, which children recognize not only from the motion picture and television screens but from many other aspects of the huge Disney marketing empire. On the other hand, although more than a hundred artists have illustrated Carroll's *Alice* books,[8] for most of us any version other than Sir John Tenniel's seems somehow just not right. To bring this problem into more contemporary times, who can even imagine *Wild Things* as drawn by any artist other than Sendak?

Some lesser known works for children have been illustrated very differently, and although two very different styles of illustration may be equally valid, they may encourage very different interpretations of the text. The Harlin Quist Company has published two quite different editions of *Gertrude's Child*—one with small, soft-colored, rather traditional children's book illustrations and the other with large, bold, surrealistic illustrations.★ The existence of these two almost opposite visual presentations of this story came to my attention midway through a rather incredulous discussion with another adult about this story; it appeared that we had read quite different works—which, of course, we had. There are also instances in which a text that has stood the test of time is rendered ineffectual, at least to some readers, by the addition of distracting illustration. The very British story poem of *The Lion and Albert* by Edgar Marriott has been around for almost fifty years and is a delight to the ear when told. It has often been included in poetry anthologies and has recently been published in several picture story book versions in England. A 1978 edition illustrated by Caroline Holden in photo album fragments slows down a text that normally moves quickly and smoothly to its conclusion. The bold and obvious humor of these illustrations is often irrelevant to and works against the subtle tongue-in-cheek humor of the text. The extraneous pictures and the captions underneath the photographs (drawings) add their own humor but draw attention away from the story itself. In addition, the placement of the illustrations does not always match the text, so the reader sometimes has to turn the page to see what is described on the previous page. Although these pictures are interesting and well executed in their own right, they do not work as illustrations for this text.

Adults concerned with the illustration of children's books have in the past spent too much time attempting to make the distinction between illustrators who are "artists in their own right" and those who are "just illustrators." Of course, there

---

★The reader may wish to compare the two editions, although the earlier version is out of print: Richard Hughes, *Gertrude's Child*, illus. Rick Schreiter (New York: Harlin Quist, Inc., 1966); *Gertrude's Child*, illus. Nicole Claveloux (New York: Harlin Quist, Inc., 1974).

are children's illustrators who have distinguished themselves in other aspects of the world of art and those who have concentrated their efforts and their talents on children's books, but as art in children's books acquires more and more importance as an art form, such distinctions become meaningless.

Early children's books, mostly moral tales and alphabets, were illustrated with simple, but often bold and dramatic, black-and-white woodcuts. Unfortunately, wood blocks were not always cut for the illustration of each particular text, and a publisher or printer might use the same print to represent both Queen Victoria and the wicked witch of the fairy tale. In addition, repeated use of the same wood blocks led to progressively less sharpness and clarity in the print.

In the nineteenth century, new techniques were introduced that stimulated the work of a number of narrative artists with very distinctive personal styles. Much of the children's book illustration of this time might be characterized as a kind of romantic naturalism in which real objects were represented with elaborate and frequently sentimental detail. Kate Greenaway's quiet, delicate, and detailed views of childhood and Caldecott's humorous drawings with bold lines and dynamic action represent two versions of this romantic naturalism. Crane and Arthur Rackham added a touch of decorative elegance to this style and, with Greenaway and Caldecott, are still pointed to as examples of excellence in children's book illustration. All of these illustrations and most of the art in picture and picture story books today are still representational in nature, and there is some evidence that children prefer it that way.[9] This preference is probably due to their difficulties in handling abstractions. The nineteenth and twentieth century movement from representational toward more abstract art has not been without influence on the art in children's books, however. It appears that nonrepresentational forms are becoming more prominent and more accepted in illustrations for young children. Artists have become as much concerned with elements of design and with their own graphic inventiveness *related to* the text as with pictorial *representations of* the narrative, and both children and critics seem to be accepting this change. Although most children's book illustration still "tells the story in pictures," more stylized and more abstract art work is becoming prominent in the field. Gerald McDermott's award-winning *Arrow to the Sun* has a primitive quality of Pueblo design that complements but does not represent the written word of the text. Some of the books published by Harlin Quist, such as Patrick Couratin's *Shhh!* are strangely surrealistic in both illustration and text. This surrealistic approach does not seem to have caught on with large groups of children, but it is unclear as yet if this is because the style does not attract most youngsters or if it is that the adults responsible for selecting children's books do not understand or appreciate these works. Whether or not these newer forms of illustration will eventually have the same appeal for children as representational art is not yet clear.

It is interesting to note that, in spite of the representative nature of much of children's book illustration and of the popularity of photography as a medium of expression, photographs have not been used very successfully to illustrate picture story books. Perhaps this is because the reality captured by the camera cannot fully convey the literary reality of story. Photography has been used to illustrate mood, concept, and information books for young children in which the material conveyed is very realistic in nature, and some more experimental photographic forms complement mood pieces or poetry quite effectively. But attempts to illustrate such works as talking animal stories have been more distracting than complementary to the written text. One has only to imagine either *The Biggest Bear* or *Winnie the Pooh* with photographic illustrations to realize the complications of making either a real animal or a toy animal behave, or appear to behave, as the character in the story must. One of the most popular of the children's stories illustrated with photographs is *The Red Balloon*, which does portray realistic characters and settings even though the story is somewhat fanciful or at least highly romantic. This is an illustrated book rather than a picture story book, however, and the stills from the film serve primarily to remind readers of or encourage them to see the outstanding film from which this book was made. As the interest in photography leads to the expansion of artistic techniques in the medium, perhaps we will see more and better examples of photographic illustrations of fictional works.

In order to create a wholly satisfying book, the illustrations must be successfully integrated not only with the text but with the totality of format and book design. The entire book in all its aspects must be an appropriate container for its contents. Many children are very sensitive to harmonious design and content and feel deceived if a particular book does not actually contain what its format and book design lead them to believe. Of course, this is most often a tacit knowing that young children could not necessarily put into words or even bring to a conscious awareness.

The most obvious considerations in this regard are size and shape. Small "Peter-Rabbit-sized" books are usually indicative of a more private, intimate, often sensitive, reading experience to be shared by no more than the two or three who can look on the pages together. Such books are to be read to a single child (perhaps a brother or sister might be invited to join in) by a loving adult or lingered over alone. In contrast, most of the Dr. Seuss books are large rectangular works to be enjoyed in the company of others in a comraderie of good cheer. * There are exceptions to this rule. *Harold and the Purple Crayon*, although small in size, is bold enough to be enjoyed by groups of children, who frequently will take up their own purple crayons in response to the reading. In general, how-

---

*This refers to the earliest and most imaginative of the Dr. Seuss books, including *And To Think That I Saw It on Mulberry Street, The 500 Hats of Bartholemew Cubbins,* and *Horton Hatches an Egg.* His later Beginning-to-Read books, beginning with *The Cat in the Hat,* are published in a smaller format.

ever, the small format that is easily controlled in the hands of very young children contains private content, while larger books are more often held up in front of groups of youngsters for public consumption. It needs to be said also that some young children, especially those not yet able to read comfortably, like to carry around oversized volumes, "heavy" in subject matter as well as in weight, as a public demonstration of their concern for books and their desire to read. For this reason, it is important that parents, teachers, and librarians do not take these books from children and force them to select only those that more closely match their age and ability levels. This is another instance in which we need not take anything away from children in order to provide them with more appropriate fare. It is important to recognize and support the symbolic significance of the large book while encouraging the child to select additional books that will give them immediate pleasure in the act of reading.

Related to the size and the shape of children's books is the consideration of the cover. In one sense, most of us do, in fact, choose our books by their covers. It is often the cover that first attracts us to a work and causes us to look more closely and consider the selection of a particular title. Children's books are likely to have attractive and colorful dust jackets, often with the illustration of the dust jacket reproduced on the actual cover of the book, or they have no jackets and the covers themselves are intended to attract potential readers and give them some idea of the contents. This is true of the mood or tone of the work as well as the subject matter. Most children (and adults) are more likely to select an attractive looking book than one that is dull in appearance and gives no clue to its contents. Beyond this, there seems to be little known about the effects of covers and book design on children's choices. In almost twenty years of working with children and books, I have encountered youngsters who won't read anything without (or with) a dust jacket, those who prefer (or absolutely hate) books with glossy picture covers and others with similarly strange preferences for the appearances of the books they select. One of the most vivid memories of my years as an elementary school librarian is of a six-year-old running my hand over an old copy of *All Aboard the Train* again and again so I could help him find another book that "felt like this one." Obviously, this young man's tactile sense was much more highly developed than my own, and I was unable to help him.

Preferences change with age, of course; and the child who selects books for their bright picture covers may, as a young adult, seek those which appear more "dignified" or "adult." This desire for the dignity of an adult format undoubtedly contributes to the popularity of paperback books with older children and young adults. Some younger children also prefer paperbacks, but it would be difficult to make a picture story book appear to be for older readers, and often young children find it easier to handle and manipulate a hard-cover book. Then too, the large full-color illustrations of these books may not reproduce adequately on less expensive paper, and the size and shape of many of them have been altered in the paperback versions.

Even when the quality of paperback editions approximates that of the hard-covers, children of any age should not be expected to subsist totally on a diet of inexpensive editions. There is something to be said for the encounter with the book itself as an art object. What is contained in the book is of course more significant than the quality of the container, and paperbacks are appropriate for most reading experiences. However, the totality of the artistic composition includes format as well as content and form, and it is sometimes of value to experience the original book—just as one wants to hear an original recording rather than a third or fourth copy.

As a child opens the covers of a book, the first thing she encounters are the endpapers. Most often these are just plain papers, usually white but sometimes coordinated with the colors of the cover or illustrations, and they go unnoticed by readers. Sometimes endpapers are decorative and pick up aspects of the illustrations to highlight the mood or spirit of the work. The Caldecott Award winners *Once a Mouse, Where the Wild Things Are*, and *The Fool of the World and the Flying Ship* have excellent examples of this type of endpaper.

At times, however, endpapers can make more critical, even startling, contributions to the totality of book design or to the content of the text. Nonfiction works frequently include maps, charts, time lines, or other such information on endpapers to assist readers in putting the contents into the appropriate perspective. Picture story books, such as *We Hide, You Seek* by Jose Aruego and Ariane Dewey, may also include informational endpapers. This book, about a clumsy rhino's game of hide and seek with some of Africa's camouflaged animals, has drawings of the animals of the East African bush, desert, and swamp on the front endpapers and of the plains, river, and forest on the back.

Bookmakers may also convey a very subtle message to readers through the use of endpapers. Virginia Lee Burton's *Life Story*, which contrasts large, colorful illustrations representing the dramatic and personalized view of the history of life on earth with small, detailed, scientifically accurate ones in Burton's typical swirling patterns, opens to a plain black endpaper and closes with a bright golden yellow one. I do not believe it is farfetched to interpret these endpapers as symbolic of the spirit of the text, which seems to imply that the world is moving out of the darkness into the light. Another example of a subtly symbolic use of endpapers is found in A. Harris Stone's *The Last Free Bird*, illustrated by Sheila Heins. This poetic reminder of the effects of man's pollution of the environment on bird life opens to an endpaper revealing a beautiful blue sky filled with bird figures; although the text ends with the statement "I am the last free bird," the final endpaper shows the same sky without a single bird to be seen. A reader might question whether this is to be interpreted as a postscript revealing the final fate of that last free bird.

Other considerations to be examined in evaluating the format of children's books are the placement of picture and text on the page, the choice of typeface, the amount of leading, and the size of margins. The first is primarily a concern in books for young children in which there is a great deal of pictorial content that may be placed at various places on the page. Peter Spier's *The Legend of New Amsterdam* has double-page spreads arranged as indicated in the diagrams below, as well as alternative configurations of these patterns.

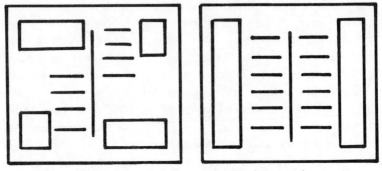

These arrangements provide variety in the visual experience, and none is confusing to young readers. However, too many different arrangements, especially those in which there is more than one segment of print on a page, may be difficult for youngsters to follow because they are unsure which segment of print is to be read first. It may also be difficult for children to decipher words that are decorated and woven into the pictures, as in *Rain Makes Applesauce*. Sometimes it is even difficult to read text that is printed on pages of certain colors if there is not enough contrast between the printed words and their background. The typeface should be clean, clear, and easy to read as well as complementary to the spirit of the text. One need not be a printing expert to observe that there are simple bold typefaces that seem to match stories in the folk tradition and more delicate typefaces for other types of fanciful stories. The size of the print, the space between the lines of print, and the size of the margins are also important in the totality of book design. Pages that appear crowded are not only difficult to read but have the psychological effect of crowding the mind of the reader.

No discussion of the format of children's books would

be complete without some comment on the "gimmick," novelty, or toy book market. The original "toy books," such as those by Caldecott and Crane, were inexpensive side-stapled paper picture books distributed as toys rather than as bound volumes. These books differed from the modern picture story book primarily in their bindings and are very different from what most of us think of as toy books today. Included in the category "toy books" are all those children's books that have some special feature of format that differs in some way from what we normally think of as a book. These may range from those works clearly books, using some special effect of format to those that are basically toys using some attribute of the book to enhance their sales to adults who want to make readers of their children. All of these forms of toy books seem to be experiencing a resurgence in the marketplace in recent years, perhaps because, as the prices of both books and toys escalate, these middle-priced half-books/half-toys become more appealing to those adults who cannot afford both but do not want to eliminate either. In addition, the current adult interest in children's literature and its history has stimulated a new look at many of the animated or movable books of the eighteenth and nineteenth centuries.[10]

Using the previous definition, the simplest form of the toy book is what has been called a "shape book," so named because it is cut into the shape of a character or object of signficance in its contents. Stamp story picture books are small-sized books that come with gummed stamps to be inserted in their proper places as illustrations of the text. Neither shape nor stamp books seem to be popular formats for modern publishers, but replicas of antique versions are currently available.★ Another relatively simple form of toy book is exemplified by Peter Newell's *The Hole Book*, in which a real hole through the pages is woven into both written

---

★The Merrimack Publishing Company in New York is one of the publishers of replicas of antique shape books and stamp books, as is Scolar Press in London (with Green Tiger Press distributing their work in the United States).

text and illustration. Newell also experimented with format and book design in *The Slant Book*, actually constructed on the slant, and in *Topsys & Turvys*, which has to be turned over and read from the opposite direction. Newell's books are also available as replicas of the turn-of-the-century originals.

More and more modern bookmakers seem to be working with other than standard page format in book design for children. John Goodall is a contemporary illustrator who makes use of cut pages or half-page inserts to change the pictures and move the action along in his wordless picture books. H. A. Rey of *Curious George* fame uses pages in *Feed the Animals* that fold in on the right side as a question is posed and then unfold to present the answer. Several recent books for the young child make use of pages cut in half horizontally so that young readers must turn them to match top and bottom to create the content or understand the concept. Eric Carle's *My Very First Book of Shapes* shows a black shape on a bright-colored background on the top half-pages and asks children to turn the bottom halves to match common objects from their own lives with the abstract shapes above. *Hit or Myth*, one of a series of British books by James Riddell, uses the same format to introduce youngsters to a number of real and imaginary animals with both the pictures and the printing of the animal's name cut in half to be reassembled properly by young readers. Graham Oakley's *Magical Changes* is one of the most beautiful and most imaginative of these horizontally split books. The top and bottom portions of the pages match so perfectly, if incongruously, in every possible combination that one is virtually compelled to go through the book again and again to appreciate each of these combinations.

Another British series of "Imagination Books" uses pages with various shapes cut out to encourage children to look through them to the next page to see familiar objects in a new way. In *A Book of Ghosts*, a child "sees" ghosts virtually everywhere but, in the end, states rather pedantically that he is not really afraid of them. In *Child's Play Magic*, a good wizardlike character and an evil witch compete for children's support in a series of events that demonstrate the evils of, among other things, playing with fire, eating sweets, and watching television. Although the content of these books is too "preachy," the format is an imaginative one that might be used to greater advantage when its creators resist trying to subvert a child's imaginative play to moralizing purposes. *Romany Free*, an unusual mood book by Vavra and Cowles, uses several cut-out pages very effectively to keep a particular illustration visible even after the page is turned.

Filip's Noisy Animal Book, another English publication, is described as a "new style board book" using a "push-out" technique. The figure of Filip (try saying his name in your best frog voice) the frog is pushed out of the inside front board and placed in the cut-out space provided for him on each page as the child moves through the book. On each page additional animals are pushed out and placed in their proper spaces beside the words for the sounds they make. On the inside of the back board is another push-out of Filip the frog, this time in black and white for the child to color. The note to adults says that this book "helps the pre-school child learn about size, shape and colour." It would be understandable to suggest that children might learn the names of some animals and the sounds they make, but since the cow, the kitten, and the kangaroo are all approximately the same size, drawn rather crudely on cartoon balloon push-out shapes, and colored with a rather narrow range of very bold colors, one must fear for the child's concepts of size, shape, and color as presented in this book.

Another popular form of the modern movable book is that in which layered scenes pop up as the book is opened or pages turned. In some instances, these pop-ups obviously are intended to give a sense of depth and dimension to illustrations as well as to attract attention to the book as toy. In contrast to a skillfully done flat illustration in which the eye can see depth and substance, however, most of the pop-ups are obvious layers of simplistic flat figures that present their contents as fragmented and fragile. This fragility is an important consideration for those who might purchase pop-up books for children. In most instances the pop-up illustrations are not really "up" until the book is fully opened and the pages flat. Many of these inexpensive bindings do not open completely, and in the process of trying to get the pages flat, one can very easily break the binding and/or tear the pop-up. Even if the illustration is successfully popped up, closing the book without destroying the illustration may require complex engineering skills. (On more than one occasion, I have sat working on an over-popped page with chopsticks, perhaps unusual but useful tools for this task, trying to refold an illustration so that the book could be closed. Most children have neither the patience nor the manual dexterity for this procedure, so many such books are destroyed at first reading.)

A number of recent pop-up books combine this type of illustration with other toy book techniques. *The Magic Castle Fairytale Book* has the text attached to the inside front cover under the endpaper and a third board, hinged to the back, that opens to pop up a castle over this board and the back cover. In addition, there are four pages of paper punch-out characters to go with the four tales but obviously not to go with the castle, because the gates into the castle are approximately a half-inch high and the characters up to five inches. *Pop-Up Fable Fun* includes doors to open, tabs to pull, and "magic glasses" with red and green acetate lenses to animate the action on the page. Some of the pages unfortunately need to open flat and others to be at a ninety-degree angle for the pop-up to work. This must be a fascinating book for any child who has at least four hands — one to hold the pages in the appropriate positions, one to pull tabs and open doors, one to hold the glasses in front of the eyes, and the fourth to pull the tab to change the lenses in the glasses.

When these books are compared with *The Children's Theatre*, a copy of an antique pop-up book, it is obvious that we have not improved on the work of previous generations. This reproduction of an 1878 German work has very detailed six-layered scenes as beautiful as they are technically sound.

What really distinguishes this and other early European movable books from most of those produced in England and the United States today is the quality of the original art work. Simple movement cannot give vitality to work that is crude, dull, and lifeless to begin with.

One of the most interesting children's books of 1979 is a large volume of pop-ups with wheels to turn, tabs to pull, and doors (and a toilet seat) to open. Jan Piénkowski's art work for *Haunted House* would entertain and reentertain readers even without its highly imaginative movable parts. From its cover— the door of the house on which a note to the reader says "Let Yourself In"— to its very end, this book is a visual and technical delight. Yet my copy, which has had only three or four handlings by an adult, already has one "movable" part that no longer moves, so one must wonder how this book will hold up in the hands of children.

Some of the more artistic pop-ups, along with many other forms of toy books, might better be considered display materials or art objects to be admired at a distance rather than handled by young children. Books like *The Changing City* and *The Changing Countryside*, with their series of detailed illustrations in poster format, are so obviously for this purpose that children's libraries that purchased them almost always posted them on a wall rather than filing them with the regular collection. Concertinas or other forms of "stretch" books, such as *I Met a Dinosaur*, are interesting novelty items that are probably of greater decorative value than of sustaining interest either as books or toys. One of the advantages of using pop-up books for display is that they can be exhibited at the proper angle for the appreciation of the picture. Most of these are fairly large books, and some, such as *Haunted House*, need to be held vertically at eye level for full effect, while others need to be placed in a different relationship to the eyes of the reader. The child who is going to manipulate one of these books on his own will most often necessarily place the book flat on the floor or table and look down into it, which may be exactly the wrong approach to such books. Carousel books are another form of pop-ups that are tied open in a circular pattern of scenes; they may sit on a table or shelf or hang as a mobile from the loop of string attached. Lothar Meggendorfer's *The Doll's House* opens to more than four feet in length, with five pop-up scenes connected by doors that open and close.* These fairly detailed scenes provide an excellent backdrop for a child's imaginative play but they may be difficult for her to set up and stabilize. There is no question that Meggendorfer was the genius of the mechanical toy book. Maurice Sendak writes of this outstanding artist: "Meggendorfer enlarged the child's visual pleasure in a way that probably will never be duplicated. His work stands alone. . . . Meggendorfer never condescended to children. He granted them, as he granted himself, a lively intellect and a cultivated visual taste. He knew, as did all the great writers and illustrators, that children observed life more shrewdly than adults; that they enjoyed with a kind of sensual gusto the delights of color, shape and movement."[11]

Many of the currently popular toy books are replicas of the eighteenth, nineteenth, or early twentieth century books, but even the contemporary ones owe a great deal to this history and are often pale in comparison with it. The harlequinades are the forerunners of all the books with flaps; *Dame*

---

*Lothar Meggendorfer's *The Doll's House* (New York: The Metropolitan Museum of Art, 1978) is a reproduction for the Museum using original books printed between 1890 and 1911 by J.F. Schreiber of Esslingen, Germany. An examination of the catalog *The Publishing Archive of Lothar Meggendorfer: Original Drawings, Hand-colored Lithographs and Production Files for His Children's Book Illustrations* (New York: Justin G. Schiller, Ltd., 1975) might be useful in understanding both the diversity and the achievement of this creator of mechanical books. It is interesting to note that Haining in *Movable Books* both discusses and reproduces a copy of *Maison de Poupée* that is identical with early versions of Meggendorfer. However, he writes "Dambuyant & Guignard of rue de Lille, Paris, were probably the leading French publishers of toy-books, and one of the finest items to come from their studios was this *Maison de Poupée*, circa 1900" (page 127) and makes no reference to Meggendorfer. The difference between *The Doll's House* and this work is found in the first panel. The first book presents an automobile and the latter a gypsy cart. However, in tracing the history of Meggendorfer's work, it is clear that early versions used the gypsy cart, and indeed the cover of the present reproduction has a gypsy cart at the side of the house.

Wonder's Transformations, a predecessor of the "hole books," and the scenic books are early versions of the pop-up. Dean and Son of London mass-produced mechanical books from the mid-nineteenth century, and by 1870 the McLoughlin and Milton Bradley companies in the United States were producing novelty items that sold to both the book and toy markets. Germany's Meggendorfer, known as the father of the pop-up book, was one of the largest and most prestigious manufacturers of toy books near the end of the nineteenth century. *The History of Little Fanny,* published by S. & J. Fuller in 1810, was not only one of the earliest toy books but was probably also the first of the paper doll books that have continued in production since that time.*

Pantomime books, toy theaters, metamorphic books, and dissolving picture books have also been with us for many years, and variations on these traditional forms are still developing. It is generally agreed, however, that the artistic quality and the technical expertise of some of those early productions has not been matched in our time.

Bruno Munari, one of the modern masters of innovative book design, has produced children's books with flaps to open, holes to peek through, and heavily inked, shiny black figures that show through layers of semi-translucent pages. With his bold use of color and sharpness of form, his sense of playfulness and discovery, and his startling visual techniques that compel readers to become involved with the page, as demonstrated in *The Circus in the Mist,* Munari is undoubtedly one of the most exciting illustrators of our time. However, it

---

* *History of Little Fanny* (London: S. and J. Fuller, 1810) was reproduced by Scolar Press in 1977 and sold in the United States by Green Tiger Press in La Jolla. *Little Henry,* a companion item, is available from the same sources. Brian Alderson in *The Times* (London) writes "The two cut-out doll books from S. and J. Fuller, 1810 (Little Henry and Little Fanny) are not quite so well colored—and Little Fanny seems to be missing an item of headgear. But even so, when you consider that you would probably spend nearly £500 on original editions of these little books today (if you could find them) these facsimiles must count as a considerable bargain. What is more, the 95p must be more or less equivalent to their original price of 1s.6d."

is also true that, as he pushes the medium of the book to its outer limits, his work is sometimes more appealing to other artists and to adults interested in book design than it is to children. One example of his extremes (never intended for children) is *Libro Illeggibile N.Y. 1*, designed by Munari for the Museum of Modern Art in New York.*

Near the other end of the scale of artistry in the toy book market are the soft cloth books with illustrations stamped on in nontoxic colors so that infants may throw, sleep on, and chew them quite safely. These books may be used as substitutes for a security blanket, a napkin, or even a handkerchief and then thrown into the washing machine and restored to their original if somewhat softer and more faded (therefore more useful?) condition. Adults who buy these books for babies often say that they do so because they want children to learn about and value books at the earliest possible age. (I agree with this sentiment, but I would not like to have them learn that books can be folded, thrown, and chewed upon and still retain their value.)

Slightly more sophisticated versions of the cloth book are those, made of very heavy cloth or plastic, that are to be braided, tied, or buttoned by the young reader. Such skills are important acquisitions for a young child, but they might be attained more easily as well as more naturally by using the actual objects to be braided, tied, or buttoned.

Story dolls are cloth story characters with several flaps attached to the neck upon which a story is printed. As each flap is turned up, the face of another character appears above while the text continues over the body. When one story is completed, the reader simply turns the doll over for a second

---

*Bruno Munari, *Libro Illeggibile N.Y. 1* (New York: The Museum of Modern Art, 1967). Many of Munari's early books for children are now reprinted by William Collins Publishers, including *The Elephant's Wish* (1980), *Animals for Sale* (1980), *Who's There? Open the Door* (1980), *Tic, Tac and Toc* (1980), *The Birthday Present* (1980), and *Jimmy Has Lost His Cap* (1980).

story on the other side. A 1979 version is a brightly colored *Pinocchio/Snow White* with four flip-over faces on each side. As an adult, I find this small and cuddly doll quite charming and have not been overly concerned with whether or not the inks are toxic. As story, however, *Pinocchio* leaves something to be desired when it is reduced to twenty-seven very short lines of text, even if the beginning of some of those lines had not been sewed inside the flap.

Mickey Mouse Takes a Vacation is a book with a hole through the pages and the cover through which a felt Mickey Mouse puppet can be manipulated in concert with the story. Because the puppet is attached to the book, it is very awkward for a child to operate, even if it fits his hand. Games, as well as toys, may be packaged as and marketed as books. A modern compilation of such games entitled *Play the Game* contains over forty board games complete with counters and detailed rules.

Another category of toy book includes those that are direct appeals to the senses of young children. These are the feel and smell and sound books common in book and toy stores today. *The Touch and Learn Book of Familiar Objects* is typical of the "feelie" book for children. The adult using this book with a child is instructed to "direct his movements so that as he traces a familiar object, its image implants itself in his memory. In this way, the child will develop mental images of the familiar object."[12] A colorful soft flocking is used on all the objects to be identified, so a man's beard, a teddy bear, a birthday cake, a duck, a bee, and a fish all feel exactly alike. (The colors of the flocking have little to do with the actual colors of the objects; so for those of you who want to implant images of blue turtles and stars, bright orange rabbits, and fuzzy birthday cakes, this is an ideal book.)

Scented Rhymes for Story Times, like almost all scratch-and-smell books, has patches of special paper that, with the first or second scratch and a great deal of imagination, may smell like the object represented but seldom do thereafter.

Out of curiosity, I recently ordered an inexpensive *Talking Animal Book* from a mail order catalog and was not really surprised to manipulate the pages and hear either a puff of air escaping or nothing at all. Another form of talking book contains a "magic" sound record that the child turns by hand to hear sound effects and excerpts of dialogue from the text. When another adult and I tried to work the magic record in *The Golden Goose*, we were able, after several tries, to make out a few words but only because we were looking at the written text at the time.

Dorothy Kunhardt's *Pat the Bunny* is probably the best-known and the all-time best-seller of this type of book. This small spiral-bound volume, which can be felt, smelled, and manipulated in a variety of ways, has for almost forty years been very popular as a first book for adults to share with very young children. It may be that this little book does encourage parents to sit down with a child to share a sort of reading experience and therefore is of value. But as a book, both the text and illustrations are insipid at best, and the sensory and manipulative experiences provided are very weak substitutes for the actual experiences they represent. For those who have never felt rabbit fur, perhaps fleecy cotton cloth is close enough to the reality, and perhaps the scent of perfumed bath powder is close enough to the smell of flowers, but I can see no value in having children experience inaccurate and misleading sensory perceptions. There are certainly enough real textures and smells available to children that we need not confuse them with false impressions.

The problems inherent in *Pat the Bunny* are typical of those of many of the toy books. What began as an awareness of sound psychological and child development principles that advocate learning through active experiences and the engagement of as many senses as possible in the process is misdirected in the execution of these books. Sensory experiences are not in themselves of value to children, especially if they are fabricated rather than authentic experiences. And what is really sad about many of these toy books is that, in their attempts to provide these active but artificial experiences for children, publishers frequently have substituted gimmicks for the kind of exciting and artistic illustration discussed earlier in this chapter. Often crude, tasteless, even inaccurate drawings are the bases upon which tactile, sound, or movable parts are appended, and these do not improve what was an insult to a child's sensibilities in the first place. A look at either the children or the bunny in *Pat the Bunny* will amply support this statement.

When turning the pages of a copy of a book like *Pat the Bunny* that has been used several times, one discovers another problem with these books. The cut-out bunny figure is torn away to reveal the square of cloth beneath; the cloth behind which Paul is supposedly hiding is permanently creased up away from him; and on the page on which the reader is asked to feel Daddy's scratchy face, is only a smooth board. The piece of sandpaper that used to cover one small segment of what would have been a beard has disappeared. Lothar Meggendorfer was aware of this built-in obsolescence and cautioned his readers with the following verse:

With this book, my own dear child,
Are various pictures gay,
Their limbs they move with gestures wild,
As with them you do play.
But still they are of paper made,
And therefore, I advise,
That care and caution should be paid,
Lest woe and grief arise;
Both you and pictures then would cry
To see what harm is done,
And sigh would follow after sigh
Because you've spoilt your fun.[13]

Most of these books are indeed graphic playthings rather than literary or artistic works. Their appeal lies predominantly in unique formats that can be manipulated in various ways by children. Some types of concept books are enhanced by these special effects or formats; but for the most part, the toy books of this century fall far short of work worthy of children in both illustration and in text. Perhaps now that there is a resurgence of interest in these books, the novelty of the gimmick for its own sake will wane and book designers will realize that good toy books, like all other books, must begin with the artistry of both illustration and text.

What is lacking in most toy books is the essential compositional unity that makes of illustration, text, and bookmaking a single and totally integrated work of art. This chapter has focused on illustration but has consistently emphasized the integration of the visual and verbal components of the children's book. It is certainly possible to apply criteria of the particular visual medium to the evaluation of illustration, and this application may at times increase our insight into the totality of the work. However, to criticize the picture story book as one would pictures hung in a gallery denies the basic unity of the artistic form. This caution applies as well to the series of illustrations in wordless picture books, which must be considered as a whole in the context of the book.

On the other hand, those who discuss and criticize children's picture story books with only brief mention of the illustrations are equally guilty of destroying the basic unity of the work—and this is a far more common practice. In part, this practice is due to the fact that those who evaluate books often have little or no understanding of the visual media and the graphic arts. Rather than risk making statements that reveal their ignorance of graphic techniques, reviewers often concentrate on the text and make only a superficial and general statement about illustration. Publishers should be urged to assist all of us in this respect by including information on artistic techniques of illustration, along with other printing and publication facts, in the colophons of picture story books. At the same time reviewers, critics, and others interested in children's books should acknowledge their responsibility to become informed about the criticism of visual media just as we now expect a knowledge of adult literature and criticism. Only when we can recognize various media, techniques, schools, and periods of works of art are we fully equipped to discuss the wide range of illustrations in children's books. Nevertheless, while we are still in the process of acquiring this knowledge, the approach to illustration used in this chapter should demonstrate that one can deal appropriately with illustration without going into detail about medium and technique. If the concentration is on the total composition of visual and verbal media as a means of communicating meaning to the child, even those who are not yet especially knowledgeable about art can comment on its effectiveness in the creation of the composed story world.

It is the obligation of adults who work with young children and their books to increase their understanding of illustration, but we cannot wait until we feel sure in our knowledge of art history and techniques to consider the picture half of picture story books. As we explore the totality of the composition of these books and open ourselves to and explore our responses to the power of illustration, we, like the children with whom we share this experience, will increase in both the appreciation and the understanding of visual as well as verbal media.

Footnotes

1. William Anderson and Patrick Groff, *A New Look at Children's Literature* (Belmont, Calif.: Wadsworth, 1972), p. 153.

2. Patricia Jean Cianciola, "Use Wordless Picture Books to Teach Reading, Visual Literacy and to Study Literature," *Top of the News* 29, 3 (April 1973): 226–34.

3. Maurice Sendak, "A Conversation with Maurice Sendak," 24th Annual Anne Carroll Moore Spring Lecture, Office of Children's Services, New York Public Library, May 3, 1979. (Tape available in listening collection of Central Children's Room.)

4. Walter Crane, *Of the Decorative Illustration of Books Old and New* (London: Bell & Hyman, 1979), p. 17. This book was first published in 1896 by G. Bell & Sons, Ltd.

5. Alvin Tresselt, *Hide and Seek Fog*, illus. Roger Duvoisin (New York: Lothrop, Lee & Shepard, 1965), pp. 5 and 12.

6. Maureen Crago, "Incompletely Shown Objects in Children's Books: One Child's Response," *Children's Literature in Education* 10, 3 (Autumn 1979): 151–57.

7. Frances Clark Sayers and Charles M. Weisenberg, "Walt Disney Accused," *Horn Book Magazine* 40 (December 1965): 602–11.

8. Graham Ovenden, ed., *The Illustrators of Alice in Wonderland and Through the Looking Glass* (London: Academy Editions, 1972).

9. Gerald Smerdon, "Children's Preferences in Illustration," *Children's Literature in Education* 20 (Spring 1976): 17–31.

10. Peter Haining's *Movable Books: An Illustrated History* (London: New English Library Ltd., 1979) provides a visually exciting examination of mechanical toy books.

11. *The Publishing Archive of Lothar Meggendorfer* (New York: Justin G. Schiller, Ltd., 1975), p. 8.

12. Ken Sobel and Sean Harrison, *The Touch and Learn Book of Familiar Objects*, illus. Associated Advertising & Design, Sean Harrison (New York: McGraw-Hill, 1966), inside front cover.

13. Lothar Meggendorfer, *Always Jolly!* (London: H. Grevel & Co., 1890).

Children's Books Cited in Chapter Four

Aruego, Jose, and Dewey, Ariane. *We Hide, You Seek.* New York: Greenwillow Books, 1979.

Bishop, Claire H. *The Five Chinese Brothers*, illus. Kurt Wiese. New York: Coward-McCann, 1938.

Bonn, Franz. *The Children's Theatre*. New York: Viking Pr., 1978. (First published in 1878 by J.F. Schreiber of Esslingen, Germany.)

A Book of Ghosts, illus. Pam Adams and Ceri Jones. Restrop Manor, Purton Wilts, England: Child's Play International Ltd., 1974.

Briggs, Raymond. *Father Christmas*. New York: Coward-McCann, 1973.

———. *Fungus the Bogeyman*. London: Hamish Hamilton, 1977.

Brown, Marcia. *Cinderella*, illus. Marcia Brown. New York: Charles Scribner's Sons, 1954.

———. *Once a Mouse*. New York: Charles Scribner's Sons, 1961.

Burkert, Nancy Ekholm. *Snow White & The Seven Dwarfs: A Tale from the Brothers Grimm*. New York: Farrar, Straus & Giroux, 1972.

Burton, Virginia Lee. *Life Story*. Boston: Houghton Mifflin, 1962.

Carle, Eric. *My Very First Book of Shapes*. New York: Thomas Y. Crowell, 1974.

Carroll, Lewis. *Alice in Wonderland*. New York: Norton, 1971. (First published in 1865; *Through the Looking Glass* in 1871.)

Child's Play Magic, illus. Pam Adams. Restrop Manor, Purton Wilts, England: Child's Play International Ltd., 1978.

Couratin, Patrick. *Shhh!* New York: Harlin Quist, Inc., 1974.

DeRegniers, Beatrice S. *May I Bring a Friend?*, illus. Beni Montresor. New York: Atheneum Publishers, 1964.

Disney Studios, Walt. *Mickey Mouse Takes a Vacation: A Puppet Book*. New York: Windmill Books, 1976.

Disney Studios, Walt. *Snow White and the Seven Dwarfs*. Racine, Wisc.: Western Publishers, 1976.

Emberly, Edward R. *Ed Emberley's ABC*. Boston: Little, Brown, 1978.

The Golden Goose, retold Jane Carmichael, illus. Mike Whittlesea. New York: A Mulberry Press Talking Book, 1974.

Grimm Brothers. *The Seven Ravens*, illus. Felix Hoffman. New York: Harcourt, Brace, Jovanovich, 1963.

Harris, Isobel. *Little Boy Brown*, illus. Andre François. Philadelphia: J.B. Lippincott, 1949.

Haskins, Ilma. *Color Seems*. New York: Vanguard Pr., 1973.

Hefter, Richard. *The Strawberry Book of Colors*. New York: Larousse & Co., 1975.

History of Little Fanny. London: S. and J. Fuller, 1810. (Reproduced by Scolar Press in 1977 and sold in London and by Green Tiger Press in La Jolla, California.)

Holden, Caroline. *The Lion and Albert*, by Edgar Marriott, pictures by Caroline Holden. London: Methuen Children's Books, 1978.

Hughes, Richard. *Gertrude's Child*, illus. Rick Schreiter. New York: Harlin Quist, Inc., 1966.

———. *Gertrude's Child*, illus. Nicole Claveloux. New York: Harlin Quist, Inc., 1974.

I Met a Dinosaur, designed and produced by Porter Productions, Inc. New York: Grosset & Dunlap, 1977.

Jarrall, Randall. *The Animal Family*, illus. Maurice Sendak. New York: Pantheon, 1965.

Johnson, Crockett. *Harold and the Purple Crayon*. New York: Harper & Row, 1958.

Kellogg, Steven. *The Island of the Skog*. New York: Dial Pr., 1973.

Kessler, Ethel, and Kessler, Leonard. *All Aboard the Train*. New York: Doubleday, 1964.

Knobler, Susan. *The Tadpole and the Frog*. New York: Harvey House, 1974.

Kunhardt, Dorothy. *Pat the Bunny*. Racine, Wisc.: Western Publishing Co., 1941.

Lamorisse, Albert. *The Red Balloon*. New York: Doubleday, 1956.

Love, Brain, comp. *Play the Game*. London: Michael Joseph & Ebury Pr., 1978.

McDermott, Gerald. *Arrow to the Sun: A Pueblo Indian Tale*. New York: Viking Pr., 1974.

The Magic Castle Fairytale Book, illus. Dale Payson and paper engineering Ib Penick. New York: Random House, 1978.

A Magic Glasses Book Pop-Up Fable Fun, based on the fables of Aesop and La Fontaine, retold Larry Shapiro, designed and illus. Roger Beerworth, paper engineering Tor Lokvig. London: Chatto & Windus, 1978.

Mayer, Mercer. *Little Monster's Mother Goose*. New York: Golden Pr., 1979.

———. *Walk, Robot, Walk*. Lexington, Mass.: Ginn and Co., 1974 (Magic Circle Book, Reading 360).

Meggendorfer, Lothar. *The Doll's House: A Reproduction of the Antique Pop-Up Book*. New York: The Metropolitan Museum of Art, 1978. (First published by Meggendorfer, *Das Puppenhaus*, in various editions from 1890 to 1910.)

Milne, A.A. *Winnie the Pooh*. New York: Dutton, 1926.

Muir, Frank. *What-a-Mess*, illus. Joseph Wright. New York: Doubleday, 1977.

Müller, Jörg. *The Changing City*. New York: Atheneum Publishers, 1977.

———. *The Changing Countryside*. New York: Atheneum Publishers, 1977.

Munari, Bruno. *The Circus in the Mist*. Cleveland, Ohio: World Publishing Co., 1969.

Newell, Peter. *The Hole Book*. New York: Harper & Row, 1908.

———. *The Slant Book*. New York: Harper & Row, 1910.

———. *Topsys & Turvys*. New York: Dover Publications, 1964. (First published in 1894.)

Oakley, Graham. *Magical Changes*. New York: Atheneum Publishers, 1980.

Piénkowski, Jan. *Colors*. New York: Harvey House, 1975.

———. *Haunted House*, assistant illus. Jane Walmsley and paper engineer Tor Lokvig. New York: Dutton, 1979.

Potter, Beatrix. *The Tailor of Gloucester*. New York: Frederick Warne, 1903.

Ransome, Arthur. *The Fool of the World and the Flying Ship*, illus. Uri Shulevitz. New York: Farrar, Straus & Giroux, 1968.

Raskin, Ellen. *Nothing Ever Happens on My Block*. New York: Atheneum Publishers, 1966.

Rey, H.A. *Curious George*. Boston: Houghton Mifflin, 1941.

———. *Feed the Animals*. Boston: Houghton Mifflin, n.d.

Riddell, James. *Hit or Myth*. London: Atrium Press Ltd., 1977.

Riley, John, and Evans, Nick. *Filip's Noisy Animal Book*. London: Foxwood Publishing Ltd., 1976.

Sandford, Ronald. *In a Sofa*. London, Ontario: Macmillan Education Ltd., 1974 (Language in Action Series).

Scented Rhymes for Story Times, illus. Benton Mahan. New York: The Mulberry Press, n.d.

Scheer, Julian. *Rain Makes Applesauce*, pictures Marvin Bileck. New York: Holiday House, 1964.

Sendak, Maurice. *In the Night Kitchen*. New York: Harper & Row, 1970.

———. *Where the Wild Things Are*. New York: Harper & Row, 1963.

Shecter, Ben. *Conrad's Castle*. New York: Harper & Row, 1967.

Sobel, Ken, and Harrison, Sean. *The Touch and Learn Book of Familiar Objects*, illus. Associated Advertising & Design, Sean Harrison. New York: McGraw-Hill, 1966.

Spier, Peter. *The Erie Canal*. New York: Doubleday, 1970.

———. *The Legend of New Amsterdam*. New York: Doubleday, 1979.

Stone, A. Harris. *The Last Free Bird*. Englewood Cliffs, N.J.: Prentice-Hall, 1967.

Story Doll: Pinocchio & Snow White. (doll) Jersey City, N.J.: Dan-Dee Imports, Inc., 1979.

The Three Billy Goats Gruff, ed. and illus. Marcia Brown. New York: Harcourt, Brace, Jovanovich, 1957.

Tresselt, Alvin. *Hide and Seek Fog*, illus. Roger Duvoisin. New York: Lothrop, Lee & Shepard, 1965.

Udry, Janice May. *The Moon Jumpers*, illus. Maurice Sendak. New York: Harper & Row, 1959.

Vavra, Robert. *Romany Free*, paintings Fleur Cowles. New York: Reynal & Co. in assoc. with William Morrow, 1977.

Ward, Lynd. *The Biggest Bear*. Boston: Houghton Mifflin, 1952.

———. *The Silver Pony: A Story in Pictures*. Boston: Houghton Mifflin, 1973.

Wetherbee, Holden. *The Wonder Ring: A Fantasy in Silhouettes*. New York: Doubleday, 1978.

Chapter Five
The Elements of Story

The import of story is given imaginative life by its author through the skillful use of literary elements in its composition, and readers re-create that imaginative meaning through their thoughtful and inquiring responses to the interaction of those elements. Such responses cannot be reduced to a series of rules but reflect the unique composition of each story as well as the individuality of each reader. Although nothing we say about story can compare with the immediate impact the reader or listener absorbs independently, the full import of story is knowable only through an understanding of its form.

One aspect of literary form accessible to children is the understanding of the various elements of story, which, in turn, increases the reader's or listener's capacity to respond more fully to subsequent encounters with literary works. The recognition of this understanding and its continuous and cumulative development in children is crucial in the process of nurturing youngsters who not only can read but do read— those who value literature as a significant source of enrichment in their own lives.

This is not to say that adults should attempt to "teach" young children about literary elements or any other formal properties of story. However, it is important for those who care about children's encounters with story to encourage the natural curiosity and the openness of response that young people ordinarily bring to such encounters. It is also essential that parents, teachers, and librarians who participate in literary experiences with children develop their adult deductive knowledge of literature so that they can more readily and more skillfully help children toward their own inductive knowing.

The development of critical literary abilities differs markedly from the reading skills commonly taught in elementary schools. Traditional reading instruction prepares one to use precise skills to decode the printed symbol and reconstruct the denotative meaning of words. Literary abilities enable the reader to use her own imaginative perception of the elements of aesthetic form to recreate the connotative meaning of a composed story world. Although literary elements and abilities are looked at separately here in order to illuminate their possibilities for the interpretation and enjoyment of story, it is in their interaction that stories come to life. Adults should not be concerned so much with a child's mastery of literary terminology or formal knowledge as with her growth in the understanding of relationships and the appreciation of imaginative works.

The child who can enter intuitively into the immediacy of story already possesses the most important literary ability. As she learns to cooperate with and follow the pattern established by the author, she maintains continuous and close contact with the work and opens up new possibilities for herself, increasing her capacity to receive and respond. Others may go before or point the way, but each reader goes alone to her experience of literature. Nothing must be done that turns children away from the enjoyment of that experience. The task of the adult working with children and literature is to help them to go beyond that personal experience to extend their knowledge about story through a dialogue with others who share their appreciation.

In order to discuss story from a truly literary point of view, the young reader must take a position in respect to what is read and recognize that while many interpretations are true, none is final. Often the child experiences literature first through her identification with character. This identification can be used to help her distinguish major from minor characters, to determine how characters are revealed by the author, and to perceive their significance in the literary world. In so doing, she comes to an awareness of the author's position, whether he speaks through one of the characters or as an all–knowing presence, and she begins to recognize those details used to build character.

As she detects details of character development, the child reader learns also to follow characters through a variety of narrative sequences and to recognize patterns of organization in literature. As she becomes more familiar with these literary patterns, she is more able to note significant details, to detect clues to mood and tone, and to predict outcomes. All of these are important and interrelated literary abilities that a child should develop as a part of her general literary experience in the appreciation of aesthetic forms of knowing. A more difficult step toward literary appreciation for most children is that of sensitivity to appropriate and artfully achieved language, although many do appreciate and interpret figurative language as well as comprehend symbols and the extended metaphor of story. The child who consciously receives as much enjoyment from finely tuned language as from the more obvious elements of character and plot is unusually well along in her development as a literary critic.

None of these literary abilities can be developed significantly without the aid of a skillful adult who is so steeped in literature herself that she is able to recognize, in all that a child says about his reading, that which is truly literary in nature. Only as a sympathetic adult helps him to formulate his responses in language are the child's discriminations among literary values sharpened. This kind of critical discussion does not tell a reader what a work means but helps him to see more in it by pointing to dimensions that might not otherwise be seen.

While the critical abilities developed by children will not necessarily serve as an entrance into the world of literary criticism as practiced by professional critics, they should lead children to point more surely to what is excellent in the literature they read. The intention of this development is not so much to evaluate for others as to clarify for themselves and to deepen their own understanding and enjoyment of a work of art. Developing critical abilities will not enable children to answer all the questions inspired by a work of literature but rather will confirm their wonder at its mystery and will make them more susceptible to its beauty.

The best known and most popular studies of children's literature for adults for the most part have discussed literary elements sketchily, if at all. For many years the basic texts used in the children's field have led readers to believe that there are only four important elements of story: theme, plot, characterization, and style. This scheme eliminates many elements that may be vital to an author's composition of a literary work, as well as to the reader's response to it. Also, two of the four elements are defined as much by the reader's interpretation as by what can be pointed to and discussed in the text. Theme is ordinarily defined as *the* main idea or *the* meaning of the work. This definition, it seems to me, is deceptive. One of the basic characteristics of good literature, whether for children or adults, is its multiplicity of meanings. Any who read regularly and discuss their reading with others know that different readers often interpret the same story quite differently. If we really value the re-creative process of reading, we must respect these differences and encourage people to share their interpretations so that we may all learn from one another. Often a young child has a great deal to offer adults in this sharing. Many authors have said that they just write stories and leave it for readers and critics to determine the themes. Of course, the author's central ideas or organizing principles do limit the possible interpretations, but they do not ordinarily reduce them to one. It is only in those stories that are so heavy-laden with thematic concerns that they are more notable as sociological theses or moral tracts than as literature that this limitation occurs.

Style, too, is an aspect of a literary work that is very difficult to define meaningfully and to point to in the composition. Some critics refer only to very specific uses of language when discussing style, while others include the total interaction of all the compositional elements used by the author.

Although each of the elements of story is treated separately here, it must be obvious that, in a skillfully written and well-developed story, all elements are so integrated into the compositional whole that readers are not aware of them as individual entities. Nor do authors necessarily consider them separately while composing. Just as painters learn first to mix colors and then so integrate the knowledge of this process in their work that they no longer need to be conscious of it, the good writer learns the craft of composition. And certainly the reader who is caught up in the made–world of the story is not aware, at least during the experience of reading, of the various elements that compose that world. It is, for the most part, only when a work is not totally integrated and believable that readers are aware of its separate parts.

Why then should we care about or want to introduce children to these compositional elements? There are two reasons. We analyze things when there is something wrong and we want to remedy the situation, as in medical analysis or psychoanalysis. On the other hand, we may analyze the things we love because we care about them so much that we want to understand how they work. Often this motive is combined with the desire to produce something similar.

It is for this second set of reasons that children should be encouraged to work with the elements of story. A comparison with one's understanding of an automobile may be a good example here. The majority of us learn only enough about our cars to insure that they will get us where we want to go most of the time; and we learn the name of the person to call when they do not. I grew up in a time and place where automobiles were so important to most young men that they insisted upon an intimate acquaintance with every element of their innards. I would hope that we could foster in children the kind of commitment to story that would encourage them to want to understand some of the complexity of the parts that make stories work. Hopefully too, they will be tempted to try their own hand at creating a story world just as a young man or woman can put together his or her own car with an accumulation of parts and the knowledge of how they work.

Character

Our world is populated as much by literary characters as by the people with whom we share our daily lives. Even those who do not read know many of the great heroes and heroines—even the great villains—of fiction because they have become so much a part of our shared symbolic society that we meet them constantly on cereal boxes, on the television screen, and in the very language we use to convey meaning to each other. How much richer then are the lives of those who do read and know characters from Peter Pan to Pericles more intimately than we know our own neighbors. Throughout life, human beings must learn to live with, perhaps even to love, those who must forever remain, at least in part, a mystery to us. Coming to know characters in story can help us to accept and understand the "otherness" of those we meet and to appreciate that, although each is the center of her own universe, we need not be alien to each other.

Children especially seem to have a very personal relationship with literary characters. Most child readers demand characters with whom they can identify. A well-developed character gives a stance from which they can proceed through the composed story world. The characters of children's story therefore must be more than just imaginably believable; they must cope with the great human concerns in images familiar and natural to the child's life. They must provide insights into human nature in appropriately child-sized actions and ideas.

Children expect characters to be plausible, whether in the plausibility of earthbound realism or that of soaring fancy. They want main characters who are not all good or all bad, so they might more easily recognize something of themselves in those characters. Children want characters to be sufficiently motivated and consistent in their actions so that readers can understand and believe in the action of the story. Character brings life to story, whether it is human life, animal life, or some more unusual form of animated or preternatural life. Story characters need not be verifiable creatures, but they must emerge dramatically through thought, dialogue, and action or they may be described directly in the author's voice as narrator and omniscient seer; that is, they may be presented either "from within" or "from without."

Various kinds of major and minor characters come to life in story. The protagonist is the hero, heroine, or main character, and it is in this character's coping with the conflict and complexities of plot that story exists. The antagonist is the opposing force in the conflict, the "bad guy" or the villain. In their identification with the protagonist of story, children are often acutely aware of the motives, ideas, and actions of that character. In fact, they may be more aware of that character's thoughts and feelings as posited by the author than they are of his appearance. Through description, the situation in which the character is placed, his reactions to and effects upon others, and through dialogue, thought, and behavior, character is developed. As these factors act upon him and in his own actions in story, the main character is revealed to readers.

Main characters are usually dynamic and round, that is, they are three-dimensional complex individuals who grow, change, and develop as a result of the events of story. Not all characters change as story develops. Static or flat characters are one-dimensional, usually representing a single idea or quality. They are not as integrated into the action as main characters and seem just to move over the surface of the story. These are often traditional stereotypes or background characters who serve any of a number of functions in story. The purpose of a static character may be to create atmosphere, to serve as a foil to the main character through traits in direct contrast to hers, to pass on information, to comment upon or criticize events as they happen, to organize and move the story along, or to receive information from others. Most children are quick to recognize that the degree of development of a character depends upon the importance of the role she plays in the total form of story, just as the real people they know have different degrees of importance in the various roles related to their own lives.

Many of the main characters in picture story books for young children are animal rather than human. The appeal of animals and the egocentricity of the young children are combined to produce characters in fur and feathers who, while retaining their animalness, represent ourselves. Frances or Little Bear reflect the conflicts and concerns of everyday life; Curious George acts out the wild adventures most children can only imagine; and Horton personalizes positive character traits by carrying them to outrageous extremes.

Point of View

Although an author's composition of story ordinarily begins with character and although many readers identify with character, it is the point of view of the characters that makes fiction unique. Characters on stage control the drama, but in story readers as audience can see inside the hearts and heads of characters and know them better than we know others either on the stage or in real life.

The point of view of story answers the questions "Who is telling the story?" and "How much can the narrator or speaker be expected to know about the persons and events of story?" Point of view is the position from which the object, scene, or action is viewed in a composition, the relationship of the narrator to the minds of the characters. The most obvious distinction in discussing point of view is the determination of whether a story is narrated in the first or third person. Each of these methods has its own advantages and limitations. A fictional "I" as the teller or narrator of story clearly can have knowledge only of that which she experiences herself. She cannot be involved in what is happening in a time or space removed from her, nor can she presume to know what another character is thinking or feeling. Most often a first-person story will have the protagonist (hero or heroine) as narrator because it is the insight into the thoughts and feelings of this character that is one of the most compelling aspects of story. A minor character, such as Dr. Watson of the Sherlock Holmes stories, may also assume this role.

Third-person narratives, on the other hand, have much more flexibility in terms of the kinds and amounts of information available to the storyteller. The totally omniscient speaker has access to all the ideas, events, and motivations of story whether they be external experiences removed in time or space or the internal workings of the minds and emotions of all characters. At the other extreme is the narrator who is merely a spectator to the action of story, recording without comment or interpretation what is observed. This is known as the objective or dramatic point of view; it leaves the reader or listener to infer what he will from the observation related. Another type of third-person narration is that of limited omniscience, in which the author remains outside yet reveals story from within a particular character, either major or minor. Often the effect of this form of narration is very similar to that of the first-person narration, since all the events of story are filtered through the chosen character. The author can also analyze and comment on events but only through his concentration on that particular character. The limited objective point of view also has an outside narrator who stays with a single character. In this case, the character merely describes what is seen rather than analyzing or interpreting.

Thus, the narrator may just be looking on as story progresses (Omniscient or Objective) or he may be looking through a character's eyes (Subjective, First Person) or he may be looking over a character's shoulder (Limited Omniscient, Limited Objective). Of course, these are not absolute categories; sometimes the point of view may shift within a story, or the combination of these categories with other story elements may change the effect of the qualities ordinarily determined by point of view. For instance, a great deal of dialogue from a particular character may reveal point of view in addition to or in contrast to that of the narrator. Story tone, setting, the choice of a formal or informal language style, or the total effect of the arrangement of all elements may also reveal the author's voice in story.

In composing story, an author creates a world and then chooses a particular position within that world from which to survey it and to be affected by it. The author's stance in that world is the point of view of story and is a major controlling factor in establishing the perimeters and the limitations of the story world.

Structure/Plot

The import of story is metaphorical; it is an author's thought about feeling revealed through the totality of the aesthetic ordering of an imagined series of events. The overall pattern or total design that gives unity and coherence to all the elements of story is its structure. The structure of story is itself a nondiscursive ordering or metaphorical expression referring to the basic shape or the way in which individual parts are ordered to form the whole. Lillian Smith defined the structure of story as "the shape or form the idea takes as it grows in the writer's mind, the way in which he wants to present his idea to the reader."[1] Structure is more than just the beginning-middle-end of story; it is the pattern of tension, movement, equilibrium, and resolution of a literary work. Within the structure of story, all other compositional elements are related and arranged, both topically and affectively, into a compositional entity with a unified aesthetic effect.

The general nondiscursive structure of story is given specific discursive embodiment in its plot. Plot is more than just a series of events arranged in their time sequence; it is a series of actions linked by cause and effect to lead the engaged reader through complications to an inevitable conclusion. The most common analogy used to distinguish between the intimately related elements of structure and plot is that of the string of beads. The string is likened to the structure and the beads to the plot. The string (structure) has some flexibility even as it remains a single closed loop, but the beads are ever fixed in their relationship to one another. The most common pattern of plot development is one of five parts: (1) a brief stage-setting or presentation of background, (2) rising action or introduction of conflict, (3) complication or the development of conflict, (4) the climax, crisis, or decisive act, and (5) the resolution or brief action immediately following the climax.

As plot develops, the many possibilities for action are narrowed through causality so that the limits are set within which the reader may anticipate an inevitable resolution. The selection of action in plot has a sort of funneling effect so that each event limits the events to follow.

Although all elements of story are interdependent, plot and character are inseparable. Plot is character in action; and, through that action, character is revealed and developed. Plot may be thought of as the ordering of events in which that character copes with some conflict. Basic conflict in plot may be between the character and (1) himself, (2) another person, (3) nature, (4) society, or (5) the supernatural. Frye's four generic plots, discussed in a previous chapter, describe the conventional powers of a mythical hero in relation to others and to the world in which he lives. In his search for identity this character has adventures (Romance), faces death (Tragedy), disappears (Irony-Satire), and returns again (Comedy).

In order to read any story, one must be able to follow a structural ordering or narrative sequence and make imaginative sense of all the incidents, scenes, and characters that occur. A reader must understand how one event builds on and is extended by another so that he will keep turning the page or continue to listen. Since plot is one of the easiest elements for readers to understand, it is often this, if anything, that adults discuss with children after sharing a story. Unfortunately, this discussion is sometimes conducted in a nonliterary manner as if one were analyzing discursive material or memorizing a grocery list. It is worthwhile for a child to be able to summarize the main events of story, but such a summary is of value only if it is done with an eye to the events' contribution to the total story as aesthetic form rather than as an exercise in outlining or a check on decoding skills.

A strong progressive plot, as developed with cause and effect through the five divisions of plot, is the most common means of organization in children's story. Less common are parallel plots or other complex plot formations such as a major plot with one or more subplots. All story does have some sense of narrative sequence, but the imaginative feel of continuity of events need not always come through a strong plot. It might also come through a developing sense of mood or from a character's mental associations as recalled in retrospect, reverie, or flashback. Even when chronological order is important in stories for children, the psychological progression may be more important and is often the thread upon which the narrative moves. Yet even the temporal ordering of events need not always follow a normal chronological sequence but may move back and forth in time as in retrospect or flashback. Spatial order may be recognized in the move from large to small or from near to far. Imaginative order may move from realism to fancy and back again. Young children particularly respond very favorably to stories with strong and obvious organizational structures that allow them to anticipate actions and participate more fully in the reading experience. A simple back and forth pattern such as that of *That's Good, That's Bad* or *Fortunately* (Unfortunately) or the recurrent refrains of *Millions of Cats* or *Caps for Sale* encourage even a preschooler to join in the telling.

Such strong patterns also help children predict the eventual outcome of the story. This does not mean that they know precisely the final events of story but that they have a general sense of how a situation will be resolved. This sense may be as simple as expecting a story that begins "Once upon a time" to end with "and they lived happily ever after." Or they can anticipate that *Call it Courage*, which opens with young Mafatu, son of a Polynesian chief, who is scorned by the other islanders because of his fear of the sea, will be resolved in his acceptance by his people after a demonstration of courage. Anticipating events does not make the reading less intriguing but rather more enthralling, as we discover the uniqueness of this author's treatment of a universal story. A totally astonishing climax to story is seldom a satisfying one for a reader. Instead readers are involved in and affected by story in direct proportion to the intensity of expectation. This is true even for a story with a "surprise" ending. The persistent appeal of

O'Henry's stories with both young people and adults attests to this. In fact, some readers find themselves drawn to rereading such stories again and again, proving that it is not the surprise itself but the quality of "surprisedness" and the author's skill in developing that quality that is compelling to the reader.

Young children often come to a story hour asking "Is it believe or make-believe?" With this question a child demonstrates his tacit knowing that one must prepare to participate in the re-creative act of "reading" differently for fiction than for fact. As he hears the opening lines, the child who has had previous experiences with story will take the next step in preparation for receiving and re-creating the imagined world. A story that begins "On a city street . . . " will quite likely set up very different patterns of expectation from one that opens with "Once upon a time . . . . " By the time most children go to primary school, they will recognize some of the basic characteristics of the fairy tale; by the time they reach the intermediate grades, they should have had enough experience with different literary genres to recognize myth, folktale, fable, legend, and tall tale as well. A good story for children may make use of these traditional forms or of more modern narrative patterns, but all events must contribute to the total meaning or effect of story so that all incidents grow out of preceding incidents and lead naturally to the next ones.

Many books for children have an episodic rather than a progressive or organic plot structure. This is especially true of books for the "middle-aged reader" who has just about mastered the decoding process of reading and wants to move beyond "easy books" to those for older children. The popularity over the years of books such as those by Carolyn Haywood and Beverly Cleary is partly due to their episodic nature. The characters and events of these books are easily recognized by most children, they are relatively easy to read, and each chapter is an episode in itself; so there are natural stopping points for those who can neither read much in a sitting nor retain details from one reading to the next.

The series books are popular with young readers for many of the same reasons, although they are more likely to end each chapter with a cliffhanging situation rather than episodic resolution. Although series such as those about Nancy Drew and the Bobbsey Twins do not measure up to most children's books in respect to other literary elements, the members of the Stratemeyer Syndicate are masters of plot development.* In fact, there is not much to recommend most of the series books beyond a rather fast-moving, highly romanticized series of events. These books are, however, excellent practice material for youngsters just cutting their literary teeth; they help children to develop that sense of confidence in their reading ability needed by those who are to make reading a part of their adult lives. The Encyclopedia Brown mysteries combine the qualities of the other series with the stylized plotting of mystery and detective stories, but they go beyond Nancy Drew and Joe and Frank Hardy by having the reader, rather than the character, solve the mystery and then check his solutions with those of Encyclopedia Brown in the rear of the book.* What better way to encour-

---

*In Russel Nye's *The Unembarrassed Muse* (New York: Dial Press, 1970), we learn "Stratemeyer usually thought up the characters and plot outlines. An assistant (often Howard Garis, who wrote 'Uncle Wiggly' on his own) filled in the outlines and passed them on to writers who did a section for twenty-five to one hundred dollars, depending on the writer's skill and the series' importance. The pieces then came back to the Stratemeyer offices where they were put together, scanned for discrepancies, and passed on to Stratemeyer, who gave final approval and sent them to the printer" (p. 77). Additional details on the output of the Stratemeyer syndicate can be found in various articles in the *Journal of Popular Culture* and in Arthur Prager's *Rascals at Large; or, The Clue in the Old Nostalgia* (Garden City, N.Y.: Doubleday, 1971).

---

*The identical technique is used in *Maximilian You're the Greatest*, by Joseph Rosenbloom (New York: A Tempo Book, 1979); but of even greater interest is the adult murder mystery written by Dennis Wheatley, *Murder Off Miami*, planned by J.G. Links (London: Hutchinson/Webb & Bower, 1930; reissued in 1979), in which "Cablegrams, original handwritten documents, photographs, police reports, criminal records, and even actual clues in the form of human hair, a piece of blood-stained curtain, etc., are all contained in this folder, each in its correct order as received at police headquarters, thereby forming the complete dossier of the crime." The solution is contained in a sealed packet at the rear of the book.

age children to follow a sequence of events, note and recall significant details, make inferences, comprehend implied meanings, and predict outcomes—all abilities necessary for the re-creative act of reading?

In informal surveys of graduate students over the past ten years, I have heard time and time again that these adults spent parts of their childhoods, often fairly large parts, reading series books. Since this is a very select population of readers and represents those concerned enough with literature to be taking a course on the topic, I can only conclude that the reading of series books is a natural step in the process of developing literary abilities in reading, just as learning the alphabet is a step in mastering decoding skills. Each activity is superseded at the appropriate time.

Distinct from the series books are the family chronicles and cycle stories in which characters, unlike those of the series, grow and change over time and from book to book. The Laura Ingalls Wilder books take readers through Laura's own life, while chronicles such as Willard's Mantlemass stories extend over many generations. In the first it is the character who provides unity throughout all the books, while in the latter it is the place, the family home of Mantlemass. The terms "chronicle" and "cycle" seem to be used interchangeably in children's literature, although there is a distinction evident in the words themselves. A chronicle is a continuous historical narrative that in discourse is presented with little or no analysis or interpretation. In nondiscourse, however, historical events are interpreted and brought to life through fictional characters. A cycle is a group of stories revolving around a central theme, event, or character, often a legendary one. Events within a cycle may recur over and over again, leading back to the starting point of the narrative. The chronicle is most closely linked with historical fiction and the cycle with highly romanticized or fanciful stories. According to these definitions, *The Chronicles of Narnia* is really a cycle, as are the books by Madeline L'Engle and Susan Cooper.

The structures and plots of some books apparently have been developed with an eye on production in some other medium. Certainly some adult novels written in this generation have been created for an easy transposition to the movies or television. Likewise, more and more children's stories have been produced in visual formats as well as in print. Well-known children's books such as *Sounder, Summer of My German Soldier, Heidi, Freaky Friday, Where the Lilies Bloom*, and *The Black Stallion* have been produced as motion pictures or television programs. The Little House books in this country and *Children of the New Forest* in England are the bases for television series. In addition, publishers capitalize on the interest in television programs to convert television scripts to children's books. Scholastic Book Services frequently issues children's books based on current television programs. Other examples include the Addie Mills books, issued simultaneously with the CBS television specials, such as *Addie and the King of Hearts*. Even the structures of many of the early classics were determined by their original publication as serials in the children's magazines of the day. *The Peterkin Papers, Jo's Boys, Eight Cousins, Little Lord Fauntleroy*, and *Master Skylark* first appeared as serials in the *St. Nicolas Magazine*, and *Harper's Young People* published an early version of Howard Pyle's *The Merry Adventures of Robin Hood*.

The plot structures mentioned to this point have been fairly conventional; however, there are some more experimental works now available for children. In fact, many forms that are conventional in adult literature are still fairly unusual in the children's field. The fictional diary is fairly atypical in stories for children, although *Go Ask Alice* and similar works are well-known by young adults and biographical diaries such as that of Anne Frank and combinations of diary and narrative as in *My Side of the Mountain* seem to be fairly popular with younger readers. Joan Blos's *A Gathering of Days* uses the format of a fictional journal to tell the compelling story of a young girl growing up in New Hampshire in the 1830s. Stream of consciousness is another common adult form almost unknown for children, although some of the modern sociological and psychological "problem" stories have characters so introspective (often egocentric) that they come close to lapsing into this form.

It must be noted that readers gradually change their expectations of plot over time. Readers of Victorian novels could know that stories would be neatly resolved by the last page, and until the 1960s most children's books were written in this same vein. In fact, this need for resolution has been the cause of one of the major difficulties of plotting in stories for children. Authors would introduce a character, set the stage, and build up a tremendous series of complications, and then resort to a highly unlikely set of coincidences to arrive at a happy, albeit unbelievable, ending. The Horatio Alger legend has survived in all those stories in which a poor but proud, hungry and homeless youngster shivering in a snow-filled gutter finds a wallet stuffed with money and, giving no thought for her own comfort, walks great distances to return the wallet to its rightful owner. An ample reward is not enough for such an act, of course, and the rich gentleman realizes that the ragged waif is really his long-lost daughter and gives her not only his heart but all the worldly possessions befitting a young princess. If such plots were as predictable as they were unbelievable, some more modern plots move so far from traditional expectations that they are almost incomprehensible to many readers. Some of the picture books published by Harlin Quist, Inc. might be included in this group, along with Chamber's *Breaktime* for older children.

Setting

As Elizabeth Ann Parker has said, "Time is the rhythm that orders the significance of story. Without the passage of time in story, there could be no development of concern for the story's characters, no development of the mystery in which story tension is created and resolved."[2] Without time there could be no story because it is the cumulative ordering of events, not the events themselves, that create story. Fictional time is not actual time; it is not measured in even sweeps of the hands of a clock but is paced according to the aesthetic import of the various events of story.

Place in story is more than just background upon which the action of story is set. It may be a pervasive environment that influences the totality of story composition. The concept of place is intimately related to that of time because story is situated in time as well as in space. Often the two are thought of together as the setting of story, but setting is also more than just time and place. Setting goes beyond period and scenery to include social, cultural, spiritual, and intellectual as well as physical background, for no character or event is uninfluenced by these aspects of the social milieu. In the arts, the country of the mind has always been more important than physical properties.

In one sense, the setting of story is always a frontier, whether this is an unexplored land or some hidden spot in the human consciousness. As external frontiers have disappeared, adult literature has turned more and more to the inner world, to "trips" into the mind. Many writers seem to believe that setting is not as important since it seldom serves a documentary purpose any longer in an age when the images of television and other media are readily available to young and old alike. But fortunately for children, they live in a world still filled with frontiers and unexplored territory. They may be able to conjure up television images of Asia, Africa, or even the moon and still be frightened or excited and unsure about their first solo trip to the local grocery store. Most of the world is still unknown to children, and one of the ways they can explore it is through stories in which they can be aesthetically engaged and involved in times and places they have only passively observed on television.

Time in story may be ordered either chronologically or psychologically. A chronological ordering generally records incidents in their order of occurrence. However, an author need not narrate his story as if it were a chronicle, keeping a strict sequential order from beginning to end. He may start at any point and then shift the focus to another time by use of the flashback, the more complex time shift, or an imaginative jump to the future. Historical time in story is somewhat different from ordinary past time in its intimate tie with actual time, place, and events. Historical time alone reveals history; the imposition of subjective or psychological time on historical time results in the composition of historical fiction.

Psychological time is most easily observed in narrative pacing or the uneven time-flow of events in story. Passage in story is measured not in hours or days or years but in human significance. What is of intense meaning to the protagonist of story may be written about at great length although it was a momentary incident, while less significant years, to the character if not the world, may be passed over in a single phrase. Such pacing or movement in time is a critical means of giving a sense of rhythm and change to story.

In addition to chronological and psychological time in story, there is a kind of universal or unbounded time. Most often this is the time of fanciful stories, those set in the magic of "long ago and far away" or "once upon a time." These are truly timeless stories in that, although all events must take place in time, there is no real evidence of the passage of time in their composition. A hundred years is a long and necessary time in story for a princess to sleep under a magic spell, yet it is as but the blinking of an eye in terms of character as she awakens with no change in her beauty to indicate the passing of the years. This is one hundred years of changeless time, a time neither chronological nor psychological, but fanciful or universal.

Sometimes time is understood only through implication in story. A twelve-year-old may recall an event that happened "years ago," but the period of time implied is likely to be quite different from that suggested if the same statement had been made by his great-grandmother. Or consider the various meanings of the word "soon" as used by a school-aged child.

"Dinner will be ready *soon*."
"The school year will *soon* be over."
"I'll *soon* be old enough to drive."
"Men will *soon* be living on the moon."

Place in story may be verifiably actual or aesthetically constructed, realistic, romantic or fanciful, constant or shifting. It may serve as either foreground or background of story, as an indication of mood or tone, as a source of customs and attitudes, or as a social or physical cause of story action. In every instance, however, the development and detail of place help to make the story world imaginable to readers and add to their ability to participate in and to follow its aesthetic form. Frye points out that cultural expectations have developed over time in which certain settings carry with them indications of far more than their immediate characteristics.[3] For instance, a story set in a garden on a bright spring morning is almost certainly going to lead readers to expect a happy story, while one that takes place at midnight in a swamp will leave them with a quite different impression. We do know that the time and place of events do not determine their emotional content, but in story we still expect that it should be so.

Tone/Mood

Tone is the reflection of an author's attitude toward her material, toward readers, and toward herself. She may write ironically, satirically, romantically, cynically, comically, tragically, or matter-of-factly. Literary tone corresponds to tone of voice in spoken language and is usually fairly obvious in a work. Without the sight and the sound of the originator of the spoken word, however, it is sometimes difficult to determine just how tone is conveyed in the written word. Literary devices such as alliteration, hyperbole, and understatement, as well as the choice and pacing of language and the nature and amount of detail, are particular means used to convey a general impression of an author's attitude. Using such techniques, the author influences the reader's perceptions of the characters, events, and settings of story and focuses attention upon those that play prominent roles in the unfolding meaning of story. Tone helps to lead a reader through the mounting and receding tension of story and, as possibilities become more and more limited, helps to shape the direction of incidents and foreshadow the resolution of story forms.

Unfortunately, tone in children's literature has too often been most obvious as condescension, sentimentality, and didacticism from authors who did not really respect the child reader. Of course, tastes have changed over time, and our tolerance for sentimentality and heavy-handed didacticism has decreased as our appreciation for children's abilities to comprehend and respond to more subtle approaches has grown. An examination of many of the rewritten "classics" or children's versions of mythical tales reveals a tone of condescension, as compelling stories are reduced to simple plot summaries and characters of awe and majesty appear as foolish buffoons. Because tone reveals the author's attitude, it is the element that comes closest to what readers refer to as theme. However, attempts to identify theme frequently lead to the oversimplification of a work, while an analysis of tone requires a careful study of techniques and the relationships with and among the other elements. One must also be aware that an author does not necessarily project her own personal attitude toward characters and events but may assume another imagined voice in the telling of story. If theme is defined as the essential idea or meaning of a literary work that leads to a clearly discernible organization, it is related to tone in terms of attitude or idea and structure as organization or form.

The mood of story refers to the overall tone that prevails in a work of literature. Various parts of a story may have unique tones, but mood is the pervasive atmosphere of the total composition that helps the reader to comprehend meaning or import beyond that actually stated. The mood of story is the aesthetic ordering of all the tones of which it is composed and is never complete until all of these tones are resolved in its total design. Mood, like tone, is created by the author in his choice of words and appropriate sounds, rhythms, and images that may be a major influence in determining the action of characters. Mood is ordinarily described in terms of human emotions (sad, serious, humorous, adventurous, etc.) and works with other elements of story to give shape to and establish the limits of the fictional world.

Language/Symbol

The life of literature is in its language. Story is rooted in words, but a reader discovers its full meaning and authenticity not only *in* words but *around* and *beyond* them. Most books have words, but no book can have emotion; it can only evoke emotion. Words do not mean anything; people mean things by words, and the essence of an author's work is in the unique molding of language so that his meanings may reach out to and evoke the meanings of others. "The truly sensitive and creative writer shapes his language. In a way which is characteristically his, he manipulates the words and syntactic structures common to us all so that his language does more than simply *express* his intended meaning—it deliberately *intensifies* or *reinforces* the essence of that meaning."[4]

Language in story may be either literal or metaphorical; it may be used to convey sense, sensibility, or just sensory impressions through sound and rhythm. An author may make assertions in his own voice or introduce ideas in the speech of his characters. Word choice and sentence structure are the basic tools with which the totality of the story world is built. These tools can also be used to develop recognizable literary devices that add structure to that building. Literary devices may be, on one level, uses of language that cause a reader to form and respond to strong sensory images or sense' an emotional reaction, or they may be more complex stylistic structures to alert the reader to a shift in the limits of the composed story world. Alliteration and onomatopoeia use the sense of sound to help the reader move through story and establish a particular mood or tone. Simile, metaphor, personification, and other figures of speech rely on the reader's recognition of relationships with objects or ideas outside the story to develop a description or make a point. Literary allusions such as "sour grapes," "Achilles' heel," and "cry wolf" depend upon one's previous experience with literature to capture a complex idea in a terse phrase. Alice's rabbit hole, Lucy's wardrobe, or Milo's tollbooth are effective means to signal the reader of the passage from a realistic to a fanciful story world. All of these are very effective literary devices that contribute to the total development of story.

All language is symbol in that it points to or signifies something other than itself. Symbol in story does more than just present and articulate meaning; it evokes a human response in relation to the imaginative idea it presents. The totality of story is itself an extended metaphor or presentational symbol of a virtual reality; that is, it does not point to something else as an image of that thing, but brings all that is of import in the object into the work itself. It does not look from story to the actual experiential world but forces the reader to look from the outside world into the composed story world and to think about what it feels like to dwell there.

Symbols vary in complexity and demand different degrees of involvement on the part of a reader to derive the symbolic concept from the reference to a concrete item. In some instances, an author may simply tell readers that an object holds symbolic meaning for a character in story. In the first chapter of *Blue Willow*, as Janey is remembering the time before her mother died when the world seemed safer and more secure, Doris Gates tells us "And because the willow plate had once been a part of all this, it seemed actually to become these things to Janey. It was the hub of her universe, a solid rock in the midst of shifting sands."[5] Or in the story of a Puerto Rican girl struggling with her new life in New York City where there seemed to be no green and growing things, Papa says of the small spider plant with its broken pot, "Our family was like your plant, Carmen. We lost our home in Puerto Rico but not our courage and strength. Our family is still whole."[6] Other symbols used in stories, such as the American flag or an olive branch, have generally accepted meanings for whole groups of people. There are also symbols that depend on previous experiences or literary allusions for their interpretation. This form of symbolization is often seen in adult literature but is not as prevalent in stories for young people because children have not as yet acquired a large common heritage of symbolic literary meanings.

Most literary symbols are symbolic only in terms of the specific actions and associations within a particular work. Such a symbol is effective to the degree that it is appropriate to its total context and is concerned not with outer resemblances but with inner qualities. For instance, the title character in *The Jazz Man* highlights a specific aspect of the Harlem community as well as the feelings of the boy Zeke. In the literary tension between Zeke and his situation, the jazz man serves as a pivotal point upon which the movement of story is based. Symbolically he represents Zeke's quest for freedom and belonging in a world that is harsh to him both physically and emotionally.

Style

An author's unique shaping of all of the elements discussed in this chapter is what many people mean by style. Style is most closely associated with language and is reflected in diction and sentence structure, but it is also revealed in the tone and point of view of the writing. In this sense, style is the personality of an author as seen in her work and can only be pointed to or discussed in reference to the composite of all other elements. On the other hand, style may refer to commonalities in literary works in a particular place or over a period of time. Using the term in this way, we may speak of an Elizabethan style, which in actuality was three styles: (1) a grand style of epic and tragedy, (2) a middle style of everyday life, and (3) a base style of satire and the pastoral. Every age has its own expectations for literary works that might be called the style of the time. For instance, much of recent adult literature has been in the ironic mode, with antiheroes defeated by the world rather than heroic characters who overcome all obstacles to achieve success. Although there are always authors and works that break with the expectations of an age, it is probably more useful to speak of style in this way than to reduce it to the particulars of a single work.

If one is to become imaginatively involved in story form, he must cultivate an understanding of literary elements, an awareness of significant detail, and a sensitivity to that which is of importance to the composition of story. He must recognize main ideas and the supporting details that help to develop those main ideas. He must note facts that reveal aspects of character and the relationships between characters or between characters and incident. As he recalls such details, the child reader is aided in the understanding of character motivation and may note incidents of foreshadowing that give literary clues for what is to follow in the narrative sequence. Details to note may be actual physical objects raised to symbolic significance, such as the blue willow plate or Carmen's spider plant, or they may be subtle clues to the emotional reactions of a character. Such details may be revealed through the author's point of view or in the influence of time, place, or mood on the events of story.

As one notes details in reading, he develops the ability to make inferences and comprehend implied meanings, an essential ability as the reader re-creates the composed story world of the author. It is in the meeting of what the author has recorded on paper and what the reader already knows about people, places, and events that story comes to life for each individual. In saying one thing, an author suggests far more, and the reading experience is a more interesting one when the reader uses all his literary abilities to interpret implied relationships. A basic relationship in story is that of cause and effect, and the ability to look at an event and know why it happened or what led up to it and to anticipate what will most likely happen as a result is both a fascinating and a necessary one for any reader.

One of the most important areas in which a reader is called upon to make inferences is that of understanding the thoughts and feelings of characters. Given a young boy in a thin torn jacket with his nose pressed against a bakery shop window on a winter evening, a reader might assume that the child is poor and hungry. Previous clues or events to follow, however, may indicate that the child is only pausing on his way home to a hot meal and a loving family after a rough football practice. Or another child's long look at a big dog may be one either of fear or of anticipation. Only through careful reading and attention to detail can one truly understand the implications that give full meaning to story.

The literary elements and critical abilities identified here are not formulas to divest story of its meaning but probative ideas to help the reader deepen and strengthen her full imaginative response to story form. If they are approached self-consciously at first, it is only that she might soon become so sensitive to their implications that such inquiry leads automatically to a deeper and more powerful understanding of story as a way of knowing.

Footnotes

1. Lillian Smith, *The Unreluctant Years* (Chicago: American Library Association, 1953), p. 36.

2. Elizabeth Ann Parker, *Teaching the Reading of Fiction* (New York: Teachers College Pr., 1969), p. 33.

3. For a discussion of this see Frye's treatment of the dialectical and cyclical rhythms and images in the *Anatomy of Criticism: Four Essays* (Princeton, N.J.: Princeton University Pr., 1957).

4. John M. Nagle, "A View of Literature Too Often Neglected," *English Journal* 58, 3 (March 1969): 399–401.

5. Doris Gates, *Blue Willow* (New York: Viking Pr., 1940), p. 23.

6. Yetta Speevack, *The Spider Plant* (New York: An Archway Paperback, Washington Square Pr., 1968), p. 35.

Children's Books Cited in Chapter Five

Alcott, Louisa May. *Eight Cousins*. New York: Grosset & Dunlap, 1971.

——. *Jo's Boys.* New York: Grosset & Dunlap, 1949.

Armstrong, William. *Sounder*. New York: Harper & Row, 1969.

Bennett, John. *Master Skylark*. New York: Grosset & Dunlap, 1897.

Blos, Joan. *A Gathering of Days*. New York: Charles Scribner's Sons, 1979.

Burnett, Frances H. *Little Lord Fauntleroy*. New York: Garland Publishing Co., 1976. (First published in 1886.)

Chambers, Aidan. *Breaktime*. New York: Harper & Row, 1979.

Charlip, Remy. *Fortunately*. New York: Parents, 1964.

Cleary, Beverly. *Henry Huggins*. New York: William Morrow Co., 1950.

——. *Ellen Tebbits*. New York: William Morrow Co., 1951.

——. *Otis Spofford*. New York: William Morrow Co., 1953.

——. *Ramona the Pest*. New York: William Morrow Co., 1968.

——. *Ramona and Her Father*. New York: William Morrow Co., 1977.

Cleaver, Vera, and Cleaver, Bill. *Where the Lilies Bloom*. Philadelphia: J.B. Lippincott Co., 1969.

Cooper, Susan. *Over Sea, Under Stone*. New York: Harcourt, Brace, Jovanovich, 1966.

——. *The Dark is Rising*. New York: Atheneum Publishers, 1973.

————. *Greenwitch*. New York: Atheneum Publishers, 1974.

————. *The Grey King*. New York: Atheneum Publishers, 1975.

————. *Silver on the Tree*. New York: Atheneum Publishers, 1977.

Farley, Walter. *The Black Stallion*. New York: Random House, 1944.

Gag, Wanda. *Millions of Cats*. New York: Coward-McCann, 1928.

Gates, Doris. *Blue Willow*. New York: Viking Pr., 1940.

Geisel, Theodore Seuss. *Horton Hatches the Egg*. New York: Random House, 1940.

George, Jean. *My Side of the Mountain*. New York: E.P. Dutton, 1959.

Go Ask Alice. Englewood Cliffs, N.J.: Prentice-Hall, 1971.

Greene, Bette. *Summer of My German Soldier*. New York: Dial Pr., 1973.

Hale, Lucretia P. *The Complete Peterkin Papers*. Boston: Houghton Mifflin, 1960.

Haywood, Carolyn. *B Is for Betsy*. New York: Harcourt, Brace, Jovanovich, 1939.

————. *Back to School with Betsy*. New York: Harcourt, Brace, Jovanovich, 1943.

————. *Little Eddie*. New York: William Morrow Co., 1947.

Hoban, Russell. *Bedtime for Frances*, illus. Garth Williams. New York: Harper & Row, 1960.

Juster, Norton. *The Phantom Tollbooth*. New York: Random House, 1961.

L'Engle, Madeline. *A Wrinkle in Time*. New York: Farrar, Straus & Giroux, 1962.

————. *A Wind in the Door*. New York: Farrar, Straus & Giroux, 1973.

————. *A Swiftly Tilting Planet*. New York: Farrar, Straus & Giroux, 1978.

Lewis, C.S. *The Lion, the Witch and the Wardrobe*. New York: Macmillan, 1950.

————. *Prince Caspian*. New York: Macmillan, 1951.

————. *The Voyage of the "Dawn Treader"*. New York: Macmillan, 1954.

————. *The Silver Chair*. New York: Macmillan, 1953.

————. *The Horse and His Boy*. New York: Macmillan, 1954.

————. *The Magician's Nephew*. New York: Macmillan, 1955.

————. *The Last Battle*. New York: Macmillan, 1956.

Lexau, Joan M. *That's Good, That's Bad*. New York: Dial Pr., 1963.

Marryat, Captain Frederick. *Children of the New Forest*, abridged and ed. Doris Dickens. London: Fontana Paperbacks, 1977. (First published in 1847.)

Minarik, Else. *Little Bear*, illus. Maurice Sendak. New York: Harper & Row, 1957.

Pyle, Howard. *The Merry Adventures of Robin Hood*. Dover Publications, 1968.

Rey, H.A. *Curious George*. Boston: Houghton Mifflin, 1941.

Rock, Gail. *Addie and the King of Hearts*. New York: Alfred A. Knopf, 1976.

Rodgers, Mary. *Freaky Friday*. New York: Harper & Row, 1972.

Slobodkina, Esphyr. *Caps for Sale*. Reading, Mass.: Addison-Wesley, 1947.

Sobol, Donald J. *Encyclopedia Brown: Boy Detective*. Nashville, Tenn.: Thomas Nelson, 1963.

Speevack, Yette. *The Spider Plant*. New York: Atheneum Publishers, 1965.

Sperry, Armstrong. *Call It Courage*. New York: Macmillan, 1940.

Spyri, Johanna. *Heidi*. New York: Macmillan, 1962.

Weik, Mary Hays. *The Jazz Man*. New York: Atheneum Publishers, 1966.

Wilder, Laura Ingalls. *Little House in the Big Woods*. New York: Harper & Row, 1932.

———. *Little House on the Prairie*. New York: Harper & Row, 1935.

———. *Farmer Boy*. New York: Harper & Row, 1933.

———. *On the Banks of Plum Creek*. New York: Harper & Row, 1937.

———. *By the Shores of the Silver Lake*. New York: Harper & Row, 1939.

———. *The Long Winter*. New York: Harper & Row, 1940.

———. *Little Town on the Prairie*. New York: Harper & Row, 1941.

———. *These Happy Golden Years*. New York: Harper & Row, 1943.

Willard, Barbara. *The Lark and the Laurel*. Harmondsworth, Middlesex, England: Puffin Books, 1974.

———. *The Sprig of Broom*. Harmondsworth, Middlesex, England: Puffin Books, 1974.

———. *A Cold Wind Blowing*. Harmondsworth, Middlesex, England: Puffin Books, 1975.

———. *The Iron Lily*. Harmondsworth, Middlesex, England: Puffin Books, 1975.

———. *Harrow and Harvest*. Harmondsworth, Middlesex, England: Puffin Books, 1977.

Chapter Six
Compositional Elements
and Genres: A Matrix

As concerned readers of any age come to appreciate and to understand the various elements of story, they begin to see relationships among these elements and other ways of viewing literary works. One of the most obvious relationships is that of the elements to genre. A genre refers to a category of literature; and, in the broadest interpretation, all imaginative literary works can be categorized as (1) Fiction, (2) Poetry, or (3) Drama, each with its own subdivisions. Difficulties in distinguishing among genres exist because they are overlapping, that is, a dramatic work may be written in poetry, and because some of the subgenres are based on content and others on form. For example, a sonnet and an elegy are both recognized as subdivisions of poetry, but the first is distinguished by its form and the second by its content.

In general, the concept of genre in literature is a means of calling attention to established conventions and of alerting readers to procedures and assumptions that have become accepted by both authors and audiences as part of their willing suspension of disbelief. This does not mean that there are strict and definite prescribed forms or purity of genre. Rather, a genre is an artistic pattern of nebulous but recognizable characteristics that establishes a framework within which a particular work of literature may be viewed and that will provide a starting point for interpretation. This framework includes organizational and structural features as well as subject matter and often even certain patterns of predictable details.

Adults concerned with children's literature have generally used genre to refer to a narrower grouping of works most often categorized according to subject. Such subjects as animal stories, sports stories, adventure stories, mysteries, humor, and fancy have all been identified as genres of children's literature. Some of these are workable categories, but others are not. In a very real sense, all stories are adventure stories in one way or another; humor may exist in any type of story; and animals, sports, or mysteries can all be approached romantically or fancifully as well as realistically. Most child readers move rather quickly beyond such broad categorical descriptions as "animal stories" to make finer distinctions. For instance, a young reader of horse stories is likely to make very clear distinctions between realistic horse stories, such as those by Marguerite Henry, and the greatly romanticized *Black Beauty*, which portrays the animal character as a thinking, feeling being and the humans as little more than stereotypes. Talking animal stories, the third and fanciful version of this type, are often not even identified as animal stories by children. Either these animals take on so many human characteristics that they almost lose their identity as animals, or stories such as Robert Lawson's tale of the horse Scheherazade in *Mr. Revere and I* are so clearly humorous versions of historical fiction that any other classification becomes almost meaningless.

The matrix that follows (Figure 4) shows the relationship of key compositional elements to genres. This matrix takes an intermediate position in its determination of genres, accepting neither the very broad categories suggested by some critics or the very narrow classifications often accepted as the genres of children's literature. Drama is excluded because there is very little truly literary drama written for children. The subgenres contained within the various spaces of Figure 4 demonstrate that there are some established relationships between particular elements and genres. It is obvious, for instance, that historical fiction is a form of realistic fiction in which setting must be a key element. This is not to say that the characters will not be memorable or the mood, powerful but that, by definition, time is the distinguishing element of historical fiction just as place is of regional fiction. Most of the subgenres included on this matrix are there because, like historical fiction and regional fiction, there is an emphasis on a particular element in the very essence of the form.

Nonsense verse differs slightly in that, although one might initially associate this form with mood, it is the nonsense language with which the poet works that creates the mood for the reader. There are also a few subgenres included to point out something about the nature of what is generally available for children rather than essential elements that must be stressed in their composition. For this reason sports stories and biographies of sports figures are listed with plot, and sex education books with mood and tone. The plots of most sports stories for children are rather thin but they are also formularized and predictable, while many of the biographies of contemporary sports figures give more attention to detailed play–action sportscasts of a person's "big games" than they do to any real development of or insight into his or her character. The most obvious differences among sex education materials seem to be based upon the tone with which they present the information to children, as will be demon-

Figure 4: The Matrix: The Relationship of Key Compositional Elements to Genres

	Traditional Literature	Modern Fancy	Realistic Fiction	Poetry	Biographical Works	Informational Works
Character	Droll or Noodle Tales Trickster Tales Legends	Ghost Stories	Psychological Story	Epic		Animal Observations—Personified
Point of View		Personifications		Lyric Ode	Autobiography	
Structure Plot	Circle Story Cumulative Story Fable	Dream Fancy	Mystery and Detective Stories Stream of Consciousness Sports Stories	Haiku Sonnet Limerick Blank Verse Narrative Poetry	Diary Sports Biography Objective Biography	Experiment Books Guide Books
Setting	Folktale	Science Fiction	Historical Fiction Regional Fiction Sociological Fiction Pastoral Romance		Fictionalized Biographies of Childhood	
Mood/Tone		Tall Tale Enchantment Tales		Elegy		Sex Education Books
Language Symbol	Myth Parable	Mystical Fancy Modern Myth		Nonsense Verse	Psychoanalytical Biography	

strated in the discussion of specific books that will follow in this chapter.

No attempt has been made to fill every space of the matrix, and it is hoped that the absence of an entry will be a challenge to readers to either complete the matrix or to discover why there is no appropriate example. For instance, traditional literature, which here means all those tales passed down in the oral tradition with no known author, has two of its six spaces in Figure 4 blank. One might attempt to fill in these spaces or, just as likely in this case, question the validity of some of the items included in the other four spaces. I have obviously stretched a point to list "Folktale" as a more generic term under setting but have done so because we normally think of whole bodies of folktales as representative of people in particular places. Virginia Haviland's series of "Favorite Fairy Tales" from many lands exemplifies this while demonstrating also the difficulties in categorizing and labeling folk literature. Fairy tale is as often used as a generic term for all of folk literature as it is for the specific type of story containing some element of faerie or magic. I have also placed myth and parable to highlight their symbolic meanings, but such meanings are transmitted to us through memorable characters. In fact, a strong case could be made for including all traditional literature under character because it is, as Alan Dundes has described it, a kind of "autobiographical ethnography" or a people's own description of themselves.[1] Since these descriptions have been preserved and passed on in a limited number of specific forms, one might say that structure and plot along with character are the basic elements of all folk literature.

This matrix was not intended to account for all that is important in children's literature but was developed for its function as a teaching tool; it went through several revisions in attempts to make it serve this purpose. For example, in a previous chapter, story was divided into realism, romance, and fancy. An earlier version of this matrix included romance, but attempts to use this category seem to do little more than verify the view that the greatest proportion of children's literature is still approached romantically. So many of the titles would need to be in that category that the usefulness of the classification would have been virtually eliminated. Mysteries and historical and regional fiction are examples of types of stories normally thought of as realistic that, in fact, are almost always highly romanticized. This is, incidentally, as true of adult books as of those for children, and the very difficulty of fitting these things into the matrix was useful in bringing to consciousness something that most readers know tacitly. Since much of what is here listed as realism would have to be moved to romance, it seems that too much attention would then be focused on the relationship between realism and romance rather than the relationship between elements and genres. The decision was made, again on the basis of usefulness, to omit romance from the matrix. In much the same way, the decision was made to include biography, poetry, and informational works and to use examples from media other than print. With these decisions, the label "Elements of Story" was changed to "Compositional Elements" to indicate their importance in discursive as well as nondiscursive compositions in several media. The nature of biographical works for children was the major impetus in bringing this about and may serve as an example here.

Biography

Biography seems to exist as a bridge or continuum between fiction and nonfiction (see Figure 5). When children define biography as "the *story* of someone's life," they are giving an accurate account of the state of most biography published for them. A large percentage of children's biographies use the importance of a person's accomplishments and a limited number of facts about that life as the basis for a story

Figure 5: Types of Biographical Works

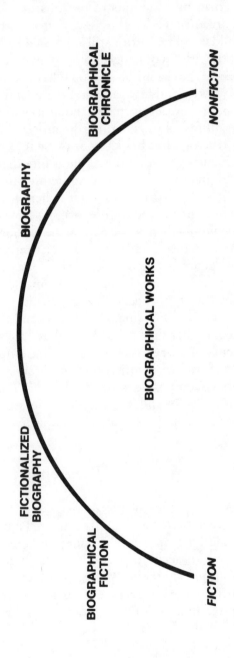

that may be entertaining but is usually not terribly informative. At least, such biographies are not very informative about the person; they may contain a great deal of detail about the time and place in which that person lived. This is primarily due to the fact that most children are more interested in the childhood than the adult accomplishments of a famous figure, and there is ordinarily not a great deal of specific information available about childhood activities. Most biographies for children are more accurate as accounts of the social history of childhood in a particular setting than they are as what we normally know as biography. These fictionalized biographies tend to invent very specific incidents and conversations in dramatizing imagined early experiences of the person.

At the one fictional end of the continuum are the biographical fictions such as *Ben and Me* that are clearly story but are also based on the facts of an actual individual's life. These stories often give as much or more information about the person as a fictionalized biography, but they move closer to pure story because of their use of a literary device, such as a talking animal, to add interest and move the action along. At the other extreme of the continuum are the biographical chronicles that attempt to present "the facts" without analysis or interpretation. Of course, it is never possible to present all the facts of a person's life and the very selection from among such facts is itself an interpretation of that life. In biographies for children, this chronicle form is most closely represented by photo essays or series of photographs and press clippings corresponding with the straight chronicle of the life of a contemporary public figure. For those who remember the early 1960s, the best examples may be some of the books about President Kennedy published shortly after his assassination. Biographies of contemporary sports figures may also make use of this form of organization.

Somewhere between biographical chronicle and fictionalized biography is what most adults normally think of as biography. These are the works that do not intentionally misrepresent or invent the facts of the person's life but do select and arrange them for dramatic effect in the reading. These contain much more factual detail about the person written about but, in their own way, they may be just as fictionalized as the "childhood" biographies. The most obvious examples of this kind of biographical writing are the psychoanalytic adult biographies that presume to analyze and attribute motives to a historical character. All of these non-story forms, poetry and information as well as biography, are included in the matrix to demonstrate that many of the same elements as are observed in fiction may be examined in their composition. It is hoped that the specific examples included in the matrices and the discussion of some of these works will bear this out.

Figure 6 uses the same matrix to cite examples of specific works that, in one way or another, may be thought of as representative of an interesting or unusual use of a compositional element in the particular genre. This matrix, like any static model of a dynamic interaction, attempts to hold still, simplify, and make sense of that which cannot really be held, simplified, or rationalized. Such a schematic represents no absolute authority, only the potential to encourage users to look at known phenomena in a new way. The value in such a matrix is precisely that — it does not pin creative works down in neat little boxes but opens new possibilities and encourages critical discussion as we share with others our perceptions of these relationships and of particular genres or literary works. In general, the more successful a work is in its total artistic composition, the more difficult it is to identify any one key element. The lines of the matrix are broken to indicate that critical support might be given to the placement of a specific work under any one of several elements, and challenging different readers to do this is indeed one of the most appropriate uses of the matrix. This challenging is precisely

Figure 6: The Matrix:
Specific Works Indicating the Relationship of Key Compositional Elements to Genres

	Traditional Literature	Modern Fancy	Realistic Fiction	Poetry	Biographical Works	Informational Works
Character	Noodles, Nitwits and Numskulls Hero Tales From Many Lands	Curious George Pippi Longstocking The Dragon Takes a Wife	Are You There, God. It's Me Margaret North to Freedom Stevie Queenie Peavy	Beastly Boys and Ghastly Girls People I'd Like to Keep A Book of Americans		Vulpes the Red Fox Maria and Ramon A Girl and Boy of Puerto Rico
Point of View		Freaky Friday The Borrowers Mouse and Tim Murphy, Molly, Max and Me	Harriet the Spy Breaktime The Pigman ...Barkam St. books The Dollar Man War on Villa Street	Prayers from the Ark	Ben and Me Poor Richard in France We Alcotts Can't You Make Them Behave King George?	Cosmic View This Is New York Behind the Wheel
Structure Plot	The Old Woman and Her Pig Arm in Arm	The Camel Who Took A Walk That's Good. That's Bad Fortunately Alice in Wonderland A Bear Called Paddington	Homer Price My Side of the Mountain Maximilian, You're the Greatest Encyclopedia Brown O'Henry's stories	Poems to Solve In a Spring Garden	Childhood of Famous Americans series Lincoln's Animal Friends	Fun With Chemistry Model-Making for Physicists
Setting	Favorite Fairy Tales Told in ...	Legend of New Amsterdam A Proud Taste for Scarlet & Miniver Traveler in Time	The House of Stairs Where the Lilies Bloom Homer's Lydia Slake's Limbo The Mixed-Up Files of Mrs. Basil E. Frankweiler Merry Ever After	Subway Swinger America Is Not All Traffic Lights Poems of the Midwest	George Washington's World A Day of Pleasure	The Story of an English Village In the Days of Dinosaurs Underground Frontier Living
Mood/Tone		The No-Name Man of the Mountain Mr. Popper's Penguins	The Chocolate War After the First Death The Snowy Day Dorp Dead My Grandson Lew	A Rocket in My Pocket Nightmares: Poems to Trouble Your Sleep Shrieks at Midnight	Why Don't You Get A Horse, Sam Adams? Pioneers in Freedom: Adventures in Courage	Life Story Green Is For Growing Story of a Baby Where Did I Come From? Wind Rose
Language Symbol	The Sun Is A Golden Earring Why the Sun and the Moon Live in the Sky	The Phantom Tollbooth Alvin Steadfast on Vernacular Island Amelia Bedelia Wind in the Willows	The Stone Book The Hundred Dresses My Special Best Words The Magic Moth	It Doesn't Always Have to Rhyme		Watchwords of Liberty Who Looks at Me

the business of criticism. There are no "right" answers to be found, only the sensitive and sound literary search that enables us to see more clearly and appreciate more fully. When we share that search with others, we cannot just *tell* them that our perceptions are accurate; we must *convince* them that our judgment is true to the spirit of the work and sound in its own response.

Character

The placement of a particular title on Figure 6 will appear to be a statement of the obvious to some readers and highly debatable to others. In general, fictional works included under character represent either those characters who are well developed and convincing to most readers or those that exaggerate a particular trait or traits to the ends of humor or to point out common human foibles. Characters who live beyond the pages of the book may be either those who are closest to our own lives or those who are striking in their disparity from ourselves. A memorable character unlike both ourselves and other story characters is the good fairy Mabel Mae Jones in *The Dragon Takes a Wife*, who greets those who come to her for help with "What's buggin' you, baby?" and may respond with "I can dig where you're coming from" or "That ain't no big thing." When her magic doesn't work for Harry the Dragon, she turns herself into a dragon to demonstrate what he should do; and, as Mabel Mae is "swishing her tail from side to side," Harry falls in love with her. She agrees to marry him because, as she says, "I never did dig fairying too much." In informational works, character seems to be used most obviously in books that tell about a specific place through an account of the life of a child who lives there or those that describe the life cycle of a species by personalizing (but not personifying) that cycle through the life of a particular animal.

Point of View

It is often difficult to decide whether it is character *per se* or the point of view of that character that is emphasized in story. For instance, is it Harriet the character or her unique view of the world that distinguishes *Harriet the Spy*? For the most part, I would choose to place such works under character. However, Harriet is developed as a character, to a large extent, through her recorded perceptions of the rest of the world. Therefore, I have included this book with point of view.

Other realistic approaches to point of view are those in which the interest comes in comparing two separate works that introduce some of the same characters and events from opposing points of view. *A Dog on Barkham Street* and *The Bully of Barkham Street* are perhaps the best example of this in that they are parallel works in which the antagonist in the first becomes the protagonist in the second. In *Dollar Man*, Marcus Rosenbloom, otherwise known as "Rosenballoon," is fat, fatherless, unpopular, and although strongly attached to his mother, very eager to find out who and where his father is. At one point in this story, Marcus is feeling sorry for himself and looks out of his window into the window of Willis Pierce, the good-looking, athletic kid at school who is sought after by others but is so sure of himself that he has no need to join the track team because everyone knows he is the fastest runner. Marcus sees Willis sitting at a table with his father in what he presumes to be a time of family closeness and sharing in stark contrast to his own aloneness at that moment. Then in *The War on Villa Street* the same incident is seen from Willis's point of view as a moment in which he has given up all hope for the drunken father who has disgraced and abused him and his mother. The incident is small and might easily be overlooked in either book, but when both stories are read, it is this moment in time that ties the two together and reminds us of the self-centeredness of our own visions of the world.

The Pigman, *The Night Daddy*, and *A Hero Ain't Nothin' but a Sandwich* are books in which the story is told through the alternating views of two or more characters. (Some might consider this structure, but I believe that it is point of view that is emphasized.) *Mouse and Tim* does the same thing in picture book format; instead of chapters that represent different points of view, Tim's account of events in roman type is alternated with Mouse's in italics. Although I have included this book with point of view, the sensitivity of the language and the warmth of Marc Simont's illustrations are compelling reasons for discussing the mood of this book as well.

Murphy, Molly, Max and Me, like Albert Cullum's other books for Harlin Quist, Inc., emphasizes a child's perspective in attempting to deal with the oftentimes absurd adult world. In this particular book, the point of view comes across most strikingly in Galeron's bold illustrations in which the teacher is seen from all angles, including from directly above, from above and behind, and from beneath her desk. Verbally the book seems to emphasize a tone and a point of view as much directed to adults as to children, forcing us, just as *The Geranium on the Window Sill Just Died but Teacher You Went Right On* and *You Think Just Because You're Big, You're Right* did, to view our actions and attitudes toward children as children themselves might perceive them.

From the point of view of *The Borrowers*, the little people in the book by that title, human beings are in the world to put down items that the borrowers might pick up for their comfort and convenience. *Freaky Friday* is another modern fanciful story that very obviously emphasizes point of view; Annabel wakes up in her mother's body one morning and has to cope with all the problems of what she had thought was an easy adult life for one whole day. Aidan Chambers's *Breaktime* is a powerful novel for young people told through a stream of consciousness technique and the move from first to third person. It is at times as difficult to follow as the disorderly mind of its narrator, but is well worth the effort.

It is interesting to look at point of view in poetry, biography, and informational works as well as in fiction. Each of the poems in *Prayers from the Ark* is in the voice of a particular animal that, in praying for those things important in its life, reveals not only something about its species but something about the human species as well. Biographies of well-known figures are frequently fascinating in terms of point of view. With the large number of works about such men as Abe Lincoln and Ben Franklin, anyone contemplating an additional book about one of these men will quite likely be eager to find a new perspective or point of view from which to write. Thus it is that we have *Poor Richard in France* narrated by Franklin's seven-year-old grandson, as well as Amos the mouse's fictionalized account in *Ben and Me*.

Informational topics are often made more accessible to children through a point of view that parallels their own. This may be the view of a city portrayed in the pictures and text of *This Is New York* or the visual detail of the presentation of what an operator of various vehicles sees from his position in *Behind the Wheel*. With humor and accurate detail, each double-page spread in this latter book shows a side view of an imaginary animal operating such conveyances as a motorcycle, a subway, a crane, and a helicopter, along with a labeled sketch of the instrument panel and a drawing of what one would see from the driver's seat. If *Behind the Wheel* shows youngsters things they would not normally see, *Inside: Seeing Beneath the Surface* and *Cosmic View* visualize that which can never be seen in actuality. The first presents very detailed cross-sectional views of all sorts of things from sandwiches to streets, houses to harbors, ocean liners to airplanes. The second opens with a girl sitting in a chair and then, in a series of pictures taken further and further away from her, moves out to infinity. Then the process is reversed to move closer and closer in until finally the view is of the nucleus of an atom.

Structure and Plot

In any examination of structure and plot in literature, the traditional patterns of folklore come to the fore, both through the original versions of these tales and in the many modern stories in the folk tradition. *The Camel Who Took a Walk* uses the repetitive structure of the cumulative tale but adds the twist of a surprise ending. The books *That's Good, That's Bad* and *Fortunately* use a "see-saw" pattern, in which the narrative is moved along by a back and forth, positive-negative balancing of events. These tightly patterned stories are very popular with young children because they can almost immediately enter into the structure and anticipate what will happen next. Often such stories have a refrain or some language that is repeated within the pattern so that young listeners can predict it and join in. Slightly older youngsters appreciate an episodic structure in a longer book such as *Homer Price* or *A Bear Called Paddington*, in which each chapter is an incident complete in itself. The "Childhood of Famous Americans" series of biographies has been read and enjoyed by readers of this same age for many years because these books are also filled with brief lively series of incidents that are related to, if not absolutely accurate about, the lives of real people.

The mystery is a fairly stylized form of story of great appeal to readers of all ages and is here represented by *Poems to Solve* as well as by *Encyclopedia Brown, Boy Detective* and *Maximilian, You're the Greatest*. One might wonder at the inclusion of *Alice in Wonderland* and *My Side of the Mountain* under structure and plot, but the first was included because it is a dream fancy that certainly contains a very lively series of events, and the second because it combines narration with a fictional diary.

Setting

Setting in story can take readers to times past, present, or future or can shift back and forth among these. It can take us to places as real as just next door or as fanciful as Narnia or Middle Earth. Realistic stories may have generalized city settings so that readers from both Chicago and Toronto can find something of their own city within, or they can be as specific as the New York City subway system of *Slake's Limbo* or the exhibits of the New York Metropolitan Museum of *From the Mixed-Up Files of Mrs. Basil E. Frankweiler.* Setting may be just a backdrop to story or it may be absolutely essential to the action and the spirit of the work, as in *Where the Lilies Bloom* or *The Stronghold.*

Sometimes the settings of stories, particularly of realistic stories, serve as the primary means by which children come to know about times and places remote from themselves. As one who grew up in "Pennsylvania Dutch country," I am interested to talk with others of my generation who formed their impressions of that area from Marguerite de Angeli's *Henner's Lydia* and *Yonie Wondernose.* Her precision of detail in both text and illustration, which I appreciate because of its familiarity, is what makes the place and its people come alive for those who have never been there. Although some authors have turned characters into caricatures with their attempts to reproduce the dialect, de Angeli somehow highlights the uniquenesses of language and customs while integrating them into a oneness with the ways of all people. It is this accuracy of detail that helps the reader enter into a story and become involved with its characters. Works of historical fiction may be the best examples of this. Not only do many of us ascertain a great deal of what we know of history from fictional works, but we are also more involved with these works as we recognize the accuracy of specific historical characters and events.

Nancy Ekholm Burkert's *Snow White* places a well-known fanciful story in a very detailed historical setting, while *A Proud Taste for Scarlet and Miniver* begins with twelfth-century English history but takes off from that to create a fanciful story. *The Story of an English Village* is a wordless informational book, while *The Legend of New Amsterdam,* which provides just as much visual information about an actual setting, is story because of its text, in which Crazy Annie sees visions of people and stones in the sky. Not until the last page do readers see modern New York skyscrapers and realize that Annie was not really crazy and that her visions were of the future. Finally there are those stories in which the settings themselves are so powerful that they exert an influence on the reader stronger than that of any other aspect of the work. The lingering horror of *The House of Stairs*, in which homeless children are confined in a window-less maze of stairs as a part of a government research project, is just such a setting for many readers.

Mood/Tone

There are as many moods in children's literature as there are in that for adults. Young readers can move from the wild hilarity of *The No-Name Man of the Mountain*, a modern tall tale, to the quiet wonder of *Charlotte's Web* to the ominous, almost nightmarish world of *After the First Death*. Along the way, one could meet Gilly Ground of *Dorp Dead* who goes to live with Kobalt, a ladder maker, whose houseful of ladders is not unlike *The House of Stairs* in its effect on the character and on readers. However, the mood in *Dorp Dead* is lightened somewhat by its almost fanciful allegorical approach and the symbol of the good hunter in the forest. One of the masters of mood and tone in stories for children is Joan Aiken, whose *The Wolves of Willoughby Chase* combines suspense with a truly funny spoof of the gothic novel and Victorian morality.

Tone, in both biographical writings and other informa-tional books, needs to be examined closely. Most biographies for children still place the person on a pedestal, point to his or her accomplishments, and in effect, say "go thou and do likewise." In the process, real people are often made into plaster saints who are of no interest to anyone, least of all children. Some recent biographical works have been more realistic in portraying people as believable human beings with faults and foibles and sometimes even with a sense of humor. Jean Fritz, in her series of books about men and events of colonial America, focuses in on a particular time or event and asks piercing questions, as indicated by her titles: *Where Was Patrick Henry on the 29th of May?*, *And Then What Happened, Paul Revere?*, *What's the Big Idea, Ben Franklin?*, *Why Don't You Get a Horse, Sam Adams?*, *Will You Sign Here, John Hancock?*, and even *Can't You Make Them Behave, King George?* These books are no less accurate than others about famous Americans, but because the information is presented with a lighter touch, I have listed them under mood and tone. The only exception is the biography of King George, included with point of view because it provides one of those rare opportunities for youngsters to see the American Revolution from the English point of view.

The tone of children's books about sex is particularly interesting to examine, and the three that follow aproach this topic in very different ways. In *The Story of a Baby* (1939) Marie Hall Ets combines scientifically accurate diagrams and text with a beautifully written and sensitively drawn, but highly sentimentalized, account of the growth of a baby from when it was "too small to be seen at all" to his first smile. Still a useful work with which many adults feel comfortable both for its sense of wonder about human life and its avoidance of the act of conception, this book has been reprinted in a smaller format in recent years.

Peter Mayle's *Where Did I Come From?*, on the other hand, is dedicated to, among others, "red-faced parents everywhere," and there is a sense in looking at these cartoon illustrations and reading the humorous asides that the creators of this book may have been trying too hard to overcome their own embarrassment in dealing with sex. Mayle does discuss conception, but the analogies and the personification have a kind of "cocktail party pseudo-sophistication" that may not be especially useful in explaining the facts of life to children. One wonders about the informational value of a work that shows a tiny tadpolelike character with top hat and bow tie sitting on a big red heart, smelling a rose, and saying, "How could an egg resist a sperm like this?" *Wind Rose* is more concerned with the parents' feelings about their daughter from the time she was conceived until her birth than with scientifically accurate information about her development. The gentle wash drawings and the joyful, poetic language combine to convey to the child addressed here the warmth and security of a caring, if somewhat unconventional, family.

Language

In most stories, language is the unnoticed medium that makes all else possible. However, there are those books in which the language itself stands out because of its special beauty, power, or inventiveness or because the nature of the work calls attention to the ways words are used. The language of *The Stone Book* is notable for its simplicity, its strength, and its metaphoric power, as seen in this description of Mary as her father lifted her to the top of the steeple on which he was working.

> Mary laughed. The wind blew on the spire and made the weathercock seem alive. The feathers of its tail were a marvel.
> Father twisted the spike with his hands against the wind, and the spike moved in its greased socket, shaking a bit, juddering, but firm. To Mary the weathercock was waking. The world turned. Her bonnet fell off and hung by its ribbon, and the wind filled her hair.
> "Faster! Faster!" she shouted. "I'm not frit!"

She banged her heels on the golden sides and the
weathercock boomed.
"Who-whoop! Wo-whoop! Wo-o-o-o!" cried Father.
The high note of his voice crossed parishes and
townships. Her hair and her bonnet flew, and she
felt no spire, but only the brilliant gold of the
bird spinning the air. [2]

Dr. Seuss uses language very differently in many of his
stories. His playfulness with words, outlandishly exaggerated
statements, and lively rhythms create a very different mood
from that of Alan Garner's *The Stone Book*, but in both cases,
the skill and craftsmanship in the use of language is evident.
John Steptoe's *My Special Best Words* is a realistic book about
the power of language in the lives of young children; it brings
out into the open some of the words normally uttered only in
private. Judy Blume, noted for her ability to get inside her
young characters and understand their concerns, does so in
large part because of her ability to capture the flavor of the
language of contemporary children and young people.

One Day It Rained Cats and Dogs illustrates the literal
interpretation of figurative expressions, while *Amelia Bedelia*
uses the distinctions between these two different uses of
language to create a humorous narrative of a maid who does
exactly what she is told — even when instructed to "dust" the
furniture or "dress" the chicken. The names of many of the
characters in *The Phantom Tollbooth* are plays on language,
but this technique is used even more obviously in *Alvin
Steadfast on Vernacular Island*, in which Alvin works with a
famous scientist to drive the Doubt from the island. Assisting
them in their battle against the Doubt and his troops (Bitter
Grudge, Purple Rage, and Ugly Rumor) are Running Commentary, a deerlike creature with red stripes who moves
around the island proclaiming the latest news; Appropriate
Gesture, who always does and says exactly the right things at
the right time; and Glowing Report, Small Wonder, Com-

mon Good, and Ultimate Aim, whose basic traits must be obvious. Eve Merriam takes her own playful look at language in *It Doesn't Always Have to Rhyme* with her poems defining "Serendipity," "Cliche," and "Onomatopoeia."

Symbol

Obviously some of the most powerful uses of language are symbolic. Garner's *The Stone Book*, for instance, has strong symbolic overtones, as does his earlier work *The Owl Service*. In these books, as in *Blue Willow*, *The Jazz Man*, *The Hundred Dresses*, and many others, the title itself refers to a symbolic element within the text. In *The Magic Moth*, for instance, the moth that has been contained in a jar flies to the ceiling and then out the window as ten-year-old Maryanne is dying. The gentle tone and religious belief that are evident throughout the story are given even greater symbolic significance in the gentle but sure ascent of the moth. Symbol is perhaps most obvious in works of mystical fancy, which, by definition, deal with symbolic or spiritual concerns. These works frequently make use of such devices as the talisman or the magic ring, which have symbolic significance carried over from the folk tradition. The writings of Alexander, Cooper, and Hunter are laden with symbolic relationships to Welsh and Celtic mythology, which add to their power and their beauty.

Genres

Although it was necessary to assign specific books to the categories of the matrix and to discuss their placement there, the matrix is best used as a guide in the discussion of a particular title. One need not decide or a group agree that the work under consideration does indeed "belong" at the coordinates of modern fancy and setting, for instance, for the use of a device such as the matrix to help focus attention on critical elements of that work. Recognizing the genre and subgenre that a work represents is important as a means of directing our expectations in a manner that is critically sound. This is especially true for those who have very strong preferences for their own reading and sometimes tend to judge all works by the characteristics of their favorite genre or subgenre.

A mystery differs markedly from mystical fancy, and a critic must be aware of those differences to discuss a work on its own terms regardless of his or her own personal preferences. Thus, one would first deal with the horizontal categories of the matrix, attempting to place a work with others most like it in genre. At times this is obvious, but at others very difficult. *Dorp Dead*, for instance, which I have included as a realistic novel, is considered to be a fanciful work by some critics. Even *Where The Wild Things Are* may be seen as either realistic or fanciful. Is it a story of a fanciful land of wild creatures or is it a very realistic story of a young boy's imaginative play? With Sendak's book this consideration may not make much difference in one's critical response, but with *Dorp Dead* it almost certainly would. Subgenres are even more difficult to distinguish. Is *A Wrinkle in Time* science fiction or mystical fancy? Does a critic's answer to this question determine in any way how he or she will perceive the book? These are some of the questions that arise in using the matrix. Then too, one begins to see changes within a particular genre or subgenre as it has developed over time. Science fiction is an obvious example of this development, in its movement from space opera, with its sweeping adventures and technological gadgetry, to a more philosophical, introspective consideration of the effects of technological developments on nature and on human beings. In this process, characterization has become increasingly important in science fiction.

The determination of genre directs our attention to certain compositional elements on the vertical axis of the matrix. If a work is historical fiction, setting is assumedly a key element and might be an appropriate place to begin our consideration. What one sometimes finds is that, although a work is identified as historical fiction, the time and place of the story do not seem to be critical to its composition. This anomaly is evident in many of the children's books set during times of war. One of the most powerful of these stories for young people is *North To Freedom*, the story of a boy's escape from an Eastern European prison camp to his mother in Denmark. But the time and place of this novel serve only as the means to introduce the boy's growing sense of himself and his gradual trust of and reaching out to others. Readers perceive only a slight sense of the war as the cause of the boy's isolation and fear of others; and the journey that occupies most of the book is more an internal than an external one, so place does not really influence content. The protagonist could have been escaping from any other institution or setting in which he was not permitted to develop fully as a human being, with no basic changes required in the work.

The same is true of many war stories that look from the specifics of a particular war to the general treatment of humankind's proclivity for war and its effects on innocent people so strongly that the specifics are no longer critical to the composition. There are, however, some novels of World War II that arrive at this universal consideration of war through the details of a particular time and place, as in Martha Bennet Stiles' portrayal of Germany in *Darkness over the Land*. In between are novels such as *Puddles down the Lane*, which describes the bombing of London from the point of view of several children who are then evacuated to the country for their safety. Details of London and the English countryside during wartime are realistic but are really incidental to what is basically a story of family life in a time of trial.

Using the Matrix to Think About Story

The use of the matrix (Figure 6) or any other schematic representing the components of artistic compositions may not add to our personal insights into particular works or types of works, but it is often useful in helping us talk about the work and share this insight with others. The considerations of the specific books to follow grew from discussions with other adults as well as with children, and these discussions added to my understanding and appreciation of these works.

Even before opening the pages of *The Secret Hiding Place*, children can anticipate a great deal about its contents by examining the cover. The front cover has a white background with rather simple black line drawings of a hippopotamus, some junglelike leaves, and a couple of smaller animals with pastel versions of the primary colors as a wash over them all. The back cover has a larger version of a hippopotamus wearing flowers on his head and apparently talking with a snake under a sunny sky, all with the same pastel wash. Children looking at these covers know immediately that this is a fanciful work and that the mood will be a light one—such is obvious from the light, airy, cheerfully colored figures of an animal that is ordinarily thought of as dull and heavy. Thus, the cover itself leads us to a consideration of the two elements that do indeed seem to be most critical in this composition.

In his search for a secret hiding place, the character of Little Hippo is one with whom most children can identify. Although the images are those of a child (albeit a hippo child) hemmed in by the protective care of the adults in his life, adults too know the need, at least temporarily, for a place to be away from but still within reach of the too-close-caring of those who love us. This story, like all literature, imaginatively comes to grips with some aspect of the common human condition. Little Hippo is true to the feelings and the characteristics of a young child but true also to his animal species. He lives in a hippo place, eats hippo food, and travels with a hippo herd. In fact, the whole story may hinge on a specific facet of hippo anatomy. Little Hippo's secret hiding place on the hill overlooking the herd is possible only because hippopotami are anatomically unable to look up. One does not need to know this fact in order to appreciate the story, but knowing it can only increase our appreciation. The portrayal of Big Charles and the other eighteen hippos who were so intent on caring for Little Hippo that they all waited for him to wake up and then "pushed and bumped each other, hurrying to bring Little Hippo his breakfast"[3] before settling down to watch him eat is exaggerated but also recognizable to both children and adults. Big Charles responds to Little Hippo's rebellion and his desire to "be by myself once in a while" by treating him as if he were ill and putting a cool leaf on his head, which also might be a recognizable pattern of behavior to some.

An aspect of characterization in *The Secret Hiding Place*, seldom even cause for consideration at the time this book was written, has become a reason for its positive reception in recent years. *The Secret Hiding Place* has been included on lists of nonsexist books for children because it is the male figure of Big Charles, rather than a female figure, who is the nurturing adult in Little Hippo's life. I do not believe that this factor is critical to the content of the book, but if it calls attention to an excellent story for children that might be ignored otherwise, I am all for it—as long as this factor is not given undue weight in the understanding and appreciation of the story.

There seems to be nothing unique or outstanding about the point of view, plot, or setting of this story. *The Secret Hiding Place* is narrated by a third-person observer but always from the perspective of the main character, and the setting is determined by the choice of the animal that is personified. The plot of the story is not unusual; young readers or listeners, especially those who keep the title in mind, will anticipate a resolution in which Little Hippo finds that secret place where he can be by himself once in a while without antagonizing those who care for him.

The mood of this story is a playful one, with a great deal of gentle humor that comes through quite clearly in language as well as in illustration. The opening page—with its picture of nineteen big hippos watching a little one sleep, and the words "Little Hippo was the pet of the herd. Every morning the big hippos waited for him to wake up so they could take care of him"[4]—sets the tone for what is to follow. On his morning walk, Little Hippo, who asks "What fun is a walk with nineteen hippos?,"[5] is warned every time he starts to venture off on his own. Often the language of these warnings adds to the fun for a young child, as in "Don't go in that tall grass where zebras hide. Do you want to catch stripes?"[6] The playfulness is reinforced in the game of hide-and-seek organized by Big Charles to put Little Hippo in a better frame of mind. Again the humor comes through in the main character's attempts to find a hiding place in the flowering trees or in the river, where, in each instance, he is greeted by half a herd of hippos calling him to "come hide with us."

The dark side of aloneness is represented by a double-page spread of the character hiding in the lion's cave, which is "filled with bat squeals and wind noises." The picture of Little Hippo, all black this one time in the book, cowering in the cave, and saying, "I'm scared. I don't want to be alone *this* much,"[7] is as powerful as it is humorous. Perhaps Little Hippo's earlier conversation with the turtle and the snail was a premonition of this scene. "You're lucky," he had said to them, "You carry your hiding places with you. What's it like inside?" And as they answered (" 'It's dark,' said the turtle." " 'It's dark,' said the snail.")[8], the usual fine-lined pastel drawing of them changes to a heavy, solid black. Of course, Little Hippo leaves the cave and after a misadventure with a "cross, old sleepy rhinoceros" comes to the top of a small hill just above the herd that is looking for and calling to him. He enjoys his freedom for a moment before racing up to Big Charles shouting, "Home free, home free." The book ends with Little Hippo having "never told anyone about his secret hiding place where he could be alone, but not too alone."[9] How satisfying a resolution to a story that speaks to all of us.

A discussion of these aspects of *The Secret Hiding Place* might lead some readers to indicate that character is the key element, while others try to convince them that mood or language are even more important. In using the matrix as a tool to get people thinking about story, such disagreements are far more beneficial than any agreed upon placement within the schematic. Any decision is a "correct" one if it is true to the spirit of the work and can be supported by evidence from it.

The cover of *na-ni* is certainly very different and not as revealing as that of *The Secret Hiding Place*. The bright yellow background has, in addition to the title in red and the author's name in black, a modernistic, somewhat stylized black-and-white drawing of a tall city building with a streetlight in the shape of an eye in front and the childlike drawing of the head of a person, as represented by a circle on a stem with an eye, a mouth, and an ear drawn on, coming out of the top. The style of the drawing may be somewhat disturbing to some, but beyond that there is little to be learned from this cover except that the contents quite likely have something to do with city life.

On the page opposite the copyright page is a visual indication of the setting represented by a street sign reading *7Ave* and *133*. The text opens to a plain white double-page spread with a tight block of print in the middle of one side that, on closer look, is made up of a series of short, declarative sentences with no capital letters to signal their beginnings. Upon reading this text, one is aware immediately of the power of the language. The first page reads:

9:00 this morning 133 street is awake.
men and ladies talk and sing on the stoops.

men and ladies are talking rainbows in the street.
they gossip with friends and yell up to the windows.
down the block a yellow garbage truck is noisy.
chocolate children on the sidewalk skip and play.
it is sweet and warm today.[10]

As the opening page indicates, this is basically a quiet mood piece against a rather stark background. For more than half the book, na-ni just sits at the curb with her fingers playing in the dirty water from a leaking fire hydrant and waits for the mailman to come. As her friend arrives, the beauty of the language reveals the contrast between the sensitivity of the character and the harshness of the environment.

lollipop says, "waiting for what?"
na-ni listens to her heart beat.
lollipop says, "waiting for what?"
"so i can fly," says na-ni.
lollipop's foot steps in a dog turd.
she sits on the curb near na-ni.
lollipop says, "where will you fly to?"
"you'll see, just wait," says na-ni.[11]

On the next page is a passage that almost repeats the first line of the book and, in so doing, not only serves as a rest does in music but also reminds us of the slowness of time when we are waiting for something we really want. Here, after pages of text, no time has passed.

133 street 9:00 this morning is awake.
old men play checkers in old clothes.
buildings sparkle in the morning light gold.
a tomcat on the sidewalk rubs his nose.[12]

As the two girls wait together and observe neighborhood activities, na-ni daydreams about her bike that flies and tells lollipop that "today the day momma's mailman bring me a bike"[13] because "today the day of welfare"[14] and "the mailman puts a green letter in the mailbox. this the last one this month. and momma promised me a bike."[15] The mail-man finally comes and, as na-ni runs to the fourth floor to get her mother, lollipop sees "a lean strange man" come into the building and break open the mailboxes with a screwdriver. By the time na-ni and her mother get there, both the lean man and the green check are gone, as are na-ni's dreams of a bicycle.

Although the story is told in the third person, there is a great deal of dialogue that helps to reveal character and makes readers care about na-ni. No matter how much we care about her, however, we are always kept at a distance and do not identify with her as a reader often does with the protagonist of story. Rather than feeling *with* na-ni, we feel *for* her and for all of us who have wanted something, waited for it, and have had it snatched away at the last moment. The aesthetic distancing is such that the story is told from the outside rather than from within. It is as if the reader is an observer listening in on the conversations of those she observes. Nonetheless, this is a very powerful and moving work. It does have a simple plot, but it affects the reader more as a mood book than as story because of this sense of being in the situation instead of inside the character.

The black line drawings that appear on approximately half of the pages of this book use a child's sense of perspective in that whatever is of importance at the moment is predominant. A fire hydrant can be as large as the house behind or a winged bicycle several times larger than a cluster of apartment buildings. In addition, the buildings in these pictures seem to be placed at odd angles as if they were falling in on one another, and their windows become eyes that continue out onto the sidewalk to the eye of the street light. All of the major characters are represented by the circle with abstract facial features reminiscent of an African mask on some sort of stem of varying lengths. Most of the minor characters in the street consist of two or even three circles, so that visually they are more complete than na-ni, lollipop, or na-ni's mother. As a seven-year-old with whom I have shared this book told me, "The people and the buildings are all broken up—like the story."

na-ni has not been especially well received by the adults who select books for children. Some believe that its subject matter is not appropriate for young readers. Others are concerned with the language, either with the specific mention of "dog turd" or the ungrammatical language of the young black child. Still others have said that this is a good book for older children; but since its format is that of a picture book, it will not be discovered and read by them. Probably the most frequent comment about this book is that it is too tied to a particular kind of city setting and would not be understood or appreciated by those unfamiliar with this setting.

It is true that the language of this book would be difficult for children, but it is also true that its poetic qualities demand that it be read aloud by a skilled reader, just as a work such as *The Wind in the Willows* seems to be enjoyed most by those not quite old enough to decode it with ease. The "dog turd argument" seems absurd in light of all the beautifully sensitive language of this story and the fact that these words are very mild compared to what most young children hear—and use—every day. Books should be a source of fine language for children, and "vulgar" words should not be included just because it is now acceptable to print them. This story, however, really deals with one's ability, through the power of language, to survive and, to some degree, even control and make sense of an environment that is in itself vulgar and unpleasant. I have shared this book with young people in junior high school, and they did enjoy it and thought it well worth reading and thinking about. Of course, they did not discover it on their own, but is it not the task of those of us who care about children's literature and believe that it cannot be restricted to narrow age levels to see that what is worth reading reaches appropriate audiences? I have also read this book, with very positive responses, to youngsters in a Harlem nursery school and to Inuit children in Nova Scotia. Although the second group did not recognize the setting or know about green welfare checks, they understood the essence of the story as well as the Harlem children because they, like all of us, knew what it is to want, to wait for, and to lose something dear to them.

A Taste of Blackberries is a realistic story for "middle-aged children," that is, for those approximately eight to twelve years old. On the cover is a softly colored illustration of two boys deep in a thicket picking berries. Again not much is revealed except that the facial expressions and soft shades would seem to indicate that this is probably a quiet rather than a bold, lively tale.

The story is told in the first person by one of these boys, a character whose name we never learn. Readers come to know the main character first through his descriptions of his friend Jamie, a clown and a showoff who is always ready to take a dare. One detects both aggravation and envy in these accounts from the quieter of the two friends. The pace of the first few pages is rather slow as one character comments on the other; neither does much. However, readers are soon drawn into the story and begin to sense that the description and the seemingly unrelated incidents, in which Jamie places himself in potentially dangerous situations, are foreshadowing some ominous event to follow. And indeed they do. Later that day when the neighborhood children are scraping Japanese beetles off a neighbor's grapevines, Jamie stops to poke a stick down a bee hole and stirs up a whole swarm. In the confusion that follows, Jamie and several other are stung, but Jamie dies from the sting.

The rest of the story deals with his friend's handling of the grief and the guilt surrounding Jamie's death in ways that are not unfamiliar to any of us who have lost those we love. First comes disbelief, the unwillingness to admit that this could have happened, then guilt that he didn't know and didn't even try to help, and then the desire to turn back the

clock so things could be as they were before. There are the
senseless little rituals in which the protagonist "kept feeling
that if I did certain things, like think about Jamie in the
bathtub, or didn't do certain things, like eat, that somehow
everything would be all right and it wouldn't be true that
Jamie was dead."[16] The entire book takes place in the few
days during which Jamie dies and is buried and then the day
after the funeral, when one could be "glad the main sadness
was over" and go on with life.

The thoughts and feelings of the main character (who
perhaps is given no name because he could be any one of us)
are the primary content of this work. There are other characters
who, in different ways, affect him and thus move the story
along. Jamie is, of course, exaggerated to make it more
believable that his friend would think he was faking and
ignore his apparent need for help when the bees stung. The
protagonist's mother is basically just a mother figure and
does not come to life even as much as Jamie's mother, who, in
spite of her own grief, recognizes the boy's need for reassurance
when "it didn't seem fair to remind Jamie's mother that I
was still alive."[17] Heather, who was next best friend to both
boys, serves as a catalyst to get the main character thinking
about what Jamie must have thought of him. As the two sit
together at the funeral, "I wondered what she was thinking.
Heather and Jamie and I, well, we'd been special to each
other. Even though Jamie and I didn't like it that Heather was
a girl. And Heather and I talked about what a showoff Jamie
was. My eyebrows arched in surprise. Never until this very
minute had I wondered what the two of them might have said
about me."[18] Mrs. Houser is the "nasty neighbor" who
children tend to invent if she doesn't exist in actuality. Probably
the two most interesting minor characters are Martha,
Jamie's little sister, and Mrs. Mullins, the "nice neighbor."
Although everyone thinks Martha is too young to comprehend,
she seems to understand better than the rest. "Jamie's
dead," she said. "Like the baby bird you and Jamie found and

tried to feed but he died anyway. Jamie's not coming home again. Not never."[19] Finally there is Mrs. Mullins, as strong as the granite seats and as quiet and gentle as the butterflies in her gardens, the person with whom the boy felt free to ask the questions for which he knew there were no answers: "Why did he have to die?," "What's it like to be dead?"[20]

Each character plays a role in the structure of this story, but it is mood and symbol that stay with the reader long after the pages of the book are closed. There is caring, there is concern, there is grief; but somehow, through it all, there is hope and a sense of renewal in spite of great loss. This sense comes through clearly in the structure: the book ends where it begins—in the blackberry patch where the berries had ripened and gotten fat since the day of Jamie's death. A thumb is pricked and one is reminded that "getting stuck was a part of berry picking." But there is also that first plump, full-to-popping berry in the mouth that makes his friend think of Jamie and wonder if somehow he can still remember the taste of blackberries. Just as nature continues in its seasons, life goes on and those who have grieved must put aside that grief and again take joy in what remains.

On first glance the picture cover of *Rabbit Island* appears to be a soft and comforting one, with the little brown rabbit very near the large grey one. A closer look reveals the features of the larger animal, and the colors of the sky seem to convey a sense of foreboding. In contrast, the title page is printed over a sunny landscape that turns out to be an island of warmth among steely gray settings. Large illustrations dominate this oversized book, and the predominance of blue-grey tones lends a cooling effect in contrast to the warmth of the little brown rabbit.

The verbal tone is also cool and matter-of-fact, as evidenced in the first two pages of text.

Factories that produce chocolate are chocolate factories. Factories that make guns are gun factories. But the factory in this story is a rabbit factory. It has no chimney and makes very little noise. Other factories have machines, but the rabbit factory just has conveyor belts rolling through it, carrying small pellets of rabbit food. Behind the belts sit hundreds of rabbits in narrow cages eating whatever comes along because they have nothing else to do. In this way they quickly grow fat. When they get fat enough, they will be slaughtered, but they don't know that. They also don't know whether it is summer or winter, day or night, for the factory has no windows, only gentle artificial light. [21]

The illustrations accompanying this text show first the outside view of the factory on a fairly stark landscape that comes to life only in the figure of a lone cow in the foreground. There is a modernistic rabbit logo on the front of the building that, even in its stylized appearance, reminds this viewer of the terror of a rabbit in a trap. All of this is in the lower half of the picture. The upper half shows a cloudy grey sky with the hint of impending storm. All in all, the effect is ominous.

The second page shows the interior of the factory and is equally ominous. From a very low angle, which adds to the fear and the awesomeness, one sees row upon row of identical cubes, which must be the rabbit cages. The same angle is used for the next illustration of two men unloading crates from a large truck bearing the factory logo. Then from the point of view of the grey rabbit, as yet unseen inside a cage, we observe, through the wires of the cage, a man bending over and reaching inside a crate full of rabbits. Although these are drawings rather than photographs, there is a sense about them of being one step from reality that, along with the changing point of view, makes one think of the eye of the camera.

On the adjoining page, it is as if the camera had been pulled back away from the big grey rabbit so that his back, as well as the hands of the man putting the little brown rabbit in the cage, is in view. Turning this page, one encounters the equivalent of three "frames" on each side of the double-page spread. In the first, the little brown rabbit obviously terrified, is pressed into the farthest corner away from the large grey one. As the eye moves from frame to frame, the little rabbit's ears rise, and he moves closer to the big one until finally they seem to be cuddling together in the opposite corner. As this movement is taking place in the illustrations, Big Grey is reassuring Little Brown that "We're all happy here. You don't have to be afraid. The men are always bringing in boxes with small skinny rabbits and they're always filling up boxes with big fat rabbits and taking them away. That's how life is; you can't change it."[22] When Little Brown wants to know what happens to the big rabbits who are taken away, Big Grey assures him that they go to a much better place where enormous White Watch Rabbits care for them. Unconvinced, Little Brown wants to know if that place has all the good things he had known on his farm and then if they can go see for themselves and not wait to be taken. So they gnaw through the walls and leave the factory through an air duct past a cross-sectional view of the factory that reinforces the sense of similarity and of control.

The next three frames are fascinating in the message conveyed through the use of perspective and point of view. First we see part of the big bulky figure of the grey rabbit close behind Little Brown, who is racing through the curve of the tunnel of the air duct to the light beyond. Then there is a straight-on shot from the rear of Little Brown, who is about to bound out into the world, and the final shot turns the viewer around to look into the eyes of Big Grey, sitting at the end of the duct, with Little Brown in the foreground seemingly urging him on. The full-page illustration on the opposite page emphasizes the smallness of the rabbits in the vast, open, untamed space, which appears even more enormous in contrast to the small, neat, orderly, and controlled spaces of the factory. From this picture until the last page, except for a double-page spread that serves as a map of the land pointing out how far they went and yet how close they remained to the factory, Big Grey and Little Brown are together in every illustration, although they are sometimes so small against the setting that we must search to find them.

The illustrations in this book are so compelling that it is tempting to go page by page and analyze each one of them. Suffice it to say that they complement and extend the written word, as Little Brown leads Big Grey through a world the former captive has forgotten and with which he no longer is able to cope. Finally, the big rabbit moans, "I can't find my kind of food anywhere, and I don't know *how* to dig a burrow. I wish I could go home. It's nicer there than anywhere,"[23] and the little one agrees to lead him back to the factory. When Big Grey tries to convince Little Brown to go home with him, the little rabbit admits that he is afraid of the road and of men and of dogs but, as he says, "You know I can't go with you." Little Brown assures Big Grey that he'll find another friend in the factory. Then, as Big Grey looks across what seems to be an extraordinarily wide space from inside his air duct, he says, "Not one like you." But Little Brown does not hear because he has not turned back and is already on his way back into his world. The final page has no text, but in the warmest illustration since the title page, it shows Little Brown as the one who has apparently made another friend.

This picture story book is a frightening and disturbing one to many adults, but it appears to be far less menacing to children. Perhaps it is that children identify with Little Brown and rejoice in his freedom while accepting the strange ways of adults, who seem to prefer to stay quietly indoors when they could be at play in the world. Most children are concerned about the rabbits in the factory, but they respond more with anger or with sadness than with the gnawing uncertainty expressed by adult readers attempting to determine "the meaning" of the story. Is this work a morality tale that speaks to us of authority, conformity, and regimentation in society? Is it an attempt to force older readers to examine their complacency in face of the prisons we accept for ourselves in this society? Must we not only accept these prisons but delude ourselves that they are for the best? Is it significant that the factory has such flimsy walls that those who have the courage might easily escape? What of the inability of those who have been in bondage to cope with freedom and the willingness, even eagerness, with which they return to the familiarity of the prison?

All of these are very big questions to come from a picture story book, but the older child or an adult could scarcely avoid raising them. Do these questions then make this any less a book for children? I do not think so. There is no book that will, or should, be read by everyone; and this book may have a less general appeal than many others. However, *Rabbit Island* is a powerful aesthetic composition that may be read on many different levels. Children who understand and enjoy this book on the simplest level have as much right to it as those who respond to its philosophical and political under-tones. It is wholly satisfying as story while, at the same time, unsettling as a statement about society and the human "is-lands" in that society.

Using the matrix (Figure 6) as a means of focusing attention on *Rabbit Island*, one thinks immediately of point of view as revealed through both illustration and the written word. The text keeps readers at a distance, almost pushes them away, while the illustrations pull them into an involve-ment with the story and force them to consider its content from different perspectives. Certainly the pictures also create and sustain a mood and establish settings that elicit strong responses. Character development in this story is interesting in that there is no antagonist, nor is there a clearly heroic figure. It is almost as if, in reading this book, we are pulled into an agreement with Big Grey: "That's how life is; you can't change it."

Of course, children are more likely to identify, at least to some degree, with Little Brown and thus get more involved in the action of the story. They have not yet learned to keep their distance, even when there is a great deal of aesthetic distancing built into the composition. If young children cannot involve themselves in story, usually through identification with a character, or immerse themselves in its mood, they will not read or listen to it at all. Given the interaction of all these elements, the resolution of the plot is completely predictable but no less powerful because of that predictability. The English translation of the text has a strength and a vigor that makes one wish to read the original German. The many interpretations of meaning in this book are witness to its symbolic power. In fact, most readers interpret the text as a whole as symbolic. Although this book certainly does not fit neatly and absolutely into any of the boxes of the matrix, the very process of considering this story in relation to the matrix brings out aspects of the work that might not be seen otherwise.

The danger of using a device such as the matrix to focus on the composition of literary works is that it may become some sort of sterile exercise in which critics try to reduce works of art to fragments that fit into neat little boxes. Any critical system or device is to be valued only so long as it increases insight into and ultimately adds to the enjoyment and appreciation of the works examined. Children should learn to approach criticism joyfully, even playfully, as a means of exploring aspects of that which brings them joy. In this way they will begin to develop the intellectual, the social, and the critical skills that will take them beyond narrow interpretations to consider possibilities of meaning that will stretch their imaginations and encourage them to open themselves to further encounters with literary works.

This is not to say that one does not work at criticism or that the ability to see literary works more perceptively comes without effort. Rather, the analysis of story should be a labor of love that increases appreciation as it does understanding. Such analysis differs markedly from the kind of plot summaries that frequently pass for criticism in the children's book field. Many children's book reviewers produce little more than the kind of book reports many of us learned to do in elementary school, the kind that, in the words of a third grader, "tell the story worser than the author did." In effect, such accounts of "this happened . . . then this . . . then this . . ." do not get at the essence of story. The basic plots of the greatest literary works are not all that different from the plots of thousands of other less successful works. There may be unique treatments of plot but, for the most part, it is not the plot itself but what one does with plot that makes great story.

In reading the analyses of the preceding books, one is informed of the events of plot, but those events are included to demonstrate something about literary form and about the way the particular author has handled compositional elements. A reviewer can be accurate in reporting plot sequences, but it is insight rather than accuracy that is needed to explore the works and one's own responses to them in literary criticism. An authentic critical approach leads not to final answers but to more insightful questions and to a more appreciative sense of wonder in the work of art. In essence, it is the critical exercise of this sense of wonder that is the literary connection between child and story.

Footnotes

 1. Alan Dundes, "Folklore as a Mirror of Culture," *Elementary English* 46 (April 1969): 471–82.

 2. Alan Garner, *The Stone Book* (London: William Collins Sons & Co., 1976), pp. 22–23. This book is one of a saga of four that trace the generations of a working class family in Chorley, a small town in Cheshire, England. The other titles are *Granny Reardun*, *The Aimer Gate*, and *Tom Fobble's Day*.

 3. Rainey Bennett, *The Secret Hiding Place* (Cleveland, Ohio: Collins & World Publishing Co., 1960), p. 2.

 4. Ibid., p. 1.

 5. Ibid., p. 5.

 6. Ibid., p. 6.

 7. Ibid., p. 19.

 8. Ibid., p. 9.

 9. Ibid., pp. 24–26.

10. Alexis Deveaux, *na-ni* (New York: Harper & Row, 1973), p. 1.

11. Ibid., p. 8.

12. Ibid., p. 9.

13. Ibid., p. 36.

14. Ibid., p. 36.

15. Ibid., p. 36.

16. Doris Buchanan Smith, *A Taste of Blackberries* (New York: Thomas Y. Crowell, 1973), p. 46.

17. Ibid., p. 45.

18. Ibid., p. 48.

19. Ibid., p. 45.

20. Ibid., p. 43.

21. Jörg Steiner, *Rabbit Island*, pictures by Jörg Müeller, trans. by Ann Conrad Lammers (New York: Harcourt, Brace, Jovanovich, 1978), pp. 1–2.

22. Ibid., p. 6.

23. Ibid., p. 21.

Children's Books Cited in Chapter Six

Adkins, Jan. *Inside: Seeing Beneath the Surface*. New York: Walker and Co., 1975.

Aiken, Joan. *The Wolves of Willoughby Chase*. New York: Doubleday, 1963.

Andrews, Roy, illus. *In the Days of Dinosaurs*. New York: Random House, 1959.

Atwater, Richard, and Atwater, Florence. *Mr. Popper's Penguins*. Boston: Little, Brown, 1938.

Belting, Natalie. *The Sun Is a Golden Earring*. New York: Holt, Rinehart & Winston, 1962.

Benet, Rosemary, and Benet, Stephen. *A Book of Americans*. New York: Holt, Rinehart & Winston, 1933.

Bennett, Rainey. *The Secret Hiding Place*. Cleveland, Ohio: Collins & World Publishing Co., 1960.

Blume, Judy. *Are You There, God, It's Me Margaret?* Scarsdale, N.Y.: Bradbury Pr., 1970.

Boeke, Kees. *Cosmic Views: The Universe in 40 Jumps*. New York: The John Day Co., 1957.

Bond, Michael. *A Bear Called Paddington*. Boston: Houghton Mifflin, 1960.

Brewton, Sara, and Brewton, John, eds. *Shrieks at Midnight: Macabre Poems, Eerie and Humorous*. New York: Thomas Y. Crowell, 1969.

Bulman, A.D. *Model Making for Physicists*. New York: Thomas Y. Crowell, 1968.

Burch, Robert. *Queenie Peavy*. New York: Viking Pr., 1966.

Burkert, Nancy Ekholm. *Snow White & The Seven Dwarfs: A Tale from the Brothers Grimm*. New York: Farrar, Straus & Giroux, 1972.

Burton, Virginia Lee. *Life Story*. Boston: Houghton Mifflin, 1962.

Carroll, Lewis. *Alice in Wonderland*. New York: Norton, 1971. (First published in 1865; *Through the Looking Glass* in 1871.)

Chambers, Aidan. *Breaktime*. New York: Harper & Row, 1979.

Charlip, Remy. *Arm in Arm*. New York: Parents, 1969.

———. *Fortunately*. New York: Parents, 1964.

Childhood of Famous American Series published by Bobbs-Merrill Co. includes:

    Parks, Aileen W. *Davy Crockett: Young Rifleman*. Indianapolis, Ind.: Bobbs-Merrill, 1949.

Seymour, Flora W. *Pocahontas: Brave Girl.* Indianapolis, Ind.: Bobbs-Merrill, 1961.

Stevenson, Augusta. *Abe Lincoln: Frontier Boy.* Indianapolis, Ind.: Bobbs-Merrill, 1959.

Weil, Ann. *Eleanor Roosevelt: Courageous Girl.* Indianapolis, Ind.: Bobbs-Merrill, 1965.

Childress, Alice. *A Hero Ain't Nothin' but a Sandwich.* New York: Coward-McCann, 1973.

Cleaver, Vera, and Cleaver, Bill. *Where the Lilies Bloom.* Philadelphia: J.B. Lippincott Co., 1969.

Cole, William, ed. *Beastly Boys and Ghastly Girls*, illus. Tomi Ungerer. Cleveland, Ohio: Collins & World Publishing Co., 1964.

Cormier, Robert. *After the First Death.* New York: Pantheon Books, 1979.

———. *The Chocolate War.* New York: Pantheon Books, 1974.

Cullum, Albert. *The Geranium on the Window Sill Just Died but Teacher You Went Right On.* New York: Harlin Quist, Inc., 1971.

———. *Murphy, Molly, Max and Me.* New York: Harlin Quist, Inc., 1976.

———. *You Think Just Because You're Big, You're Right.* New York: Harlin Quist, Inc., 1976.

Cunningham, Julia. *Dorp Dead.* New York: Pantheon Books, 1965.

Dayrell, Elphinstone. *Why the Sun and Moon Live in the Sky.* Boston: Houghton Mifflin, 1977.

De Angeli, Marguerite. *Henner's Lydia.* New York: Doubleday, 1936.

———. *Yonie Wondernose.* New York: Doubleday, 1944.

De Gasztold, Carmen B. *Prayers From the Ark*, trans. Rumer Godden. London: Macmillan, 1967.

Deveaux, Alexis. *na-ni.* New York: Harper & Row, 1973.

Dragonwagon, Crescent. *Wind Rose.* New York: Harper & Row, 1976.

Estes, Eleanor. *The Hundred Dresses.* New York: Harcourt, Brace, Jovanovich, 1944.

Ets, Marie Hall. *The Story of a Baby.* New York: Viking Pr., 1939.

Fisher, Aileen, and Rabe, Olive. *We Alcotts.* New York: Atheneum Publishers, 1968.

Fitzhugh, Louise. *Harriet the Spy.* New York: Harper & Row, 1964.

Fleming, Alice. *America Is Not All Traffic Lights: Poems of the Midwest.* Boston: Little, Brown, 1976.

Foster, Genevieve. *George Washington's World*. New York: Charles Scribner's Sons, 1941.

Freeman, Mae E., and Freeman, Ira F. *Fun with Chemistry*. New York: Random House, 1967.

Fritz, Jean. *And Then What Happened Paul Revere?* New York: Coward-McCann, 1973.

———. *Can't You Make Them Behave, King George?* New York: Coward-McCann, 1977.

———. *What's the Big Idea, Ben Franklin?* New York: Coward-McCann, 1976.

———. *Where Was Patrick Henry on the 29th of May?* New York: Coward-McCann, 1975.

———. *Why Don't You Get a Horse, Sam Adams?* New York: Coward-McCann, 1974.

———. *Will You Sign Here John Hancock?* New York: Coward-McCann, 1976.

Galdone, Paul. *The Old Woman and Her Pig*, illus. Paul Galdone. New York: McGraw-Hill, 1961.

Garner, Alan. *The Owl Service*. New York: Henry Z. Walck, 1968.

———. *The Stone Book*. London: William Collins Sons & Co., Ltd., 1976.

Gates, Doris. *Blue Willow*. New York: Viking Pr., 1940.

George, Jean. *My Side of the Mountain*. New York: E.P. Dutton, 1959.

George, John L., and George, Jean. *Vulpes: The Red Fox*. New York: E.P. Dutton, 1948.

Goodall, John S. *The Story of an English Village*. New York: Atheneum Publishers, 1979.

Grahame, Kenneth. *The Wind in the Willows*. Cleveland, Ohio: World Publishing Co., 1966. (First published in 1908.)

Gripe, Maria. *The Night Daddy*. New York: Delacorte, 1971.

Haviland, Virginia. *Favorite Fairy Tales Told in France*. Boston: Little, Brown, 1959.

———. *Favorite Fairy Tales Told in Denmark*. Boston: Little, Brown, 1971.

———. *Favorite Fairy Tales Told in Greece*. Boston: Little, Brown, 1970.

———. *Favorite Fairy Tales Told in India*. Boston: Little, Brown, 1973.

Hazeline, Alice, ed., *Hero Tales From Many Lands*. Nashville, Tenn.: Abingdon Pr., 1961.

Henry, Marguerite. *King of the Wind*. Skokie, Ill.: Rand McNally, 1948.

———. *Misty of Chincoteague*. Skokie, Ill.: Rand McNally, 1947.

———. *Justin Morgan Had a Horse*. Skokie, Ill.: Rand McNally, 1954.

Henry, O. *The Four Million and Other Stories*. New York: Airmont Publishing Co., 1965.

Holm, Anne. *North To Freedom*, trans. L.W. Kingsland. New York: Harcourt, Brace, Jovanovich, 1965.

Holman, Felice. *Slake's Limbo*. New York: Charles Scribner's Sons, 1974.

Hunter, Mollie. *The Stronghold*. New York: Harper & Row, 1974.

Jacobs, Frank. *Alvin Steadfast on Vernacular Island*. New York: Dial Pr., 1965.

Jordan, June. *Who Look at Me*. New York: Thomas Y. Crowell, 1969.

Juster, Norton. *The Phantom Tollbooth*. New York: Random House, 1961.

Keats, Ezra Jack. *The Snowy Day*. New York: Viking Pr., 1962.

Kohn, Bernice. *One Day It Rained Cats and Dogs*, pictures by Aliki. New York: Coward-McCann, 1965.

Konigsburg, E.L. *From the Mixed-Up Files of Mrs. Basil E. Frankweiler*. New York: Atheneum Publishers, 1967.

———. *A Proud Taste for Scarlet and Miniver*. New York: Atheneum Publishers, 1973.

Koren, Edward. *Behind the Wheel*. New York: Holt, Rinehart & Winston, 1972.

Lasker, Joe. *Merry Ever After: The Story of Two Medieval Weddings*. New York: Viking Pr., 1976.

Lawson, Robert. *Ben and Me*. Boston: Little, Brown, 1939.

———. *Mr. Revere and I*. Boston: Little, Brown, 1953.

———. *Watchwords of Liberty: A Pageant of American Quotations*, illus. Robert Lawson. Boston: Little, Brown, 1957.

Leach, Maria. *Noodles, Nitwits and Numskulls*. Cleveland, Ohio: Collins-World Publishing Co., 1961.

Lee, Virginia. *The Magic Moth*. New York: Seabury Pr., 1972.

L'Engle, Madeline. *A Wrinkle in Time*. New York: Farrar, Straus & Giroux, 1962.

Lewis, Richard, ed., *In a Spring Garden,* illus. Ezra Jack Keats. New York: Dial Pr., 1976.

Lexau, Joan M. *That's Good, That's Bad*. New York: Dial Pr., 1963.

Lingren, Astrid. *Pippi Longstocking*. New York: Viking Pr., 1950.

Lubell, Winifred, and Lubell, Cecil. *Green Is for Growing*. Skokie, Ill.: Rand McNally, 1964.

Macaulay, David. *Underground*. Boston: Houghton Mifflin, 1976.

McCloskey, Robert. *Homer Price*. New York: Viking Pr., 1943.

McNulty, Faith. *Mouse and Tim*, illus. Marc Simont. New York: Harper & Row, 1978.

Mayle, Peter. *Where Did I Come From?*, illus. Arthur Robins. Secaucus, N.J.: Lyle Stuart, 1973.

Mazer, Harry. *The Dollar Man*. New York: Delacorte, 1974.

———. *The War on Villa Street*. New York: Delacorte, 1978.

Merriam, Eve. *It Doesn't Always Have to Rhyme*. New York: Atheneum Publishers, 1964.

Monjo, F.N. *Poor Richard in France*. New York: Holt, Rinehart & Winston, 1973.

Myers, Walter Dean. *The Dragon Takes a Wife*. Indianapolis, Ind.: Bobbs-Merrill, 1973.

Norton, Mary. *The Borrowers*. New York: Harcourt, Brace, Jovanovich, 1953.

O'Neill, Mary. *People I'd Like to Keep*. New York: Doubleday, 1964.

Parish, Peggy. *Amelia Bedelia*. New York: Harper & Row, 1963.

Parker, Alan. *Puddles Down the Lane*. London: W.H. Allen & Co., Ltd., 1977.

Prelutsky, Jack. *Nightmares: Poems to Trouble Your Sleep*. New York: Greenwillow Books, 1976.

Randall, Ruth P. *Lincoln's Animal Friends*. Boston: Little, Brown, 1958.

Rey, H.A. *Curious George*. Boston: Houghton Mifflin, 1941.

Rogers, Mary. *Freaky Friday*. New York: Harper & Row, 1972.

Rosenbloom, Joseph. *Maximilian You're the Greatest*. New York: Grosset & Dunlap, 1979.

Sasek, Miroslav. *This Is New York*. New York: Macmillan, 1960.

Schloat, G. Warren. *Maria and Ramon: A Girl and Boy of Puerto Rico*. New York: Alfred A. Knopf, 1966.

Schonborg, Virginia. *Subway Swingers*. New York: William Morrow Co., 1970.

Sendak, Maurice. *Where the Wild Things Are*. New York: Harper & Row, 1963.

Sewell, Anna. *Black Beauty*. New York: Charles Scribner's Sons, 1952. (First published in 1877.)

Singer, Isaac B. *A Day of Pleasure: Stories of a Boy Growing Up in Warsaw*. New York: Farrar, Straus & Giroux, 1969.

Sleator, William. *The House of Stairs*. New York: E.P. Dutton, 1974.

Smith, Doris Buchanan. *A Taste of Blackberries*. New York: Thomas Y. Crowell, 1973.

Sobol, Donald J. *Encyclopedia Brown: Boy Detective*. Nashville, Tenn.: Thomas Nelson, 1963.

Spier, Peter. *The Legend of New Amsterdam*. New York: Doubleday, 1979.

Steele, William O. *The No-Name Man of the Mountain*. New York: Harcourt, Brace, Jovanovich, 1964.

Steiner, Jörg. *Rabbit Island*, pictures Jörg Müller and trans. Ann Conrad Lammers. New York: Harcourt, Brace, Jovanovich, 1978.

Steptoe, John. *My Special Best Words*. New York: Viking Pr., 1974.

———. *Stevie*. New York: Harper & Row, 1969.

Stevenson, Janet. *Pioneers in Freedom: Adventures in Courage*. Chicago, Ill.: Reilly & Lee, 1969.

Stiles, Martha Bennet. *Darkness Over the Land*. New York: Dial Pr., 1966.

Stolz, Mary S. *The Bully of Barkham Street*. New York: Harper & Row, 1963.

———. *A Dog on Barkham Street*. New York: Harper & Row, 1960.

Swenson, May. *Poems to Solve*. New York: Charles Scribner's Sons, 1966.

Tunis, Edwin. *Frontier Living*. New York: Thomas Y. Crowell, 1976.

Tworkov, Jack. *The Camel Who Took a Walk*. New York: E.P. Dutton, 1951.

Uttley, Alison. *A Traveler in Time*. New York: Viking Pr., 1964.

Weik, Mary Hays. *The Jazz Man*. New York: Atheneum Publishers, 1966.

White, E.B. *Charlotte's Web*. New York: Harper & Row, 1952.

Withers, Carl A. *A Rocket in My Pocket: Rhymes and Chants of Young Americans*. New York: Holt, Rinehart & Winston, 1948.

Zindel, Paul. *The Pigman*. New York: Harper & Row, 1968.

Zolotow, Charlotte. *My Grandson Lew*. New York: Harper & Row, 1974.

Chapter Seven
Planning Encounters with Story

In planning children's encounters with story, one must appreciate as a reader and inquire and explore as a critic while maintaining the basic relationship with children as parent, teacher, or librarian. Each of these roles and activities supports the others and helps the adult expose children to possible engagements with story in ways that encourage them to find in their reading a greater source of enjoyment, of insight, and of satisfaction. Those who work with children compose their own ideas about young people, about literature, and about criticism to establish a position in relation to story that is different from that of either the casual reader or the literary scholar or critic. They conceptualize a way of thinking about story that enables them to make decisions based on more than prescribed guides or their own "feel for" literature. They must become confident in their own judgments about literature and accept the responsibility for their own decision-making in this field. Those who plan literary encounters for children must focus on key ideas about literature and structure possible learning sequences in which children may discover more and more about the nature of story as an imaginative means of shaping the experiential world.

In planning children's encounters with story, adults must release them to read and listen to a wide variety of stories with no obligation to report back or respond to others. We must be willing both to "teach more less" and to "teach less more." That is, we must give up the notion still held by some teachers and librarians that children have not really read a book until they submit some proof of the fact, usually in the form of an oral or written book report. It is far more important for children to turn to books often for their own reasons than to write beautiful plot summaries to be filed with their cumulative record or to add another segment to the bookworm on the library wall. In most instances, we know more about the comprehension of a child who catches our eyes during the reading of a particularly vivid image, laughs uproariously at an incongruous exaggeration, or shares a moment of silence after a moving incident than we do about one who writes numerous book reports. This is not to say adults should not encourage children to respond to and share their reactions to story in whatever ways are appropriate. However, if we have in mind an internal and coherent structure for increasing children's sensitivity to story, it is that which should be used to evaluate literary encounters rather than traditional forms of children's responses. The literary climate of the home, classroom, and library; the opportunities provided for reading and sharing books; the selection of materials available to children; and especially our own responses to and enjoyment of story are more important means of encouraging children's interactions with and valuing of story than any responses we demand of them.

On the other hand, in "teaching less more," we must be

prepared to go far deeper into the discussion of those few books to which children really respond than we have been used to in the past. Even young children are far more able than we have given them credit for to look insightfully into a work of literature and re-create not only the content but the spirit of that work. In fact, young children are often freer and more imaginative in their interaction with story before they become bogged down in the process of decoding; youngsters almost always develop literary abilities before reading skills. Our task as adults working with children and story is to recognize literary abilities at their earliest stages of development and to acknowledge the importance of their development, side-by-side with reading skills, in the life of every child.

Children are often the most emphatic critics of the literature available to them, but adults do not always recognize the beginning stages of literary criticism in a child's responses, nor do they always help children towards a more intelligent appreciation and a just estimate of the literary work. The first evidence of critical judgment on the part of a child is often a physical one. The young girl who squirms or is easily distracted during the reading of a story is indicating the inappropriateness of that story for her at that particular time. Although this is not always a response to the literature itself, it may be, and consistent reactions of this sort from children should cause us to examine that work more closely for its literary quality. Of course, what children like does not define good literature any more than their taste for candy corresponds with its nutritional value. On the other hand, the rapture of a young listener should not be totally disregarded in the evaluation of literature. The experience of enjoyment or of awe in response to a work of art is not just an emotion but a way of understanding. It usually indicates that the whole of the work is comprehensive and illuminating. In addition, there are other forms of physical criticism that one might observe in a young listener. Often a child literally moves with a story, joins in a refrain, anticipates the action, or reenacts its characters. These activities, the moment of silence at the end of a story, or the perennial "Read it again" may be the kind of involvement that can become the beginning of criticism.

Just listening to a story all the way through requires the mastery of many critical literary abilities by the young child. In order to make "story sense" of what is heard, children must be able to hold in their minds a sequence of events, respond imaginatively to relationships among characters, use significant details to anticipate events and predict outcomes, and detect clues to mood and tone. Most children have an intuitive feel for literary form.[1] Whether this is innate or learned is not of prime importance at this point; what is important is that it exists. An adult often unwittingly proves that this feel for form exists when attempting to tell a story to a child. If too many characters or events are included without tying them into the basic fabric of the story, even a young child will often challenge with "What ever happened to . . . ?" Somehow a child seems to sense that story must have unity and coherence, that a character or event belongs in story only when it is necessary for the resolution of the whole. As children hear more stories and learn to read and write themselves, they begin the gradual development of these critical abilities. It is through the example of fine literature and the discussion with knowledgeable and sensitive persons that their own literary standards are raised.

Another way in which the young child exercises critical judgment even before reading independently is by evaluating the illustrations while listening to the text. Most children are quick to notice if a picture does not correspond exactly with the author's description, and many are also able to distinguish those that do not go with the text in more subtle ways, such as mood or tone, although they are seldom able to express this in any way other than "I don't like it."

We all read with what we have read before. It is only through comparison that children can begin to make critical evaluations. At first these will probably be choices among books that have been read to them previously. From there, they might go on to distinguish one kind of story from another and to ask for a "Once upon a time" or a "Believe" story. As soon as boys and girls can do this, they are beginning to understand the uniqueness of various literary forms.

Young readers are ordinarily quick to say whether they liked a particular story but reluctant to go beyond that to discuss what it was in the literary work that they liked or disliked. Since "liking" is not a literary judgment, adults must find ways to help children get beyond that point in their discussions of literature. Sometimes just the additional question of "Why?" will encourage a child to relate original responses to something in the work itself. Subjective judgments must be valued, for, in fact, all judgments are subjective. However, children should also realize that subjective judgment without explication is more autobiography than criticism.

Rather than responding to literature by asking children "Did you like it?," we might begin by asking "What is it about?" This shifts the emphasis more toward the work itself and leaves an opening for the introduction of almost any literary element.

For example, one October several years ago, a six-year-old boy brought a book to me and asked me to read it aloud to him and his friends. It was not one I knew and appeared to be more the "supermarket" variety than "good" literature, so I was reluctant to do so. My young friend was insistent, however, and because it seemed so important to him to have *his* book read, I agreed. It turned out to be a rather uninspired story about a brother and sister in a small town who set out trick or treating on Halloween and ended up paying a very brief and very frightened visit to the inevitable "haunted house." I believe that the children were more enthralled with the impending holiday than with the power of this story; nevertheless, they seemed to enjoy it. After listening to their spontaneous responses, I asked each of them to tell me what the story was about, and their answers demonstrated that we each make our own meaning from a story. They also referred to very different literary elements in their responses. Of course, they did not use the words character, plot, setting, mood, and point of view, but they did speak of these things when they said:

"It's about a big boy and his little sister on Halloween."
"It's about all the different things kids do on Halloween."
"It's about a big haunted house with cobwebs and ghosts and strange noises."
"It's about how scary it is on Halloween."
"It's about how a boy feels when he has to take care of his little sister instead of doing what he wants to do."

In my early years of working with children, I would quite likely have been concentrating so much on what I was going to do next that I would not have made the correspondences between what the children said and what I had learned in my own study of literature. Until we have built up experience and confidence with both children and literature, most adults find it difficult to decide when we can give up leading children through whatever we had planned for them in order to follow their responses. Often this hesitancy reflects our fear of losing control of the situation, either in terms of group behavior or in intellectual content, because certainly the smallest child can ask questions that the wisest adults cannot answer. Consequently, when adults ask children questions, we tend to listen *for* the answers we have predetermined will move our plan ahead rather than really listening *to* new possibilities opened up by children's responses. This is not to say that those who work with children should not plan activities very carefully to provide the richest experience for all involved, but we need to develop the ability to recognize when giving up the plan and living in and of that moment with children is the most beneficial for all.

Following up on their comments, we might ask questions that encourage children to extend their responses further into the work itself and to seek some balance between their subjective experiences and the limits and possibilities of the literary form. It is the insightful second or third question that leads children more discriminatingly into the literary work and helps them to achieve the aesthetic distance required to separate themselves from the work of literature. Children are, in one sense, evaluating as they select elements to remember and discuss and allow their personal reactions to be noted by others.

Although this kind of reaction and discussion seems to come quite naturally from even very young children in a responsive environment, adults cannot just sit back and wait for it to happen. In their selections of stories for use with children and in their own imaginative responses to them, they encourage the children's own reactions to and experiences of literary forms. If after reading one of those frightening Halloween stories most children love, the reader can honestly say— "Wow, the descriptions of that haunted house and all those weird sound effects really gave me the chills. I always enjoy reading a story that gives me a good scare"— one is doing several things. The adult is legitimizing the sharing of immediate personal responses to literature; helping to sort out the differences between the imaginative life of story, in which one may enjoy the thought of being frightened, and the actual everyday world, in which fear is no enjoyable matter; and pointing to major elements of mood and setting. Such a comment of course should not be planned in advance for its "teaching" content but must be a sincere response to a work of art. Only in an atmosphere of trust in which both adults and children are free to share their thoughts and feelings with others will youngsters allow themselves to be affected by story, to reveal the state of their own knowing, and to begin the process of critiquing their own knowledge that is what learning and growing is all about.

Even if we do not immediately follow up on children's responses, we should be listening carefully enough to them that we can store their ideas in our own consciousness and return to them when appropriate. Thus, in hearing the responses to the Halloween story, we might encourage children, using whatever labels are right for them, to discuss any or all of the elements of that story or we might use what we have learned about their reactions to story in planning further encounters with literary works. If, for instance, we decide that children could benefit from and enjoy developing their understanding of mood or point of view, we might, without mentioning these terms, select stories to read to them over a period of time that convey different moods or points of view. Then, when the moment is right, children might be encouraged to compare and contrast several stories they have heard. In most instances youngsters find such discussions fascinating, feel good about themselves because they are so knowledgeable (which indeed they are), and at the same time increase their abilities to respond to and appreciate good literature. And recognizing "when the moment is right" is not really a subjective or intuitive knowing granted only to a gifted few working with children. It is the result of dedication, concern, and hard work. It is the result of learning far more about literature than we would ever share with children, of studying children and their social, emotional, and intellectual development, and of caring enough about the youngsters with whom we work to take them seriously, respect them as human beings, and give them the very best that we have to offer.

The selection of stories to be shared with children should be based primarily on the capacity of these works to stimulate enjoyment. The adult should also insure that there is a variety of stories read so that children may begin to identify types and patterns of story. We have already mentioned the child's ability to distinguish between "Believe" and "Make-Believe." This is not a distinction between fact and fiction (which is also a necessary distinction to make) but one between realistic and fanciful story forms. It is the difference between *Crow Boy*, which could really have happened, and *Curious George*, which could happen only in the imagination.

Parents, teachers, and librarians who have in their own minds a clearly articulated deductive structure for helping children understand story can be alert to a child's own discoveries about the nature and elements of story. They can hear the child's big ideas about literature even when the comments are couched in appropriately child-sized language, which may bear little resemblance to that of the literary critic. The task of the adult is not to push children too soon into the "proper" language about literature but to encourage them to increase their own understanding and appreciation of story forms. At times, the more disciplined language of literary criticism will help them to do this, but the use of literary terminology is certainly not to be valued for its own sake. Only that which adds to an appreciation of literary works is to be valued in children's encounters with story. The foundation of one's whole life experiences with story is built at a very young age. It is far better for a youngster to enjoy the reading of story without having developed sophisticated skills as a critic than to use the language of the critic without really enjoying the experience of literature. For one who is truly a critic must love that which he critiques. Fortunately, this is not an either–or proposition. The natural extension of literary appreciation is through the appropriate development of literary criticism.

In order to take full advantage of the literary opportunities and experiences provided for them by adults, children must be taught how to carry on a discussion so that their understanding and appreciation of story can be shared and extended. The size of the group is often a crucial factor in the productivity of the discussion. A group of six to eight children seems to be an ideal size to share in-depth interpretations of story. Such a group is large enough to encourage a variety of responses but small enough to allow each child to participate. Although these small groups are optimal for most critical discussions, larger groups are possible and even to be desired for some purposes. An introduction to a new story form or literary element might easily take place in a large group in which the enthusiastic response of one or two children may stimulate the interest of the entire group.

The role of the adult in a literary discussion is to help focus the responses on what children have read, experienced, and observed in story without exerting so much control over what happens that previously unexplored ideas or avenues of discussion are not given the opportunity to be explored. The primary role of the teacher or librarian is often that of a recorder and one who urges children to clarify and amplify their critical comments. The adult encourages them to return again and again to the story to look sympathetically at what the author was attempting to do. Most important, the adult creates an atmosphere in which the discussion of the bases for criticism is far more important than any critical conclusion that can be reached.

An interesting encounter with story shared by this author with five- and six-year-olds demonstrates young children's sense of story and their developing critical abilities. After a reading of *And to Think That I Saw It on Mulberry Street* to a group of about eight children, we began discussing the difference between believe and make-believe in story. Soon one five-year-old boy jumped up and went to the blackboard behind me and drew a line something like this.

My first impulse was to tell him to sit down and listen to what one of the little girls was saying about the story, but instead I waited until she was through and then asked him what he had drawn on the board. He replied, "It's the story." He did not have the words to explain how or why this line represented the story for him. However, one of the most verbal little girls in the group said, "Yeah, it's how it goes from believe to make-believe." Another child pointed to the left side of the line (they knew stories are read from left to right although most could not yet decode the printed symbols for words) and said, "This is where he started to school, and it's believe. Then it gets more and more make-believe until the end when it's believe again." Of course, this was a very apt diagram for the particular story but one which I had never thought of and would probably not have introduced to children of this age if I had.

After a bit of discussion in which it was explained to me that there is "like a bottom line"on which things occur that could really happen and that "make-believe things jump off that line," we took turns composing stories orally by following a "story line" drawn on the board by one child. It was immediately obvious that this means of identifying and discussing story was useful to children as authors as well as in their early work as critics.

As we looked again at the story, the children discussed the relationship between the build-up of story incidents and the illustrations that accompanied them. They noticed immediately that Seuss had used simple black and white line drawings for what corresponded to their "bottom line for believe" and that detail and color were added as Marco's imagination saw more and more on Mulberry Street. While we slowly turned the pages to follow this sequence of events visually, one child began anticipating the structure of the story with movements of her body and her hands. She swayed from side to side and put her hands up in front of her alternately as the pattern of the narrative developed. She was saying with her body that she was aware that the changes made from one page to another were dependent upon and in contrast to what had gone immediately before. For instance, when Marco decides that a plain horse and wagon on Mulberry Street are too tame to report, he imagines that the wagon is pulled by a zebra. On the next page the wagon is imagined to be a gold and blue chariot so as not to be too tame for the zebra. Then the zebra is too small for the chariot and is replaced by a reindeer who would be happier pulling a fancy sled. When the reindeer is replaced by an elephant with a rajah perched on his back, the sled is too light and so on and on and on until all of Mulberry Street is filled with a huge imaginative parade. The animals doing the pulling are always on one side of a double-page spread and that which they are pulling on the other. A change on either side of the page demands a counterbalancing change on the other. After some groping for language, the children were able to say, "The story goes on because one side has to go with the other." Such a statement might sound nonsensical to some adults, but the adult who is tuned in to children and to story can recognize in it a very mature understanding, for ones so young, of the patterning of story.

All of this discussion, including the reading of the story, took place in approximately twenty to twenty-five minutes. Then the group was asked if they could think of any other stories that were like . . . *Mulberry Street* in some way. After a few minutes deliberation, they agreed that *Where the Wild Things Are* "looked like" the line still on the blackboard, that is, the relationship between "believe" and "make-believe" was similar in the two stories. We had no more time that day but decided to look more closely at . . . *Wild Things* . . . at our next meeting as well as to search for other similar books. Later that day, one of the girls in the group rushed into my office to tell me that we had been all wrong about . . . *Mulberry Street*. In comparing it with *Where the Wild Things Are*, she had discovered that the "story lines" (as we were using the term) were not identical. In fact, the line that we had used to represent ... *Mulberry Street* was incorrect for that book but right for the Sendak story. She drew the following two lines for me and explained that the Seuss book "got more and more make-believe and then just came down fast to believe," while Sendak's story "backed down slowly to where it started."

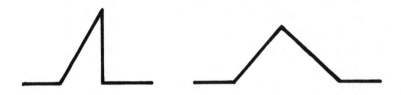

And to Think That I Saw
It on Mulberry Street

Where the Wild Things Are

The next day when we met again with the group, this little girl recounted her discovery to the other children and then went on to refine it even further by saying that "there is like a step that goes up for everything that happens and sometimes there are steps back down." At this point she drew her story lines to include these steps.

This young lady was certainly very bright and more articulate than the other children in the group, but all of them understood immediately what she was talking about and became very excited by the idea. They went on to find several other books for which they could discern a similar pattern and, at the same time, continued to "assign" each other compositions (oral or in pictures, for the most part) that followed a particular story line they had drawn.

I also searched for other stories that would carry this idea a bit further. Two of the best examples I found were Karla Kuskin's *Just Like Everyone Else* and Joan Walsh Anglund's *The Brave Cowboy*. The Kuskin book is basically a sequence of very mundane events in which a young boy gets out of bed, gets dressed, eats breakfast, and does all those ordinary things "just like everyone else." The story moves, however, to a fanciful realm in the final incident when he flies off to school under his own power, "not like everyone else." It was evident that the students really understood what they had been doing when they agreed upon the following story line for that book.

The Brave Cowboy is unlike any of the other books we had used in that what is "believe" and what is "make-believe" go on simultaneously in the illustrations. A young boy in the story is playing cowboy, and what he is realistically seeing and doing is illustrated in black while what he imagines is happening is drawn in red. For example, the black lines show that what he is carrying is a stick; the red ones convert it to the gun he imagines it to be. I'm reasonably sure that the children increased their enjoyment of this story because of the discussions that had gone before, and their comments indicated that they understood what the artist was doing. They were able to draw the following story lines with the dotted line representing the red "make-believe" drawings.

None of the children risked trying to use this model for their own story writing because the interplay between word and picture was just too complex for them to handle.

Compelled by my own curiosity, I decided to try to take this study one step further and introduce one more book. Ellen Raskin's *Nothing Ever Happens on My Block* is similar to *The Brave Cowboy* in that the story really exists neither in words nor in pictures but in the interplay between the two. In Raskin's story, however, Chester Filbert just sits forlornly in black and white lamenting the fact that "nothing ever happens on my block." Meanwhile, all sorts of exciting and colorful things are going on behind him without his ever noticing. We compared the use of illustrations in this book with Anglund's and then compared the total composition of story with that of . . . *Mulberry Street*. The contrast in characters was immediately mentioned and at least three of the eight children discovered that in all three books, the stories grew out of the contrast between what "really" happens around the character and what he imagines to be happening to him.

Often this contrast is the very essence of story. A factual

report of an event quickly moves to story when one crosses the line between "what happened" and "what happened *to me.*" Almost as soon as one allows one's own feelings about an event to enter into the recording of that event, story is composed. Thus, the children not only use their literary abilities to increase their understanding of these stories; they also began to see some of the relationships between story and real life experiences. They saw how story can develop from a factual narration of events and began to experiment with transforming a report of something that actually happened to them into an imaginative story of what might have been.

These incidents are but a few illustrations of the necessity for adults to remain open to children's responses to story rather than listening only for specific answers. Of course, one must also know enough about the essence of story and its elements to channel these responses into literary ideas appropriate to the children's stage of development. It is not uncommon for young children to be able to discuss literature in this way.

Early childhood school and library programs are usually rich in literary experiences for children. The young child is read to frequently, and good books are obviously valued contributors to a child's life. Unfortunately, this is not as likely to be true as children grow older. It seems as soon as children master the skills necessary for reading, adults deemphasize the value of reading for enjoyment and channel reading activities almost exclusively to discursive or instructional ends. This is a real disservice to children. Literature is a way of knowing about the world as much as the sciences are, and children have as much need to develop aesthetic modes of inquiry as scientific ones.

Literature is an exploration of life and living, a chance to try on various lives as a confirmation, an illumination, or an extension of one's own life experiences. Children in the later elementary grades are beginning to expand their interests beyond themselves and appreciate opportunities to reach out to the world from the safety of their own chairs. To help them do this through story, parents, teachers, and librarians ought to continue many of the same activities used with younger children. Chief among these is reading aloud. Even the best readers enjoy being read to, and adults do far too little of this for older children. Reading aloud not only gives all children in a group an opportunity to know the same story regardless of their individual reading levels; it demonstrates the reader's valuing of literature, exemplifies good oral reading, and provides opportunities for the sharing of books that would not ordinarily be selected by children because of strange language patterns, unfamiliar content, or difficult reading level. Children should also be encouraged to read independently for their own pleasure so we do not take away the primary purpose for reading as soon as children develop the skills that enable them to read on their own.

Literary discussion remains the primary means of helping children develop as critics of story. The enjoyment shared and the interests stirred in the interchange of ideas about story are the bases upon which critical abilities grow. As children increase the breadth and depth of their reading, they are able to move from simple reporting of the events of story to reviewing or looking anew at some of the literary elements of a particular book, to the kinds of criticism that puts one story in perspective among all the others that they know. Small book discussion groups ought to be a regular part of the school or library program, but there should also be opportunities for children to talk together about their reading more informally at other times. Parents should read children's books themselves and encourage such discussions in the home. In an atmosphere where literature is valued, discussion encouraged, and children's knowledge and opinions respected, literary abilities flourish.

The following transcription of an excerpt from a taped discussion among a group of ten- and eleven-year-olds demonstrates these abilities in action. The voice of the adult leader is notably absent in this segment of the discussion of *The Jazz Man* by Mary Hays Weik, but there is ample evidence that these youngsters have participated in previous discussions with the guidance of those who respected their opinions as well as the integrity of literary works. *The Jazz Man* is an excellent book for discussion because it is one of the few children's books with a deliberately ambiguous ending. In the story, Zeke, a lame child from Harlem, is deserted by his parents and left in a tenement without heat or food. Cold, hungry, and despairing, he seeks the comfort of his bed and enters into a dreamlike state in which he imagines that all is well with him and his family. Then there is the impression that he awakens from his dream and is reunited with his parents in the scene of warm security. Literally, that is what happens, but the literary clues seem to indicate that the boy's dream is actually a final delirium from which he is released only by death.

You will notice that this group of children had the problem of their intellectual powers and their literary abilities outreaching their emotional maturity. They could point to literary clues in the story and acknowledge the possibility of the boy's death, but they could not really accept this ending and preferred to believe the literal, if contrived, view of the ending.

> Danny: I liked the book because it had a lot of feeling.
>
> Betty: What makes you feel?
>
> Danny: Not the facts. It's the way the author writes it, the words she chooses — what the boy thinks.
>
> Ed: I was confused at the end. Was that a dream?
>
> Monica: Did his pain just go away all of a sudden?
>
> Betty: I didn't expect his parents to come back because of the way they acted, but it could happen.

Jon: I expected it to end happy because books always do . . . or with the hope of happiness. It should be like that because you get to like the character.

Erica: It should be both ways, but I like happy endings.

Jeff: Sometimes you just don't know, you are up in the air about an ending. It may not stay happy, but that doesn't leave you up in the air because it's really over.

Bill: Endings are happy because you build up the character so that you feel for him and want the ending that you think is best for him.

Jane: Do you think he could have died? If you look back at the way his father acted and at his pain, dying might go with the ending. I don't think so, but it could have.

Jeff: Wow, maybe he did die. A lot of the descriptions use images that are like death. She's always talking about "dark" and "cold" and even says things are "as still as death." She uses a lot of death language.

Danny: The movie *White Mane* has a sad ending, but he has to die, so it's a good ending.

Martha: I don't think Zeke could have died.

Ed: Adult books have sad endings, why not kid's books.

Betty: Because kids get a different idea in a book. If you read a book on marriage now and then read it when you're married, you'll get a different feeling. It will be almost a different book.

Danny: If you read that book and the marriage didn't turn out that happily and then you realized that everything doesn't always turn out o.k. and then your mother's and father's marriage doesn't turn out happily, would it be better if it just came out of the blue and you think you're the only one that ever happened to?

Monica: You don't need a book to tell you that everything doesn't always turn out happy.

Danny: Yeah, but if a book gives you the feeling of the bad thing . . .

Bill: How does that compare with the statement that the character you identify with should have a happy ending?

Ed: Younger kids need a happy ending?

Jon: The ending has to fit with the book. What are you reading it for?

Betty: We talked about this before when we said a book had to be complete or whole. Each part has to be good and the putting together is good.

Jeff: I still like to use the word "sound." If it's complete, it can still fall apart on you, but if it's sound, it's sturdy. I don't know how to describe it any other way, but if you're building a building and don't rivet the beams or whatever together real tightly, the building can be complete. But then if someone gets in the elevator, the shaft breaks and there goes the whole building. So I think story can be complete or whole but not good. If it's good, it's sound.

Danny: O.k., o.k., but could he die at the end?

Jeff: . . . well, he could . . .

Martha: I don't think he could.

Betty: The writer built it so that he could, and the clues look like that, but I don't think he did.

Jan: They're beginning to write books now where people die. Bill died in *Across Five Aprils* and in all these books about drugs and stuff, kids sometimes die.

Betty: But you don't ever feel for them like you do the boy in this story.

Erica: You know it has to end happy because you really want it to.

Monica: Yes, even with a happy ending, the book is sad; and you can have too much sadness.

Ed: Anyway, it's sure good the way the author wrote it so you're not really sure. Usually they just tell you everything plain out. He could have died, but I don't want to believe he did, so I don't have to.

In this discussion, children touched upon many important literary ideas. They were primarily concerned with the role of the reader in the re-creation of story and with their ability to predict outcomes through the recall of significant detail and the interpretation of implied meanings. However, this discussion illustrates the interrelationships of all elements and abilities as children struggle with critical questions that emphasize literary form and structure.

An excellent means of encouraging children and young people to become involved in literary discussions and in their own work as writers is to provide opportunities for them to meet the authors of some of the books they have read. Almost every area of the country has some authors or illustrators nearby, and many of these people enjoy meeting and talking with their readers or at least responding to letters from those who are sincerely interested in their work and not just completing an assignment for their teacher or librarian. Adults concerned with children's literature must also be alert for opportunities to attend conferences, workshops, and other special events where they can hear figures from the children's book world talk about their work. In some instances, such as Children's Book Week or National Library Week programs, youngsters might be participants as well. Even when young people have access only to secondhand information about such events through the adults with whom they normally discuss books, authors' comments about their works can give an added dimension and sometimes new insights to literary discussions.

On one occasion some years ago, I had the opportunity to arrange a "Writers' Conference" for a group of upper elementary grade students with whom I had been working. In this instance, my students were the writers. Leland B. Jacobs, Madeline L'Engle, Jean Merrill, John Neufeld, Ronni Solbert, and Charlotte Zolotow came to talk with them about their (the students') work as authors. Of course, the youngsters had studied the work of their consultants and were prepared to raise questions about specific techniques used and decisions made by them in their work. Although much of the work of these published authors was for readers younger than this group, our authors had found that they could learn much by studying shorter and less complex works than those they normally read for their own enjoyment.

Leland Jacobs talked with a group of struggling poets about some of the sources for his own poetry in everyday life, explaining how, for instance, the shape of "The Bridge"[2] grew as he commuted from New Jersey to New York City across the George Washington Bridge each day. He listened attentively to the work of the other poets in the group and joined in the discussion with questions and comments about what he had heard. Finally, he shared some of his own work in progress, pointing out a word he was working on or where he was at a loss for a line, and he accepted critical suggestions from the others. Jean Merrill also talked with our authors about how real characters and events that she had observed in her Greenwich Village neighborhood became fictionalized in *The Pushcart War*. This was especially interesting to those in the group who had spent some time in the Village and could discuss with Merrill the differences between General Anna in the book and the real woman they had observed. All were fascinated by the skill with which Merrill used incidents from her own experiences and not only told a fast-moving and humorous story but also made some very powerful satirical statements about humankind's proclivity for war. This led to a discussion of an author's need to be very specific about the particulars of his or her composition yet at the same time to embed those unique characters and events with more universal appeal and significance. Ronni Solbert, who illustrated *The Pushcart War*, joined this discussion and told the youngsters how she worked with a manuscript, in this case an author, to decide what illustrations should be created to highlight the text. Both Merrill and Solbert listened to some students read and discuss their own work and then Merrill worked privately with a series of individual authors while Solbert met with a group of budding illustrators.

The discussion with Madeline L'Engle seemed to be as scientific as it was literary. One or two members of the group knew enough about physics to be intrigued with L'Engle's ability to include very complex scientific information gracefully within the context of *A Wrinkle in Time* and were impressed with the amount of time and effort she had spent on getting that information "just right." Other authors shared their experiences of having to do a great deal of research on a topic that showed up only marginally in their final compositions, for as Leland Jacobs had said to them earlier, "It's what you know that isn't on the page that makes what is there ring true." Most of these students had not been aware of the religious symbolism in *A Wrinkle in Time* and were interested in getting some clues that would unlock this new aspect of the story in a subsequent reading. The references to the Christian symbolism in this story took the group back to a question they had raised with Jean Merrill a few days earlier. They wanted to know if the authors thought it was "all right" if readers didn't "get" everything that they had put into a story. Was it acceptable to read *The Pushcart War* or *A Wrinkle in Time* solely as an adventure story without understanding the deeper or more complex meanings? They finally agreed that almost any reading was acceptable as long as the reader realized that any work of real literary value is worth rereading. Those who had been studying picture story books as a means of analyzing the craft involved in the composition of story reinforced that notion with reports of their added insights as more mature readers into the stories they had enjoyed when they were younger.

I recalled also a fifth and a sixth grader some years before who had challenged Leland Jacobs to a public debate at Teachers College, Columbia University, because he had commented to his graduate class in children's literature there that children just had not lived long enough to really read adult novels. The two young men in question were unusually bright and very interested in politics. As a part of their study of political systems, they had read Huxley and Orwell and several other Utopian novelists and knew far more about the relationship of these works to political history than I had ever cared to know. (It was these same two boys who had been not-so-patiently waiting for me to get through *The Rise and Fall of the Third Reich* so I could discuss it with them when the children's version, *The Rise and Fall of Adolf Hitler*, was published. They generously brought this version to me and suggested that, if I could at least read that, we would have a little something in common to talk about.)

The two students agreed with Jacobs that they might not have lived long enough to understand and appreciate all the intricacies of human relationships and emotion as portrayed in these books, but they also doubted that he knew enough of the political history of the USSR to interpret some of the specifics of Orwell's work with as much political insight as they could bring to bear. He allowed as how this might be so and listened as they went on to explain that they were aware that theirs was not the only way to read these works or even the only way in which they would ever read them. Because these youngsters too were rereading books for very young children at the same time that they were reading those intended for their own age and beyond, they could talk about this experience and were very convincing in their argument. The public debate never took place.

John Neufeld's visit to this group spurred a great deal of discussion of character development and motivation in story as well as the different roles that characters play in story structure. The youngsters had read and been moved by Neufeld's *Edgar Allan* and were interested to learn that this story had grown from a very small snippet of information about an actual event. In this case, the author had no firsthand experience with characters or events but used the little he knew of a real situation to create the totality of story. The story, told from a perspective of Michael, the twelve-year-old son of a white minister who decides to adopt a black child but, after a year, returns the child, is a poignant account of the effect of that year on all the members of the family.

Students noticed that the title character was little more than a "cute kid" who existed in the background as the cause for changes and concern in others. The first-person narrator seemed brighter, more observant, and more introspective than most boys his age, but it was agreed that he was "not too unusual" and that his observations and insights were necessary to move the story along. In contrast, his teen-age sister seemed almost too typical in her overconcern for what her friends would think, but it was pointed out that this was quite likely the way Michael would have perceived her. The younger brother and sister are only slightly more developed than Edgar Allan and seem to represent childhood innocence and acceptance in the face of adult prejudice.

We all agreed that the parents were the most interesting characters. The narrator points readers to the key character in the first lines of the book: "This is a story about my father, and about God. Neither is very easy to understand."[3] We see Rev. Fickett first as an almost godlike figure in Michael's eyes and then watch the son's distrust, disillusion, and disapproval grow as his father fails to live up to his convictions. The father's final plea for compassion, if not for understanding, forces readers to face their own hidden prejudices as well as their views of these fictional characters. Mrs. Fickett is not as well developed as some of the other characters, but as we discussed this book we came to the realization that the mother was the pivotal character around whom the lives of the whole family revolved. She was the sounding board against which the views of all other characters resonated. Although she did not surface as a major character in our early discussion, the mother assumed greater importance as we went along, and Neufeld admitted that, to some extent, the same thing had happened in his writing of the story. After this discussion, the young authors took advantage of the opportunity to seek Mr. Neufeld's advice in respect to some of their own problems of characterization.

The final consultant to this extended Writers' Conference was Charlotte Zolotow, who shared with these young people some of her work as a children's book editor and in addition responded to questions about her own books for young children. The group was especially interested in Zolotow's ability to capture a mood and what appeared to them to be a bit of that special essence of childhood they remembered only vaguely from their early years. They questioned whether her books are as much for adults with fond memories of childhood as for young children themselves, but agreed that all ages responded to the poetic quality of her language. Those who had read her books aloud to younger children did share with Zolotow the fact that their favorite of all her books, *The White Marble*, although enjoyed by most younger children, did not seem to have the almost universal appeal of some of her other work. They considered the possibility that they might have read more into the symbolism of the white marble or that this particular book was more about younger children than for them. This brought us back again to the multiple layers of meaning in a literary work and the reader's role in the re-creation of story. Finally, the members of this group were fascinated to hear about the role of the editor in the publication of a book. (They all knew what it is to be an author.) Zolotow was the hit of the conference when she agreed to work with individual students on their manuscripts and demonstrated that she respected their work enough to make tough editorial comments about it.

This writers' conference was a unique experience for this group of youngsters, but it was not all that different from other opportunities we might provide for the children with whom we work. These were not unusually bright or talented young people; they had just had what are, unfortunately, all too unusual opportunities to discuss their reading and writing with concerned adults. For most of them, this was the first time they had met the authors of books they had read, and they were eager to talk with these people. However, if they had not had many previous discussions about literature among themselves and with parents, teachers, or librarians, they certainly would not have been able to respond as they did to the visits of these authors. Many of us have sat through too many of those painful encounters in which young people ask authors a series of questions such as:

- When did you begin to write?
- Where do you get your ideas for stories?
- How do you get a book published?
- Do you have any brothers or sisters?
- How much money do you make for a book?

Some of these questions may elicit interesting responses, but they do not necessarily lead to any literary discussion nor do they even indicate whether the authors' books have been read. Children need practice not only in the act of discussion but in the process of revealing new aspects of a work of art through questions that take one into rather than outside of the work. Literary questions are those that cause us to enter again into the structure and form of story. They take the reader back into what has been read rather than out into discussions that are peripheral. The latter type of discussion sometimes has its place, but too often such questions as "Have you ever felt as this character did?" or "Did your parents ever treat you like this?" are more invasions of a child's privacy than means of increasing literary comprehension or understanding. Questions such as those below not only allow children to test their understanding of literary ideas and elements, but also encourage them to evaluate their own abilities to make inferences and judgments based upon their reading and ultimately may help them toward becoming more critical and more appreciative readers.

- What is this story about? (Responses may be in terms of character, plot, mood, etc., and should help students to focus on the most important literary elements in a particular story.)
- What idea or ideas does this story make you think about? How does the author get you to think about this?
- Do any particular feelings come across in this story? Does the story actually make you feel in a certain way or does it make you think about what it is to feel that way? How does the author accomplish this? (This is intended to help students become more aware of the distinctions between literary and "real life" experiences.)
- Is there one character you know more about than any of the others? If so, who is this character and what kind of a person is he/she? How does the author reveal this character to you? (Description, dialogue, behavior, other characters' reactions to him/her?) What words would you use to describe the main character's feeling in this book?
- Are there other characters who are important to the story? Who are they? Why are they important in this

story?
- Are all the characters the same at the end of the story as they were at the beginning? If not, how and why are they different?
- Is there a lot of action in the story? How is the plot arranged? (Chronological order, individual incidents, flashback, etc.)
- Did the story end as you expected it to? Did the author prepare you for the ending? If so, how?
- What does the author do to get the story going? Suppose the incident were changed or removed, how would the rest of the story be changed?
- Suppose the order of events were changed? What would happen to the story? Would it be a new story or not a story at all?
- Suppose we thought of a different ending for the story. How would the rest of the story have to be changed to match the new ending?
- Where and when does the story take place? Could it have taken place in another place? In another time? Why or why not?
- Does the story as a whole create any particular mood? If so, what is this mood and how does the author establish it?
- Is there anything that seems to make this particular author's work unique? If so, what?
- Did you notice any particular patterns in the form of this book? If you are reading this book in more than one sitting, are there natural points at which to break off your reading? If so, what are these?
- Were there any clues that the author built into the story that helped you to anticipate the outcome? If so, what were they? Did you think these clues were important bits of information when you first read them?
- What signs and signals indicate that a story will be fanciful rather than realistic? Funny rather than serious?

- Does the story language seem natural for the intent of the story and for the various speakers?
- Who is the "teller" of the story? If the teller is one of the characters in the story, how is the story different from one that is related by a narrator who is not a character in the story?
- Every writer creates a make-believe world and peoples it with characters. Even where the world is far different from your own, how does the author make the story seem possible or probable?

It may be useful here to report a literary encounter with young people that was not so carefully planned. When *Flowers for Algernon* was first published as an adult novel,* I found it absorbing and read it through at one sitting. The next day I was telling one of my students about it, and before long, I was convinced to read it aloud to a group of fifth and six graders. They were especially interested in comparing the educational program in which Charlie participated in his move from mental retardation to genius to their own schooling and delighted in quoting such statements as " . . . Dr. Strauss said do anything the testor telld me even if it don't make no sense because thats testing."[4] Since I was not thinking of reading this book to the children, I had not been aware of any potential "problems" in my first reading. And as I began to read aloud, I was again so caught up in the story and the students' enthusiasm for it, that, without thinking, I read a passage that I might have avoided if I had been more alert.*

---

*It had previously been published as a short story and produced as a television drama; later it was made into a movie.

---

*Athough there is nothing in this book that would have caused me to hesitate in giving it to any of these children for their personal reading, there are some topics about which, I believe, the wise teacher or librarian does nothing to initiate public discussion with children. Frequently these are topics that some parents may find objectionable for their children even if the teacher or librarian is both accurate and comfortable in his or her discussion of them.

This passage dealt with Charlie's growing awareness of women. After a night in which his co-workers give him a great deal to drink in order to make fun of him trying to dance with a young woman, Charlie "dreamed about that girl Ellen dancing and rubbing up against me and when I woke up the sheets were wet and messy."[5] It was not until I was through with that sentence that I realized what I had read and tried to hurry on. However, one young girl was puzzled by the words and insisted upon an explanation; so, against my better judgment, I found myself explaining wet dreams to a fifth grade girl. Fortunately for me, I not only knew all of these children quite well, I also knew their parents. Because of the very open and honest relationship established with these youngsters in two years of discussing their reading and writing with them, I felt I could not avoid the question. I also was fairly certain that their parents would be more amused than upset about my dilemma—which indeed they were. After that, I was very careful to doublecheck anything that I read aloud to children.

Once we got beyond our initial experience with this book, the group enjoyed discussing its more literary aspects. They were fascinated by Keyes's ability to handle point of view so that we as readers could see and feel Charlie's intellectual progress and then his heartbreaking regression. The structure of this book, written as Charlie's journal, was difficult to read initially; but before many pages had turned, we were so involved with the character that the misspellings and grammatical errors of his mental retardation days seemed almost natural to us. This was a very powerful realization to many of these intelligent young people—that they could so closely identify with someone of such limited mental capacities. They thrilled as Charlie's I.Q. grew and the language of the journal became more polished and complex, and they shared the character's panic as his mental powers began slipping away again. We all entered into the experiencing of this story so completely that I doubt if any one of us will ever again see someone who is mentally retarded without feeling a great deal of compassion for the little bit of Charlie we find in that person. Moreover, each of us confronted a bit of Charlie in ourselves as we acknowledged that there were things we longed for and would probably never achieve. What began as an uncomfortable, certainly nonliterary, sharing with children grew into one of the most powerful reading experiences I have ever shared with children.

In all of these discussions of story, children tested their own comprehension, interpretations, and criticism of a particular work or works against those of others. As they compared and contrasted different stories and different interpretations of those stories, they sharpened their literary perceptions and came to appreciate more fully the uniqueness both of the individual stories and of themselves as readers and critics.

The primary role of the adult remained that of guide and facilitator, one who turned children back to the story again and again so that their critical comments remained rooted in what was really there. Adults should not attempt to tell children what is on the page but rather make them look for themselves. In that looking and with some guidance, children are assisted in the move toward a clearer understanding of the relationship of the particular story elements to their own critical abilities, and to the unfolding implications of story as an aesthetic whole. The most important outcomes of these literary discussions with children are not the conclusions reached, but the developing bases upon which the criticism is founded.

Footnotes

1. Kay E. Vandergrift, "Children as Critics," in *Literature with Children*, ed. Monroe D. Cohen (Washington, D.C.: Association for Childhood Education International, 1972), pp. 24–27.

2. Leland B. Jacobs, "The Bridge," in *Is Somewhere Always Far Away?* (New York: Holt, Rinehart and Winston, 1967), p. 25.

3. John Neufeld, *Edgar Allan* (New York: S.G. Phillips, 1968), p. 9.

4. Daniel Keyes, *Flowers for Algernon* (New York: Harcourt, Brace & World, 1966), p. 4.

5. Ibid., p. 41.

Children's Books Cited in Chapter Seven

Anglund, Joan Walsh. *The Brave Cowboy*. New York: Harcourt, Brace & World, 1959.

Geisel, Theodore Seuss. *And to Think That I Saw It on Mulberry Street*. New York: Vanguard Press., 1937.

Hunt, Irene. *Across Five Aprils*. New York: Follett, 1964.

Jacobs, Leland B. *Is Somewhere Always Far Away?* New York: Holt, 1969.

Kuskin, Karla. *Just Like Everyone Else*. New York: Harper & Row, 1959.

L'Engle, Madeline. *A Wrinkle in Time*. New York: Farrar, Straus & Giroux, 1962.

Merrill, Jean. *The Pushcart War*, illus. Ronni Solbert. Reading, Mass.: Addison-Wesley Publishing Co., 1964.

Neufeld, John. *Edgar Allan*. New York: S.G. Phillips, 1968.

Raskin, Ellen. *Nothing Ever Happens on My Block*. New York: Atheneum Publishers, 1966.

Rey, H.A. *Curious George*. Boston: Houghton Mifflin, 1941.

Sendak, Maurice. *Where the Wild Things Are*. New York: Harper & Row, 1963.

Shirer, William. *The Rise and Fall of Adolph Hitler*. New York: Random House, 1961.

Weik, Mary Hays. *The Jazz Man*. New York: Atheneum Publishers, 1966.

Yashima, Taro. *Crow Boy*. New York: Viking Pr., 1955.

Zolotow, Charlotte. *The White Marble*, illus. Lilian Obligado. New York: Abelard-Schuman, 1963.

Chapter Eight
Composition: The Child as Storyteller

Even the very young child should experience the feeling of power and satisfaction that comes with the ability to impose one's own order on the world through the composition of original stories. Children who have read widely and developed critical abilities in the comprehension of their reading have already built a sound basis for their own composition. As adults help children to enjoy and to comprehend various forms of literature, we help them also to understand the basic forms and patterns of composition. The ability to aesthetically order some components of existence in story form is developed gradually through many encounters with fine literature and through practice in the compositional arts. Youngsters who recognize common patterns of story and archetypal characters and symbols are building a reservoir of literary elements that may be used in their own compositions, and it is in those compositions that their understanding of story is most readily and most convincingly revealed. It is important to note here that such composition begins before writing begins. Most children are able to create fairly complex stories before they are able to put a single word on paper. Adults who have been on the receiving end of explanations of how a favorite toy got broken or of the need for a pet in the home are well aware of the originality with which the young compose their world.

Even before the age of television, the child's development of compositional skills was a multimedia experience, and one of our aims ought to be to continue and refine that development of compositional ability in all media throughout childhood, indeed throughout life. Dramatic play, which involves various forms of sound, movement, gesture, and oral language, is one of the child's earliest means of composition. When we ask children to compose in written language, we are, in effect, depriving them of many of the elements of their most effective means of communication. Thus, we might think of written story as coming fairly late in the compositional process and as a more artificial and fairly restricted means of expression. This is not to say that it cannot, with the skillful manipulation of its restrictions, be one of the most powerful artistic forms, but it is certainly not a replacement for other forms.

As pre-readers move in the cumulative developmental process toward critical appreciation of story discussed previously, pre-writers move through progressive stages in the development of written story. Because the pre-reader and pre-writer are dealing with the same basic concerns and because they ordinarily come together in one child, these two cannot be separated. The child's tacit understanding of the form of story is necessary both for comprehension and for composition. Young children develop their abilities in written communication from a beginning in scribble writing that demonstrates an awareness of the fact that those strange squiggles on a page represent meaning. They then move from picture writing through dictation to adults, to word stories in which they label their drawings with a single word symbolizing a whole story, to an imitation or revision of known stories. In this last stage a child may copy another's story, making minor changes to reflect themselves and their beginning attempts to compose.

Adults must recognize these stages of written development and encourage them just as we encourage the development of oral language skills. Admittedly, it is easier to appreciate a child's first babbling attempts to speak than it is to praise scribbling, especially if it happens to be practiced on walls. Later we must realize that imitation, even copying of a sort, is not just plagiarism but a natural stage in the development of writing skill. Instead of condemning this practice, we ought to bring it out in the open as a form of modeling and use it to help children move toward the creation of their own original imaginative compositions.

Frye stated it most emphatically when he said that literature grows out of itself; that while each work is new, it is also recognizably the same as the old, just as each new baby is both a unique individual and a recognizable human being.[1] He and other archetypal critics have emphasized the recurring patterns of literary images (archetypes) that are common to the "one story" of the mythical hero's quest for identity. The archetypes or structural patterns of imagery are most easily seen as they are embodied in the simple but powerful mythical stories of primitive societies. These symbols or images have persisted, with some variations, from age to age as a means of exploring personal and communal responses to phenomena of nature and human existence. Archetypes are often defined as first forms or original models that are repeated, consciously or unconsciously, in the literature of many cultures over time and in many different media. They may be characters (hero, scapegoat, enchantress), events (rites of initiation, sacrifices), topics (coming of age, love, guilt, death, redemption), settings (wastelands, gardens), or even whole story shapes (the "Cinderella" story, slaying of the monster).

A motif is similar to an archetype in that it is a recurring literary image, but it is less universal. It is most frequently used to refer to an image repeated within a single work or in the body of work of a single author. (The recurrence of images of birds within Betsy Byars's work might be called a motif.) Stith Thompson defines motif as "the smallest element in a tale having a power to persist in tradition"[2] and identifies three categories of motifs as (1) actors, (2) special customs or beliefs, and (3) single incidents. Thompson makes a distinction between "types" or complete tales such as the "Cinderella" tale, and "motifs," which are combined in relatively fixed combinations to make up those types. He goes on to identify motifs in the same way that most critics define archetypes, demonstrating that these terms have been used almost interchangeably in different approaches to literary criticism. A third literary term, "convention," refers to widely known and accepted devices, techniques, or artistic contrivances used to achieve a particular effect in a composition. Conventional endings such as weddings or the death of a character have also been confused with archetypes and motifs.

If the lack of absolutely precise distinctions among these definitions has not been a major concern for the critical community, it need not trouble those of us primarily concerned with the literary connection between child and story. What is important is our ability to help children recognize that stories do come in a limited number of shapes and that similar characters, images, and patterns of action occur over and over again in our literary heritage and become common elements in literary creations. The rags to riches story, the struggle between good and evil, and the triumph of the underdog are examples of literary patterns that most of us became familiar with in early childhood. The quest, the journey, the test of the hero, the triangle, the twist, goodness rewarded, the tempting of fate, and the use of the magic numbers three and seven are all so ingrained in our culture that they can be identified in many stories and used to shape one's own compositions. The use of these patterns helps children compose stories with greater ease, more plausibility, and a ring of authenticity that is often absent when they have little conscious awareness of these forms.

The necessary first step toward composition is the collection of impressions and experiences, both actual and vicarious. This may be done directly, as when the author sets out consciously to collect ideas and information or when a parent, teacher, or other adult points out specific objects or events and encourages a child to use these items in composition. Indirect collection is taking place all the time as one picks up ideas and impressions and stores them for possible future use. Many of these indirectly collected impressions will be vicarious ones that grow out of contacts with other art forms. This is why a child's first stories are as likely to be set in forests and castles as in her own neighborhood and to have a cast of characters from fairy princesses to the Incredible Hulk as well as family and friends. Then too, these characters and settings may come together in recognizable patterns because the process of collection is one of both content and form.

One of the best ways for adults to assist young children in this beginning stage of composition is to make them aware that they are already actively composing many aspects of their world and pointing out to them when they do it most powerfully and most beautifully. A child's unique vision of the world is a way of composing (putting oneself with) the world and often this is done metaphorically and very expressively. Just saying to a child, "That is a lovely way to say that," reinforces both this imaginative vision and an appreciation for the language that captures that vision. The love of language and the desire to use it both effectively and affectively blossoms in a climate where both literature and the child's own language and compositions are valued. Adults who care about these things might repeat especially apt sayings back to children and perhaps even write them down for them.

In my years as an elementary school librarian, teacher, and principal, I collected many such sayings. Children were fascinated by what I chose to record and often came back to have me read to them what they had said. On one occasion, a group of four-year-olds came into my office to report that they had just returned from a funeral service for a pet turtle. There were more long faces and silent shufflings than verbal comments, but one child finally said, "We buried our turtle in the park. The grass was sharp." I responded that what she said about the grass made me feel how sad they were and asked if I might write her words down to save them. In the weeks to follow, she and several others from that group came in to share with me what they thought was a special way of saying something—just in case I should want to write it down. Some of them also asked me to read some of my collection of special sayings to them and discussed, revised, and added to what others had said. They also listened for such sayings in the words of family and friends and in the stories read to them and thus increased their sensitivity to and appreciation of language. Children of this age still have some of that "primitive" belief in the magic of words and sense that they can somehow exert power over things they can name or in some way capture in language. If this belief in the power of language is retained, it can be one of the most influential factors in the child's desire to read and to write, that is, both to borrow and to create some of that magic of meaning.

After collecting impressions, one must reflect upon and develop a personal attitude toward those experiences in order to shape them into unique compositions. The actual composition of story is the mental manipulation of elements to create an order and relationships that are aesthetically pleasing. In order to share this composition, mental images must be captured and recorded in sound, pictures, movement, or written words. Each of us probably has certain idiosyncratic practices that help us to translate these mental images to a medium observable by others. In dealing with the written word, for instance, this might have to do with the size, shape, or color of the paper, whether it is lined or unlined, and with the type of writing instrument used as well as with the writing environment. Some writers compose at the typewriter while others must do a complete first draft in pencil. I have a friend who writes on the backs of used sheets of paper, while I must have a fine point ball point pen and nice, clean letter-sized lined yellow pad. A legal-sized yellow pad and a pen with a regular point just will not do.

I once taught a young girl who had an amazing ability to adapt the content of her composition to the conditions of the writing act. Beth loved to write and would pick up any scrap of paper, including paper towels and old envelopes, to practice her craft. When her teachers noticed that the content of her writing somehow seemed to "match" what she wrote on and with, we experimented by giving her different kinds of paper and as many alternative writing instruments as we could find. Size, shape, and color of paper did not seem to have much effect on content, but different textures and kinds of lines on the paper (graph paper, primary school manuscript paper, etc.) did seem to stimulate her imagination. When writing on tightly lined graph paper, for instance, she broke out of all the little boxes into a highly imaginative science fiction story in which the dialogue of each character was written in different colored felt tipped pens. Beth was unusual in her versatility in the act of writing; most of us have habitual times, places, and conditions that seem to make the difficult process of writing somewhat less difficult, and we need to encourage children to capitalize on these idiosyncracies. The power of ritual is great, especially with young children; special writing places, materials, and practices may, by their very repetition, take on some of that ritualistic power.

Once the mental composition is captured in written

form it can be criticized by its author, at least, and perhaps by trusted others. One of the easiest and best ways for young writers to get a critical perspective on their own written work is to read it aloud. Often they can hear in the reading what they cannot see on the written page. An interval of time or even the transformation from the handwritten to the typed manuscript may also provide the distancing necessary for critical evaluation. Critical comments from others ought to be encouraged as well, but this is possible only in an atmosphere of support, encouragement, and trust. Composition is a very personal endeavor, and the youngster who is beginning to discover and express his own inner voice in writing cannot be expected to share this shaping of his own ideas and experiences with just anyone upon demand.

This is as true in respect to parents and teachers as it is with other children. Any adult who becomes involved in a child's compositions must respect that child, his sense of the world, and also his sense of privacy, knowing that none of us shares with others all that we write. The child who dares to open his own mind and heart to others through his writing does so with some sense of personal risk, and the adults who ask that of children must be willing to risk revealing their own perceptions of and feelings about the world as openly and honestly as they ask it of others. This takes place, in part, in the critical dialogue with a child concerning her work, but adults should also participate in the writing experiences and share their works-in-process with children. Rather than discouraging children who might compare their work with that of adults, most frequently young people are surprised and encouraged to see that those with much more experience and assumedly greater skill in the craft of writing still struggle with language, do a lot of rewriting, and even then do not always come out with a satisfying composition. In fact, children should realize that even well-known and successful authors often go through many versions of a work, and that a first draft is almost never the final composition. [3]

I once worked in an elementary school library where there was a very active "Algonquin Club" modeled after the stories of the writers who used to meet and discuss their work at the Algonquin Hotel in New York. Such small groups of children who are all concerned with composition are often helpful to each other in shaping and refining their compositions in all stages, from the idea in the mind to the final manuscript. The members of the group must first learn to listen carefully and appreciatively to the ideas and works of the others, and they must have an acquaintance with a wide variety of fine literature so that they might recognize that which is fine in their own compositions.

Adults who are concerned with children's writing could learn much from the way such groups of child critics operate. Once they establish a sense of caring and trust among themselves, they are usually very tough with each other and generally appreciate the harsh criticism of their work. Of course, each author knows that she must make the final decisions in the compositional process and can accept, reject, or modify whatever critical suggestions are made by others. The kind of false praise with which too many adults respond to children's compositions is certainly not helpful to them and may even be insulting because it reveals that we do not respect the work enough to deal with it honestly. Children who care enough to write want to have some sort of standards for their work, and they are often more aware than anyone else when what they have written does not measure up to these standards. Those who praise every effort have no means of recognizing real excellence.

What we need to do is to point to the best of a child's work so that she will continue to develop her own critical judgment as well as her craft as a writer and will have some sense of achievement and of direction for future efforts. This should not be interpreted as "red-penciling" everything a child writes. Teachers are not the only adults who spend too much time "correcting" children's compositions when we should be "reading" them, although they are probably the worst offenders. And it is offensive to respond to another human being's thoughts and feelings by pointing to what is wrong in the presentation of them.

As a teacher interested in the development of the child's ability to express his or her thoughts in written language, I insisted that each student turn in some piece of writing to me every day. This writing could be random thoughts on a topic, a portion of a work in progress, a note that what was written was too private to share, or even an excuse for not writing, as alternatives to a finished product. I read and responded to the students' work each day, but I did not edit it unless I was specifically asked to do so. A word or two of encouragement, a question, or a brief suggestion was more valuable to them than editorial corrections. That comes later. What a child needs to know first is whether or not the expression of the idea is worth editing and putting in final form to share with others. I was concerned that each child complete and polish some works, although the insistence that one finish everything begun whether or not it is of value to the person makes no more sense in writing than it does in reading. In addition, I asked each child to experiment with a variety of both discursive and nondiscursive forms over the course of the year. Some children needed more personal dialogue and assistance than others in order to accomplish this, but they also criticized and assisted each other, and I communicated with each one daily, in writing if not in person.

Adults should encourage children to write, help them collect ideas for writing, provide opportunities for them to reflect and to compose, help them set critical standards for their compositions, and dignify the best of their work by having it edited, typed, bound, recorded, or in some way shared with others. Most of all, we must value each child and respect what he has to say about himself and his world.

The matrix discussed previously (see Figure 4) that depicts the relationship of key compositional elements to genres may be useful in the collecting process by helping children focus on ways of modeling their own compositions on favorite stories composed by others. Obviously, the understanding of literary elements and genres is itself helpful, but the matrix may assist youngsters in thinking about different forms of literary modeling. As an author manipulates one or two elements of another's story, she invests her imagination and experience in that story and makes it her own. All story begins when one looks at the world and asks "What if . . . ?" If, in looking at someone else's composed story world, one asks "What if I used or changed just this one element . . . or this . . . or this," the result is frequently a genuinely new story. No one creates a totally original story. In fact, if such a story could be created, readers would probably be unable to understand it. Both our composition and our comprehension are dependent upon our previous experience and our knowledge of the world, especially the world of story.

The characters of children's literature, from Mother Goose to Madeline to the magical beasts of the fairy tales, are as much alive to boys and girls as are the people down the street. These fictional beings make them laugh and cry and shape the way they see and understand the world. Many children know the ways of elves and gnomes far better than they understand their own parents. Adults may speak of the "little people" of fiction, but children know that elves, fairies, trolls, leprechauns, hobbits, and gnomes are beings very different from one another and may be able to describe some of the characteristics of each. They know that unicorns and dragons and griffins have very special mystical and majestic powers. It is the mystery of these characters and their ability to take children beyond the everyday into an unknown but a totally knowable world that is as appealing as the reflection of their own world seen through the eyes of Henry Huggins or the "me" characters of Judy Blume.

Such fanciful characters are fairly consistent from story to story so that a child with a rich literary background may know enough of their characteristics to create a new but totally believable story world for them. An appreciation of an involvement with particular fictional characters may also lead young readers to take those characters beyond the book into places and situations of their own creation. Those who "get inside" story characters are often reluctant to let those characters go after the final page and may imagine them in settings from the reader's own lives.

A writing group of nine- and ten-year-olds from New York City wrote a series of sequels to *The Wind in the Willows* in which Ratty and Mole visited the Empire State Building, Coney Island, and other places in and around their homes. Although the settings were unlike their original home, Ratty and Mole stayed in character and behaved just as readers of *The Wind in the Willows* would expect. Even the flavor of their speech was captured in such titles as "Forgotten About Christmas? That's Absurd, Preposterous, etc., etc."

In this instance, the characters remained constant while the settings were changed, but the converse might also occur by introducing new characters into familiar settings. In fact, it may be amusing as well as instructive about the nature of story to attempt to mix and match characters and settings from various stories. Obviously these elements are not interchangeable, but the incongruity of Little Georgie of *Rabbit Hill* exchanging places with *Anatole* or *Babar* from Paris or even of Alice and Dorothy exchanging Wonderland and Oz reinforces the sense of the total integration of all elements of story.

Children may also wish to explore the effect of setting in story by moving characters and events forward and backward in time in order to determine what changes would need to be made to transform a contemporary story to historical or science fiction. They might even experiment with setting as the starting point of their own composition of story. Elementary school social science teachers sometimes use the creation of imaginary environments as an activity to help children understand how societies work. In one version of this activity, each child is asked to imagine a single person in a relatively small, self-contained setting and to describe that person's activities there. New elements and new people are gradually introduced into the environment to demonstrate the effects of physical and social surroundings on human life. Although the intention is to get youngsters thinking about how and why people create complex social and economic systems, one of the benefits of this activity is the composition of some very imaginative stories as children attempt to create the most unusual place for a human being to live. As they describe this person's survival as the sole inhabitant of the setting, they are coming to a literary, as well as a social scientific, understanding of the relationship of person and place.

A child can also increase his capacity to understand and to create character by attempting to capture archetypal or stereotypical characters in as few words as possible. Once the "typical" cowboy or movie star has been created, the author could experiment by placing these characters in various settings and situations to explore how our expectations for such characters affect story. If this typical figure remains "in character," the writer is aided by reader expectations and can be more economical in character development and the total composition of story. On the other hand, children familiar with the cowardly lion or the reluctant dragon may wish to heighten interest in their characters by breaking with expectations to create a fainthearted cowboy or a bashful movie star. None of these characters is new to fiction; in fact, recent stories have probably revealed more friendly dragons than fierce ones and at least as many shy movie stars as bold and vain ones. Nevertheless, the basic expectations have not changed, and readers are still caught off guard somehow when they encounter such characters.

Children might also be encouraged to compose short written descriptions, what I call "snapshot images," and compare these with the visual representations of characters on film or television. They may find that, in some instances, it is faster and easier to present a typical character pictorially rather than in words. A few deft strokes can portray a cartoon-like image of a dark-haired villain with a long face, narrow eyes, a drooping mustache over a tight mouth, and a thin sharp chin when many lines of text would be required to present as complete a picture. The very process of attempting to describe favorite television characters in language helps young writers appreciate both the care with which authors observe or create characters and the techniques that enable them to convey their characters most fully to others.

A tacit knowledge of many of the basic archetypal characters and plots will often enable a child to predict what the whole shape of story is likely to be from the identification of major characters. If the characters are, for instance, three brothers and a beautiful princess, most children will anticipate that the three brothers will compete for the hand of the princess. If asked which one is likely to win the princess, many will know that it is likely to be the youngest. Some may go even further to characterize the oldest brother as wise, the middle brother as handsome, and the youngest as somewhat foolish although very kind and know that each of the three will probably have to set out on a journey and pass some tests (often three) in their attempts to win the love of the princess. Thus, through this one story children can anticipate the traditional patterns of the quest, including a journey and a series of tests, the triumph of the underdog (the young and "foolish" brother), and the use of the number three, with perhaps a hint of the rags to riches story.

If the characters identified are a king's son, an orphan, and a beautiful girl, most young people will expect a story making use of the triangle, mysterious birth, and loss-recovery motifs, along with the patterns of good versus evil, rags to riches, and the quest through a perilous journey with at least three tests to a safe return. Often there will be some sort of a talisman involved that brings about the final resolution or recognition of the origins of the hero. These stories have been told over and over again in many versions and in many cultures, and one of the greatest challenges for the writer is to breathe new life into these traditional forms. One of the most used patterns in stories for children is that of the defiance of rules or the heedless mocking of power in which a young character is given instruction to do (or not to do) something and then acts in opposition to those instructions. As a result, the protagonist is threatened, but he or she is eventually saved from harm and is welcomed home to safety—even if there is some punishment for the disobedience. *The Tale of Peter Rabbit* is an obvious example of this pattern, but many other children's stories follow this same basic structure.

Young writers might wish to investigate the use of an archetypal story form as it appears in modern literature and in the mass media. The "Cinderella story" is one of the most popular of these basic story shapes and can be seen several times each half hour on television. Television commercials may well be the Mother Goose of the modern child, and they are certainly some of the best examples of the most powerful and most efficient use of archetypal story patterns. The producer who has only thirty seconds to sell a product must rely on the recognition and expectation factors built into traditional images to bring the message home in so little time. Thus, the Cinderella story is repeated hundreds of times each day, only it is told in modern dress; instead of the fairy godmother with the magic wand, it is the new brand of toothpaste or soap powder or breakfast food that turns events around and improves the fate of the protagonist.

Children may also experiment with structure and plot in their own composition by creating cumulative or circle stories, those that are told through questions and answers, or stories with a twist or surprise ending. They may also modify the basic idea or structure of a modern story to create a sequel or a totally new story. For instance, Jean Merrill's *The Push-*

cart War inspired an eleven-year-old to write a story called "The Soda-Pop War" in which New York City's bicycle messengers waged war against the cars and buses in the city. This story inspired by a book its author had read made use of some of the same images and literary devices from its model, yet it was truly an original story.

Children may also practice their own compositional skills by attempting to translate the content of one form to that of another, that is, to rewrite a short story as a play or vice versa. What they usually discover in the process is that one cannot really translate from one form to another because, in the doing, one is forced to change or to transform the content. Thus, the imitation of a literary model is, in some instances, a demonstration of its author's critical understanding of the elements and forms of literature.

Often children will convert a story idea to a cartoon format or a story board, such as is used in preparation for making a film, as a way of following a sequence of events visually and noting the significant details that move the story from one "frame" to the next. Another means of doing this is through the use of simple literary flow charts. The flow chart that follows (Figure 7) was devised by a ten-year-old to aid him in the composing act and clearly indicates some of the possibilities considered in developing his story. Although it is not clear in this chart how he decided to end the story, those ideas that were rejected are clear, and either of the two possible endings demonstrates the traditional cyclical pattern of story. Such visual representations of the pivotal events of story help children to bring order and direction to their ideas and to see the overall design of their composition.

Another diagram designed by a group of children to illustrate the funneling together of several literary elements in the composition of story is reproduced in Figure 8. The funnel shapes indicate the way in which the many possibilities open to an author are narrowed further with each choice of an element until there is a kind of inevitability in the

Figure 7: Child's Diagram of a Specific Composition

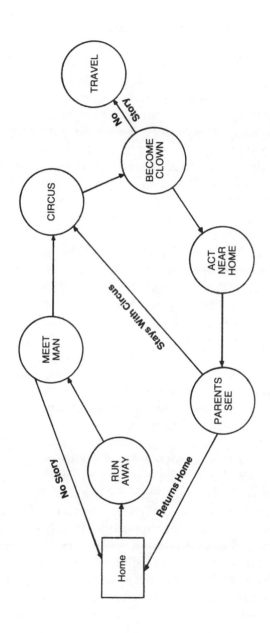

movement of story as these elements converge. Again you will notice the cyclical pattern of the events of the narrative.

The visual representations of story in Figures 7 and 8 were invented by children as they discussed their reading and prepared for their work as authors. An idea from the critical theory of Northrop Frye, cited frequently in this book, lends itself naturally to a simple diagram, which has been reproduced by many of Frye's students and which is easily understood by even very young children. This idea is Frye's belief in the two basic patterns or structures of literary images, the cyclical and the dialectical. The dialectical, which points out the struggle between opposites, is very easy for children to work with and use in their own compositions. Most often they will think of these opposites as a division between "good" and "bad" people, places, and things in story. Beginning with the placement of the four seasons of the year in relation to the dialectical structure, many children will be able to go on to use Frye's cyclical pattern to select images for their own writing that will carry with them the power of traditional expectations.

The diagram of Frye's theories of the basic rhythms of story (reproduced here in Figure 9) helps students bring some order to common metaphorical connections made between the human world and the world of nature. Children as young as second graders are able to place archetypal characters, events, stories, images, and themes in their "rightful" place within this schema and are able to use it to add depth and universality to their own writing. Even young children have enjoyed playing a literary version of twenty questions with this diagram, placing various animals, vegetables, and minerals in the appropriate quadrant, often making a collage of magazine illustrations in the process. The questions beneath Figure 9 are samples of those asked by children in the later elementary grades while using this diagram as a kind of "game board" in their imaginative play with literary archetypes.

Figure 8: Child's Diagram of Story Form

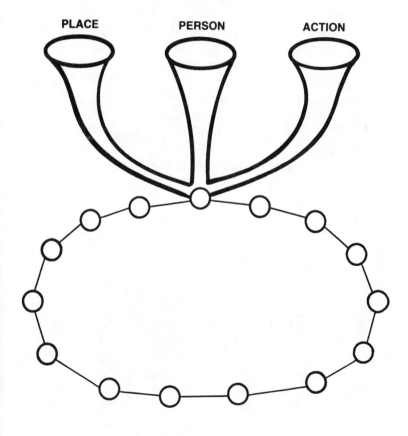

The introduction of Frye's dialectical and cyclical rhythms is a very effective means of helping young authors create mood in story. In fact, my first use of the diagram with children came as the result of the dismay of a seven-year-old who was trying to write a "scary story" and had not been able to frighten her audience. When other children laughed when they should have screamed, she was close to tears, and immediate assistance was required. We talked about specific times, places, characters, and objects that seem to be in themselves frightening, and we then discussed the diagram in Figure 9 before looking at some scary stories to see how other authors had made use of these images. Frye's dialectic was employed to oppose "scary" and "nice" qualities in this instance, but it did prove very useful for this child. After the success of her revised story, she was eager to explain to the rest of the second grade "how all the things in stories are divided in half."

Language and symbol are probably the most difficult literary elements for children to deal with in their own composition, but there are some techniques that may prove useful in helping them handle these elements. A playful approach to language usage might be to encourage children to experiment with alliteration, onomatoepoeia, and other literary devices in story or poetry.

A quite different approach begins with the fact that even young children are well aware that one of the reasons they are forbidden to attend certain movies is because of the language used and that some television programs are preceded by a warning to parents about dialogue that may be considered "objectionable." Most readers, by the time they are nine or ten, have discovered some words in print that they or some of their friends are forbidden to say aloud. Rather than just ignoring the pointing and tittering that go with such discoveries, an adult may decide to use these events to examine how language, particularly dialogue, contributes to character development.

Figure 9: Frye's Dialectic and Cyclical Patterns

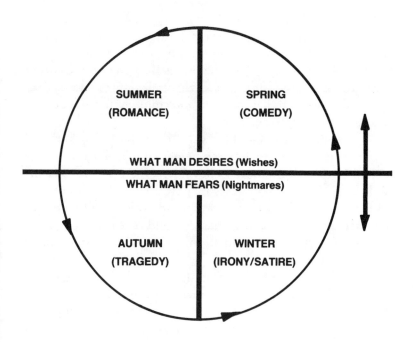

If you wanted to write a very happy story, in what season would you most likely set it? (Spring)

In which of the quadrants would you probably find
       . . . a unicorn? (Summer—Romance)
       . . . a snake? (Autumn—Tragedy)
       . . . a lamb? (Spring—Comedy)
       . . . a buzzard? (Winter—Irony)

What colors could you associate with each of the four seasons or types of stories? (Spring—yellow, Summer—green, Autumn—red, Winter—black)

Would a lion most likely fall above or below the horizontal line? (Below) What of Baum's cowardly lion? (Above. The break with literary tradition emphasizes the characteristic.)

It is obvious that "street kids" do not talk like college professors, but it is also true that college professors do not always talk like college professors. Each of us, no matter what our age, educational background, or experience, uses many different levels of language, each of which is probably appropriate in its own context. The street kid most likely changes his language when he leaves the gang on the corner and enters a classroom, just as the college professor speaks quite differently to her husband and children than she does to students in the lecture hall.

An understanding of the various levels of language used by all people in our society can help young people make their own compositions more believable. One need not get involved with language that is inappropriate to the home, the library, or the classroom in order to do this. Children might be encouraged to create a character and reveal something of that character's age, occupation, or regional origins solely through language.

The overuse of dialect or slang should be avoided because these may limit communication and may even appear to be a means of making fun of a character. An authentic use of a dialect may not be understood by outsiders; anything less may not capture the flavor and the spirit of the language and thus be offensive to people. Slang is also regional and becomes dated so quickly that it too may not be understood and may appear more strange than apt to future readers. However, children enjoy the challenge of revealing certain aspects of a character's life through language.

Those familiar with allegorical works such as *Pilgrim's Progress* may also enjoy creating names for characters, such as Patience and Trueheart, that represent human traits, while others attempt to find more modern or more common names that, because of sound or association, seem to indicate certain characteristics. In the process they may ask, would you rather buy a used car from a Bill or a Horace or go to a movie with a Gertrude or a Kathy? It is important for youngsters to realize the effects of these names in story, but even more important for them to realize that the characteristics they represent do not carry over into life and that people should not be trapped into making superficial judgments about others because of their names.

Symbol is even more difficult for children to cope with in their composition. Although they recognize the use of symbol in the stories they read, most young people find it almost impossible to convey symbolic meanings in their own work. Those who are interested in the use of symbolism might be encouraged to think of an object that has symbolic significance in their own or in a character's life, elaborate on the meaning of that symbol, and then try to communicate that meaning through the placement and the use of that object in story. This works for many children because the problem often is that they have not clearly thought through what an item is symbolic of or what they are attempting to do with a particular symbol in story. Identifying some common cultural or national symbols and determining how they are used in literary compositions might also be helpful. The differences between private and public symbols and the various perspectives from which one may view those symbols may be critical to story. For instance, what represents warmth and security and love to a parent may represent authority and unnecessary restrictions to a child, and the American flag flown over a battlefield may stir up as much hatred on one side of the line as it does patriotism on the other. Many of these uses of symbol are very complex, and few children will become involved with them in their compositions, but, as adults concerned with both children and literature, we must be prepared to help those who are ready to deal with this element.

Point of view, on the other hand, is quite easily handled, at least on some level, by most children. The primary interest of much that they read comes from the introduction of points of view both like and unlike their own. A large percentage of the stories for young children have personified objects or animals as protagonists; although most of these characters do represent human beings, they may also give readers or listeners some indication of what it must be like to be that particular object or animal.

A twelve-year-old who was enthralled with *Ben and Me* used this story as a model for his own lengthy historical novel entitled *J. Rutherford Rat and the American Revolution*. He even outdid Lawson by having "J.R.R." manipulating not just one character but all participants on both sides of the conflict, as if he were moving figures on a giant chess board. Those who have read Stolz's Barkham Street books may be inspired to follow her lead and try to rewrite a favorite story in such a way that the antagonist becomes the protagonist or even to create several different versions of the same story as it might be told by various characters or observers. This is not only excellent experience for a youngster interested in composition, it is an activity that all of us should engage in from time to time to help increase our sensitivity to other human beings. Too often we are so bound by our own private points of view that we have no patience or sympathy for those who see the world or a particular incident from a different perspective. If an appreciation of different points of view in literature can carry over into everyday living, this might well be the focal point of all literary learning.

Point of view can often be seen quite clearly in the illustrations of picture story books. Again one might compare the visual and verbal presentations of the point of view or attempt to tell in words what is revealed only in picture. In fact, critical analysis of picture story books, looking at all the elements on the matrix, is often a very useful method of getting at the essence of story, artfully achieved.

Many of these stories are very beautiful ones, worthy of being shared with a wider audience than their format would indicate is appropriate. One way of legitimizing their use with older children is as a focus of discussion for the analysis of story patterns and elements. The simplicity and clarity of their use in these books may make it possible for the reader to see relationships among the elements of story and to reflect upon the author's and illustrator's craftsmanship in the aesthetic composition. Once older children accept the use of picture story books in this way, these books may take their place beside the books for more mature readers in their total literary experience. Not only are these books fine literature but they provide a means for less able readers to participate more fully with others in literary activities and discussions. Books for young children are also very helpful to all youngsters looking at the various types of literary works across the horizontal axis of the matrix (Figure 4) used here. The differences between and among genre can be seen and held in mind more clearly when dealing with shorter works. In addition, the child who wishes to begin composition with the total structure of a particular genre will probably find one of these books to be a better model than a much more lengthy and complex work.

One of the things that adults need to realize in helping children with composition is that young people are often not aware of the genre they are creating. Most of what we read to children is story, and that is what we ordinarily expect in their compositions. However, children often write as they live and as they speak—in dramatic form. What appears at first to be poorly constructed story might, in fact, be perfectly adequate drama if it were presented on the page in that form. The child who tells stories by repeating "and he says and then she says" may also write that way and could probably be shown in a matter of minutes how to write a play with its settings, stage directions, and characters' speeches clearly delineated. There are also those children whose compositions, although written as if they were prose, are much closer to poetry; these authors too need to see how to arrange their words on the page to give them the most power and the most impact. It is only when a child understands the literary form in which he is writing and feels successful in that form that he will continue to improve his compositional work.

Finally, in discussing the matrix (Figure 4), I would like to mention the composition of informational materials. Too often we speak of "creative writing" as if only fictional works could be creative, and most of what children learn about informational writing is confined to changing a word or two from an encyclopedia article. Here again, books for young children can be both instructive and inspirational. Many of these books contain a great deal of factual content, but they are also beautifully written and convey concern about the topic as well as knowledge of it. Such works are certainly worthy models for the compositional efforts of children.

One of the most natural responses to the enjoyment of story among children is their transposition or recomposition of some of the elements of that story into another art form. A child's playacting—sometimes many days after the sharing of a story—a crayon drawing of a favorite character, or a song and dance capturing the mood of story indicate quite clearly the response to and understanding of literary elements. Evidences of children's productions in music, dance, drama, the graphic arts, and filmmaking indicate that children have been concerned with and actively involved in giving their own personal shape to the world of their experiences. The skillful and sensitive adult helps them to see the similarities in the compositional process as well as the uniqueness of the different media of expression.

All of these activities help children see from inside the skin of a composer what it is to create an original aesthetic form. Through their own struggle with mood, character, detail, and imagery, they increase their sensitivity to these elements well-used by others. In other words, they develop those critical abilities that enable them to approach story more sensitively and more joyously. At the same time, they increase their capacity for control and connection in the world.

Footnotes

1. A theme throughout all his work, see especially Northrop Frye, *Anatomy of Criticism: Four Essays* (Princeton, N.J.: Princeton University Pr., 1957).

2. Stith Thompson, *The Folktale* (Berkeley, Calif.: University of California Pr., 1977), p. 415.

3. Louise A. DeSalvo, "Writers at Work," *Media & Methods* 16, 4 (December 1979): 12–18+.

Children's Books Cited in Chapter Eight

Bemmelmans, Ludwig. *Madeline*. New York: Viking Pr., 1939.

Blume, Judy. *Are You There, God, It's Me Margaret?* Scarsdale, N.Y.: Bradbury Pr., 1970.

Cleary, Beverly. *Henry Huggins*. New York: William Morrow Co., 1950.

De Brunhoff, Jean. *The Story of Babar*. New York: Random House, 1937.

Grahame, Kenneth. *The Wind in the Willows*. Cleveland, Ohio: World Publishing Co., 1966. (First published in 1908.)

Lawson, Robert. *Rabbit Hill*. New York: Viking Pr., 1944.

———. *Ben and Me*. Boston: Little, Brown, 1939.

Merrill, Jean. *The Pushcart War*, illus. Ronni Solbert. Reading, Mass.: Addison-Wesley Publishing Co., 1964.

Potter, Beatrix. *The Tale of Peter Rabbit*. New York: Frederick Warne, 1902.

Stolz, Mary. *The Bully of Barkham Street*. New York: Harper & Row, 1963.

———. *A Dog on Barkham Street*. New York: Harper & Row, 1960.

Titus, Eve. *Anatole*, illus. Paul Galdone. New York: McGraw-Hill, 1956.

Chapter Nine
Large Screen and Small:
Media and the Child

Never has story been so pervasive in the lives of children as it is today. Fiction has always been a powerful force in society, but never have stories been so available to so many on so regular a basis. Of course, most of these stories are part of the barrage of sounds and images from television, motion pictures, popular music, and other mass media that are so constantly a part of our lives. Such stories may not always be of the highest quality, but they do offer an immediacy, an intimacy, and an accessibility that can exert a powerful influence on the way children perceive and understand the world. Children in some areas of the country can even go to the telephone each day and "dial-a-story" recorded especially for them.*

---

*I dialed this number three successive days and heard one story (a brief version of a legend) and two biographical sketches. In order to complete the work in the allocated time, the "storyteller" spoke so rapidly that she was halfway through before I began to understand. Repeated queries to the New York Telephone Company asking about this program and its criteria have been unfruitful. It is unfortunate that children's fascination with the telephone is not used to better advantage in furthering their appreciation of story.

Only a few of these media require the child to rely on her own personal vision to convert words to mental images. The others present all children with the same repertoire of shared images. There may be some advantage in these shared images if they provide a means of uniting the community of children through a common symbol system. The mass media can provide unique opportunities to extend the power and the range of the person and to amplify the force of that person's creative, human potential. They are additional ways of reaching out to others and of gaining new meanings from them through more divergent opportunities for communication. The mass media present possibilities of new forms of confrontation between the meanings made by children and those of others, new ways to structure and restructure one's relationship with the rest of the world. As Marshall McLuhan has said, "The medium is the message . . . it controls and shapes the scale and form of human association and action."[1]

On the other hand, there are dangers inherent in the reliance on the various mass media for our metaphorical connections to the world and to each other. One's point of view in relation to film and television images is usually very different from that conjured up from one's personal reading or from listening to story. Owing to the nature of the media, these visual images are much less open to interpretation then is one's subjective rendering of a character, setting, or event through the medium of print. Although any process of making meaning from a symbol system is a re-creative process, a television or movie image must be too definite and too complete to allow the viewer the degree of personal re-creation experienced with the printed page. It is for this reason that some types of stories are more powerful on radio than they are on television and that viewers often resent seeing characters on the motion picture or television screen previously seen only in the imagination. For the most part, we are all too accepting of television views of the world. Young children sometimes do not even distinguish between news footage and story on television. The bombardment of both informational and imaginative images, all with their own values and opinions, may be confusing to children; although today's young people are often more informed than previous generations, the images, information, and ideas collected may have been imperfectly absorbed or interpreted.

Common media experiences may also set up new role models or new classes of authority figures and exert undue pressure for conformity. Adults need to realize that, although a child's horizons are no longer bounded by the limited world in which she lives, her ideas and opinions are often unrelated to either the quantity or the accuracy of the messages absorbed. What Lawrence Cremin said of the role of the school in an age of mass media is equally true for all of us concerned with children and their metaphoric as well as intellectual connections to the world. Our task "is to make youngsters aware of the constant bombardment of acts, opinions and values to which they are subjected; to help them question what they see and hear; and ultimately, to give them the intellectual resources they need to make judgments and assess significance."[2]

Today's children are undeniably influenced by television and motion picture images. Adults, who are often themselves too close to the source of this influence, must develop the capacity to help children discriminate among these images, that is, to sort out, select, and bring order and perspective to all that is seen and heard. In order to do this, we must approach these and all media with respect for what they are uniquely able to do rather than with condescension or reproach. The elitist approach to media, all too common among "literary" adults who just want television to go away, is not at all useful. If television is indeed, as Marie Winn has called it, a "plug-in-drug,"[3] should we not help children deal with it rather than just hope it will not affect them? One might draw an analogy here and conjecture that the proportion of "bad" books may be no greater than the proportion of "bad" television shows. Should we then attempt to do away with all books to protect children from contact with those that do not meet our standards? And whose standards are "our" standards? Granted, television is more readily and more easily available to children, but it is adults who provide this resource for them and it is adults who must exercise some control over it.

The most effective means of controlling the power of the media is the development of critical abilities that will enable children to select and appreciate the best that is available to them. Action for Children's Television[4] has been lobbying for the elimination of commercials from all children's programs because they encourage young viewers to ask for nutritionless food and expensive toys that neither look nor perform in actuality as they do on the television screen. It seems to me, however, that from the point of view of story and its connections, the commercials are often at least as good as the programs they interrupt. Of course, a great deal of money is put into the creation of these thirty-second spots, but so too is a knowledge of traditional story forms and the elements with which they communicate. For this reason and because they are so much a part of the child culture, we might compare and contrast television commercials with the older and more established forms of folk literature very early in any treatment of story. In the process, as Jeffrey Schrank has noted, adults can help children look closely at the informational content and the techniques of persuasion[5] used and attempt to educate discriminating consumers for the future.

Attempts to encourage children to develop a more critical approach to film and television are certainly not new. During the middle and late sixties, there was a great deal of discussion among educators of the need to develop visual literacy as well as print literacy. To a large extent this movement was a response to major works on the topic by McLuhan, Rudolf Arnheim, and Gyorgy Kepes published between

1964–1969.[6] John Debes, keynote speaker at the First National Conference on Visual Literacy held in 1969, defined visual literacy as follows:

> Visual literacy refers to a group of vision–competencies a human being can develop by seeing and at the same time having and integrating other sensory experiences. The development of these competencies is fundamental to normal human learning. When developed, they enable a visually literate person to discriminate and interpret the visible actions, objects, and symbols, natural or man-made, that he encounters in his environment. Through the creative use of these competencies, he is able to communicate and enjoy the masterworks of visual communication.[7]

A number of the components of this visual literacy are learned naturally as the child lives and grows in a media-saturated world. However, many of the proponents of visual literacy in the late sixties approached the development of more complex visual abilities through film production. An alternative approach concentrated on the viewing of many films so that youngsters might begin to understand the art of filmmaking through the analysis of specific works. At the same time, a small community of scholars were involved in a semiological study of cinema, which looked at the language and the grammar of film as one studies linguistics.[8]

None of these attempts to promote visual literacy seemed to have any major impact on the education of children in the sixties and seventies, although semiotics seems to be exerting some influence on film study today, perhaps as a way of including mass media in education amidst cries of "back-to-basics." Probably the key factors in the lack of enthusiastic response to the other two approaches to visual literacy were the cost factors and the lack of qualified and committed adults who had the necessary competencies. Both the hardware and the software required for the kind of filmmaking programs advocated by Debes and others of the "Rochester School" were, in spite of the generous government funding of the sixties, too expensive for many schools, as was the provision of films for the alternative approach. The lack of expertise on the part of adults was an even greater deterrent, and it remains one even today. Only when adults are willing to invest the time and energy to become truly literate in the visual media can we help children to develop critical abilities in their evaluation, selection, and comprehension.

It is important that young people become producers as well as consumers of the visual media, just as they increase their comprehension and enjoyment of the printed page by shaping their own written work. It is not necessary to invest in elaborate or expensive equipment in order to become such. At least at the beginning stages, children can sharpen their visual abilities through the use of what is already in the environment. They can learn to analyze individual pictures from magazines and book illustrations, as well as their own drawings, to determine what the messages are and how they are communicated. Children can then isolate a particular segment or segments of a picture through cropping and thus alter its message. This activity is similar to the modeling of the child's written compositions on the finished work of others. Using groups of pictures, children can arrange and rearrange these into various narrative sequences that tell a story or convey information.*

In such activities, it is important for the adult to select pictures that will carry different messages when arranged in different sequences so that it becomes evident that it is the

---

*A number of story sequence card sets are available, among them Educational Design Associates' *MUST: Multi Story Sequence Cards*, Unit One: Around the House (East Lansing, Mich.: Eastman Kodak Co., 1972) and *Photo-Story Discover Set, No. 1* (Rochester, New York: Eastman Kodak Co., 1967; available at this time through AECT); Developmental Learning Materials' *Sequence Pictures, No. 1* (Chicago, Ill.: Developmental Learning Materials, 1968.)

relationship among pictures as well as the elements of a particular picture that communicates to viewers. Cartoons and comic strips may be especially useful tools in this kind of manipulation and analysis of still pictures. The creation of an original comic strip is often enjoyable for children and may also be one of the best tests of a child's understanding of the components of visual literacy. With just a small investment of funds, adults can work with children using inexpensive cameras to photograph their own pictures to be used in these ways. Motion can be added, still very inexpensively, by making use of simple filmstrip-making kits, drawing on film leader, or using a simple home movie camera, which many children may already have available to them. For little more than the cost of taking a group of children to a movie, we can have them shooting and editing their own movies.*

One need not be an "expert" in order to begin some of these activities with children. Too often we spend so much time getting ready to do some of these things that we never get around to actually doing them. Of course, expertise is to be desired and those who share these activities with children should work toward that expertise. But the lack of it is no excuse for not allowing children to get more actively involved with the media that are such powerful influences on their world. All that is needed is a willingness to begin, an openness to exploring ideas and materials, and an acceptance of the fact that children may well be more adept at many media activities than we as adults are.

At the same time that children are learning simple production techniques, they should be increasing their critical

---

*There are many excellent sources of information that will help adults begin filmmaking and other media production activities with children, such as Yvonne Anderson's *Teaching Film Animation to Children* (New York: Van Nostrand & Reinhold, 1970); Kirk Smallman's *Creative Filmmaking* (New York: Collier Books, 1969); Editors Kit Layborne and Pauline Cianciolo's *Doing the Media* (Chicago, Ill.: American Library Association, 1979).

abilities in response to the media that are already so much a part of their lives. There are a number of ways of helping them to do this, even for those adults more comfortable with the printed page than with other forms of media. Comparison of different presentations of the same story in print and on film helps children to sort out the differences in the media and to see the value of both. *Mary Poppins* in print focuses on a close-up view of the eccentricities of the title character and her influence on Jane and Michael. The Walt Disney movie version moves back from the main characters somewhat to present a broader view. In fact, the motion picture is an extravaganza of musical numbers and special effects. Both are interesting compositions, but the reader's re-creation of Mary Poppin's world is probably very different, and much more intimate, than that of the motion picture viewer.

The Weston Woods Company provides an opportunity for children to explore the differences both in a story itself and in their own responses to that story as it is converted from one medium to another.[9] This company produces both sound filmstrips and motion pictures/videocassettes from many well-known children's books. A group of eight children, ages nine to eleven, tested these relationships for themselves by selecting several stories available in book, filmstrip, and motion picture/videocassette formats for each by (1) reading the story privately, (2) having an adult read it to the group, (3) looking at the story as a filmstrip with an accompanying recording, and (4) seeing it as an iconographic, or animated motion picture/videocassette. The group decided that, although the stories and the pictures were the same in almost every case, both the works themselves and their experiences as readers and viewers were very different. In their own personal reading, most of the group became very involved in their identification with the main characters; the members felt that they were very intimately "a part of the story." When an adult read to them, they seemed to enjoy the warm social contact almost as much as the stories. They mentioned the sound of the reader's voice, their eye contact with him and with each other, and the fact that they all gathered together "in a tight little group." Of all the media of presentation, the filmstrip was the most difficult for children to attend to. The group did not seem to maintain its cohesiveness, although physically they were as close together, when they were asked to focus on a screen outside of the group instead of on a book and reader within the group. In addition, the movement from one frame to another seemed "jerky" and arbitrary or, as one child put it, "It always moves, but I can't tell when or why. I spent my time guessing and forgot to watch."

The experiences with the motion pictures then were more like that of the child reading alone, "only we don't have to do the work." The position of the group facing the screen, the darkness of the room, and the holistic character of the presentations encouraged individual involvement. This kind of involvement was not as intimate as that of the individual child's own reading because the verbal interpretation, the pacing, and even the eye movement were no longer under the viewer's control.

Although this particular group of children was more intrigued with exploring their own responses to various media, they did compare and contrast different formats to some extent. They tried to analyze their dissatisfaction with most of the filmstrips and decided that it might be due, to some extent at least, to the fact that they are so used to the smoother movement and faster pace of television. Then they tried to determine how the decisions might have been made to produce *Andy and the Lion* and *Make Way for Ducklings* as iconographic films and *Patrick* and *Pierre* as animated films. In the process of selecting these films, they discovered that Weston Wood's live-action films were not available as filmstrips and decided to compare the film *The Doughnuts* with the corresponding chapter from *Homer Price* and the print and film versions of *The Sorcerer's Apprentice*. Although this group of children had no previous experience either with the analysis or the production of visual media, they were used to talking about story and very quickly began to identify how literary elements and conventions were conveyed or adapted in another medium.

Another motion picture that helped the group sort out some of the essential characteristics of story, by comparing it with a newspaper report of an auto accident and a poem as well as the film version of that poem, is *What Is Poetry?* The motion picture compares an objective, unemotional, and impersonal account of an automobile accident with the highly personalized and emotional version of Karl Shapiro's poem "Auto Wreck." The major portion of this motion picture is a powerful and beautiful visual representation of "Auto Wreck" that some children found frightening and "horribly fascinating." The feeling, the imagery, and the raw beauty of the film were so real to them that they could accept, many for the first time, that the subject matter of literature is not as important as its composition. Many of these children were the same ones who had discussed *The Jazz Man* several weeks before (see Chapter Seven), and when they realized that a beautiful poem could be written about a tragic accident, they began to reconsider the possibility of that story ending with the death of the main character.

Since this film presents both the newspaper report and the poem, children discussed the possibility of using the same incident to write or film a story. They experimented orally with composing the story from different points of view and decided that the stories would be very different depending upon whether they were narrated by one of the victims, an observer from the sidewalk, one of the policemen, or the wife of one of the drivers. Each of these narrators represents a different emotional distance from the accident and would necessarily use different details, incidents, and ideas in their composition of story. In addition, the differences between film and print require different approaches to composition; through the exploration of these differences came an increased understanding of the nature and possibilities of various story forms.

It may be helpful in examining film and television with children to use the same matrix (Figure 4) relating key compositional elements to genres that was discussed in Chapter Six. Although some film and television critics object to the imposition of critical language and techniques from the world of print onto these visual compositions, it is probably better to begin our critical analysis with what we already know than not to begin at all. And, of course, it is impossible, even for a beginner, to discuss the compositional elements of film and television without discovering, or realizing what has already been known tacitly about, the techniques used to portray these elements visually. The films and television programs identified in Figure 10 include works of varying lengths and subjects and using a variety of visual techniques. It is obvious that many of these visual compositions are new versions of works that originally appeared in print. Full-length feature films made from children's books have both increased in number and improved in quality in recent years. Many of these are fine family films that can be enjoyed by parents as well as children, and are, shortly after their appearances in the first-run theaters, available for rental. It is important to children's understanding of the language of film that they see and discuss a number of full-length films, just as they need to read full-length novels as well as short stories.

This is not to say that only feature films made from children's books are worthy of critical attention. They are, however, usually more available to schools and libraries and more easily justified in a time of tight budgets. On the other hand, one could scarcely ignore the influence of a film such as *Star Wars* on child culture in this country. Large numbers of youngsters saw this film more than once and then were the recipients of millions of dollars worth of *Star Wars* games and toys, costumes, bed sheets, and virtually anything else that could be imprinted with the image of Darth Vader or R2D2.

Figure 10: The Matrix:
Specific Media Indicating the Relationship of Key Compositional Elements to Genres

	Traditional Literature	Modern Fancy	Realistic Fiction	Poetry	Biographical Works	Informational Works
Character	The Golem The Wave A Story, A Story	Mork and Mindy The Muppets The Incredible Hulk Claude Superman	Laverne and Shirley Thank You, M'am The Tramp David and Lisa Rocky	The Face	Nanook of the North Eugenie The Autobiography of Miss Jane Pittman	The Holy Ghost People
Point of View		Freaky Friday	Bad Dog The Perils of Priscilla Eye of the Beholder Occurrence at Owl Creek Bridge	Lopsideland Bridges Go Round	I Wonder Why	Pigs This Is New York A Child's Eyes
Structure Plot	The Fisherman and His Wife The Owl and the Lemming Just Say Hic!	The Mole Films Unicorn in the Garden Roadrunner Cartoons		Danced Squared		Clay In the Beginning Overture/Nyitany The Story of a Book
Setting	Hansel and Gretel An Appalachian Version	Star Trek	Where the Lilies Bloom The Waltons Little House on the Prairie	Sea Fever Spring Color	Children Adrift My Own Yard to Play In	City of Gold
Mood/Tone		Patrick	Sounder White Mane	Dream of the Wild Horses Begone Dull Care Le Merle	Flavio	Tops The Old Mill Day After Day
Language Symbol	The Loon's Necklace	Star Wars The Red Balloon The Birds Jabberwocky Toys	The String Bean	Hangman Boiled Egg		American Time Capsule

Adult fans of this film were probably much more aware of its spoofs of the hero/quest myth of romance and of various filmic conventions, but this only enhanced their enjoyment. Whether or not adults consider *Star Wars* and *Mork and Mindy* to be worthy of children's attention, the fact remains that such works are a very important part of child life and therefore need to be examined from the point of view of both their appeal to and their influence on children. In order to do this, we must begin to look more critically at these nonprint media, that is, to seek out the best of what is available. At the same time we must recognize that, in films and television, just as in print, what is popular does not necessarily represent the best that is available. We cannot expect children to give up the popular any more than we as adults do, but we can help them to be more discriminating so that they will recognize and appreciate the best of film and television. The use of the matrices that follow may be the first step in helping them, and us, to do this.

Character can be conveyed through size, shape, lighting, posture, motion, and the relationship between figure and ground in a scene. Certainly one of the most memorable characters of the seventies was the title character in *Rocky*, whose run up the stairs and dance symbolizing the victory of the symbolic underdog has been replicated in television commercials and other forms of popular media. This scene was given added impact by its stirring musical sound track. Another survivor against all odds is Claude from the short animated film of that name. Claude is a very simply drawn cartoon figure, literally an egghead, whose private existence is pictured in smooth, slow movements against an almost empty background, in contrast to the cluttered and symbolic opulence against which the jerky motions of his parents are seen. The title character of *The Incredible Hulk* is a modern television hero who, like some of the mythical characters of traditional literature, is the "beastly" side of an ordinarily mild-mannered young man. The Hulk is characterized by his bulk, his green coloring, and the quizzical, uncomprehending expressions on his face as he observes the beastly behaviors of the "bad guys" of the human world. Miss Piggy of *The Muppets* is one of the most glamorously detailed puppets ever to appear on film and television. She appeals to adults at least as much as to children because of her "hammy" caricature of all media-made sex symbols.

Point of view is seen most obviously through the use of camera angles that allow us to see the world through the eyes of the main character. When this character is a dog or a cat as in *Bad Dog* or *The Perils of Priscilla*, the very eye level of the viewer is so changed that the world is seen in ways it is not normally seen. Even the child's eye view of New York City in *This Is New York* reminds us of what it is to look at all things from less than four feet from the ground, just as *A Child's Eyes* shares children's interpretations of the events surrounding President Kennedy's assassination. *Pigs*, by moving the camera in closer to a barnyard full of pigs than most of us ever want to be, focuses on particular pig activities and parts of pig anatomy in a way that makes many viewers see and care about them in a new way.

The most obvious aspect of the structure of television programs is that they are discontinuous. The many commercial interruptions in each hour of television broadcasting makes viewing something on the small screen very different from seeing a continuous showing of the same work on the motion picture screen. Because overt actions are more easily conveyed in a half-hour visual presentation than are more complex forms of story conflict, plot is a key element in many television programs. Many of the children's cartoons on Saturday morning television, for example, are almost totally dependent on very short and very active, often violent, episodes. Motion picture technology now allows filmmakers to use microphotography, time-lapses, and other means of visualizing what is normally invisible to structure their work according to a natural, but accelerated, temporal sequence. Informational films such as *In the Beginning* and *Overture/Nyitany* use these special photographic techniques to reveal the stages of development of an animal within an egg. *Story of a Book* condenses time through traditional cutting to take viewers step-by-step with the Hollingses from their initial research to the final production of one of their children's books.

Although it may appear that the filmmaker or television producer has an advantage over the writer in establishing the physical setting of a work because she only has to find an appropriate place to film, this is almost never the case. In the first place, it is far easier to create with language precisely the setting required than to find or create it in the real world. Viewers may not be especially aware of place in many visual compositions, but settings may subtly influence the interpretation of and response to the total work. Set designers, knowing this, spend a great deal of time, money, and effort making certain that the sets are just right. This was brought home to me quite forcefully when a portion of a feature film was shot in an apartment next to mine.[10] Although this was not one of the primary sets of the film, a quarter of a million dollars worth of furnishings were moved into two rooms, and a week prior to shooting was spent in preparing the set. The attention to detail was astounding to those of us unfamiliar with professional filmmaking. Very deliberate decisions were made about such things as the precise position of an ashtray on a table, which demonstrated to me that the details of set dressing are every bit as important to the total composition of a film as detail is to painting or book illustration. My awe increased when I realized that, owing to the nature of the filming required, a portion of this set had to be replicated exactly in the studio.

Physical locations are very important in television programs such as *The Waltons* and *Little House on the Prairie*. It is interesting to note, however, that it is the specific setting of Walton's Mountain that is used symbolically in the first and the more generalized sense of "frontier" in the second. Time is also important in both of these shows, which look back nostalgically at ways of life unknown to most of us. *Hansel and Gretel: An Appalachian Version* transforms the fanciful timelessness and the generalized setting of the original tale to the period of the Great Depression in a very specific region of the United States. *Children Adrift* and *My Own Yard to Play In* show young children growing up in France and New York City respectively and give very powerful visual evidence of the effects of environment on their development. *City of Gold* is a motion picture that intersperses live action with shots of still pictures of the gold rush days in the Yukon. For this reason structure might be identified as a key element, but it presents such a vivid picture of a particular time and place that I have included it here. All of these works demonstrate the manipulation of time through editing that alternately expands and contracts clock time.

Visual artists can do a great deal with lighting, special filters, music, and sound effects as well as with pacing to create a mood. The film made from the picture story book *Patrick* creates a different, and more engaging, mood than the print version by the substitution of a very lively musical sound track for the words of the text. The film version of *Sounder*, although true to the original book, seems to be lightened somewhat by seeing the harsh realities of the character's lives against the beautiful, if unyielding, setting in which they live. *Dream of the Wild Horses* uses slow motion, a musical sound track, and soft focus to romanticize a frightening experience.

One of the most powerful uses of symbol in a visual medium is that of the birds in the Hitchcock film of that name. Viewers of *The Birds* quickly change their perceptions of these creatures so that a bird that might ordinarily be thought of as lovely and peaceful strikes fear in their hearts. *American Time Capsule* is a fast-moving montage of visual symbols that runs through the whole history of the United

States in three minutes. The title objects in *The String Bean* and *The Red Balloon* are both symbols of hope for the characters in these films, and both films use color symbolically. The first moves back and forth from color to black and white; in the second, the bright red balloon stands out against the drab shades of most of the boy's world.

Even using a matrix designed primarily for print, a sympathetic viewer can gain many insights into the properties and the characteristics of media other than print. One might then go on to revise this matrix to look specifically at the elements and genres of a particular visual medium. Figure 11 was designed to examine the nature of television programs. Although others might identify either the compositional elements or the genre differently, the Figure is one means of focusing attention on some critical aspects of this most pervasive medium.

As it is used here, visual composition refers to the arrangement, placement, and framing of objects within a scene. Arrangement is the relationship between objects or persons in the foreground and between the foreground and the background. Placement has to do with the distance and angle of the camera in shooting the arrangement, whether it is a close-up, middle distance, or long shot seen from eye level, above, or below. Framing controls what is seen by drawing attention to subjects; it forces viewers to see them separated out from the rest of a scene into the rectangular frame. In some instances, this frame may be divided to show more than one image on the split screen. The use of line may also be an effective factor in visual composition. Vertical lines often convey a sense of power, majesty, or awe while long horizontal lines are restful and diagonal lines indicate action or dynamism.

Light is the basic substance with which a photographer works. It is light that makes the actual world visible on the television or motion picture screen and draws attention to the central action. It is also the skillful use of light that changes

Figure 11: The Matrix: The Relationship of Key Compositional Elements to Television Genres

	Situation Comedies	Situation Dramas	Children's Programs	Musical & Variety Shows	Soap Operas	News Documentary
Visual Composition						
Lighting						
Color						
Movement						
Sound						
Editing						

viewers' perceptions of that world to correspond with the filmmakers' personal or artistic vision. Natural lighting may lend an immediacy and a warmth to a scene while artificial lighting may be manipulated to a greater extent to produce various effects. The position of the lighting sources in relation to the scene may also be used to interpret characters and events by the intensity of the light and the interplay of light and shadows.

Although color is often thought of as a means of adding realism to a visual image, early movies used it primarily for fanciful sequences. For example, the Kansas scenes in *The Wizard of Oz* were shot in black and white and the scenes of Oz in color. Black and white is often used today to convey a kind of harsh reality that cannot easily be achieved with color, which often brightens and flattens what is seen. The use of color may be (1) descriptive, (2) decorative, (3) expressive, (4) diagrammatic, or (5) symbolic.[11] Color may be necessary to recognize certain objects in which color is a distinguishing feature or it may be used for purely decorative purposes. The expressive use of color is most powerful in film and television images. Sometimes the film stock itself is tinted with either a "warm" or a "cool" color in order to convey a subtle emotional tone. At other times, different colors within a scene are chosen either to "harmonize" or to "clash" in ways that add to the impact of the total aesthetic composition. A diagrammatic use of color highlights or emphasizes a certain segment or clarifies relationships among such segments of a visual image. Finally, the symbolic use of color refers to international color coding as in electrical wiring or map-making, not used to any great extent in film and television except in certain informational contexts.

Movement or the illusion of movement is obviously the essence of the television and motion picture industries. Central action is the movement of the actors or objects being photographed, but the background behind that central image can also move, as can the camera itself. One need not be especially sophisticated in the understanding of photographic techniques to recognize camera movements such as panning, tracking, tilting, or zooming. Even more obvious is the use of slow motion, often as a means of conveying mood, or the use of accelerated action for humor.

Although film and television are primarily visual media, sound is often critical to communication in these media. In fact, it is far easier to follow most television programs by listening to them without the visual image than it would be to watch the picture without the sound. Many television "viewers" do, in fact, have their television sets on even when they are in another room and just go to check the visual image when they hear something of interest to them. Sports broadcasts lend themselves especially to this style of viewing since one can ordinarily depend on a series of instant replays showing any critical action from several different camera angles. Dialogue, music, sound effects, and voice-over or commentary are the basic categories of sound in motion picture and television. Sounds may move from the background to the foreground of the total composition as they increase in intensity or volume just as images fade in or fade out on the screen. The theme song is one of the most obvious uses of a musical sound track because of its repetition throughout a work or from episode to episode in a series. There are also musical conventions which, on their own, conjure up images of suspense or the action of the chase, as well as more subtle musical transitions from one scene to another. The speed, the pitch, and the character of the sound, whether it is harsh or soft or hollow, are often used to direct emotional responses and create dramatic impact. Perhaps the most dramatic use of sound is the interval of silence that arrests action and draws viewers into a more intense emotional response with the subjects and actions on the screen.

Editing is the process of selecting and ordering all the shots and putting them together into a unified composition. It is probably fair to say that almost all movies are made in the editing room; and, to a somewhat lesser extent, this statement is true of television as well. Certainly most films are shot discontinuously as it would be economically disastrous to go back and forth from one setting to another as the action of a story indicates. All the shots that occur in one place are therefore shot at the same time regardless of their actual sequence in the final composition. Editors then use straight cuts or various forms of gradual cuts (fade-ins, fade-outs, wipes, dissolves, or overlaps) to reorder and dramatize a series of visual events. It is important to note here that more sophisticated techniques and technologies are regularly developed that increase the possibilities open to camera operators, laboratory technicians, and editors. Advances in film and television technologies have made significant changes in these media; however, it is still the collective imagination of all the creative human beings involved that results in excellence for either the large or the small screen.

The horizontal axis of this matrix contains a fairly limited selection of genres or types of television programs. Others might wish to include sports events, talk shows, quiz and game shows, cultural specials, or additional forms of general or family drama such as miniseries, docudramas, and motion pictures. One might look individually at the various types of programs that are combined here as situation dramas. These include the westerns, police and detective stories, medical programs, war or military shows, and other forms of formulitic fiction seen on the home screen.* It may even be possible to look only at various types of children's programs, from cartoons to the recent magazine news formats especially designed for the young viewer. The genres included here were selected because they seem to be the ones that consume a

---

* Some fine examples of application of formulitic theories to various media may be found in *The Journal of Popular Culture* and *The Journal of American Culture*. See also John G. Cawelti, *The Six-Gun Mystique* (Bowling Green, Ohio: Bowling Green Popular Pr., 1970).

great deal of the viewing time of children, whether this is by their active choice or simply by the chance of their being in the same room with adult viewers.

Although television commercials are not included on this matrix, they are very important in the child's total viewing and should be examined for both their aesthetic and their advertising content. Therefore, rather than attempt to examine all of the program types included in the matrix, which will be left to the reader to complete, I will discuss the various compositional elements as they are most commonly used in television commercials. The overall visual composition of most commercials features sharply focused close-ups of the product so that potential purchasers will be able to distinguish it among many similar products in the store. A low camera angle is often used to make the product appear larger, and scenes that convey the kind of image the advertisers wish to project may appear in the background. Titles are frequently superimposed on the screen to reinforce the recognition factor, and a split screen may be used to compare the product to the infamous Brand X or to show more than one product from the store advertised. Lighting is ordinarily bright and of high intensity because most advertisers do not wish to have shadows of doubt or suspicion cast on their product. Some commercials, however, use soft lighting to create a romantic mood to correspond to the image associated with the product. Color is most often used descriptively or diagrammatically to identify the product more precisely or to point to particular aspects or characteristics. A key color or color scheme from the merchandise is sometimes picked up and duplicated in subtle ways or a color wash may be used to create an emotional tone. The most obvious and most controversial use of color in television advertising is the adding of color or "touching up" a product, especially a food product, to make it more appealing to consumers. The movement within these thirty-second spots is necessarily fast, with a great deal of action and information compressed into very little time. Time lapse photography and other forms of time manipulation and special effects are used to get the message across to viewers most efficiently and most effectively. The sound level of commercials is now regulated so that volume does not increase noticeably when there is a cut from program to commercial. The speed of the sound track and the use of special sound effects may have the same result, however, that is, to draw attention to the screen. The character of the sound is often matched with the nature of the product, and musical themes or jingles or slogans may accompany the visual representation. One of the most impactful of these themes was Coke's mountain full of children singing "I'd like to teach the world to sing in perfect harmony." Children have sometimes even incorporated old commercial jingles such as "You wonder where the yellow went when you brush you teeth with Pepsodent," into their culture in the form of jumping rope rhymes, chants or taunts. All of these sounds, movements, and colors come together in a very sophisticated editing process that makes use of fades, dissolves, and overlaps as well as many straight fast cuts to move the action and the identification with the product along.

A much more complex analysis might be made of any one of the various television genre or of a specific program; and, with the concern about children's viewing habits, both of these are being done. Teachers Guides to Television[12] is a New York–based organization that, as its name indicates, publishes guides to specific programs of interest to children. More recently this group is also conducting Parent Participation TV Workshops to suggest ways in which parents might become more involved in their children's television activities. My concern with these materials and programs is that they are too much dependent on the content rather than the language or the form of the medium and do not really help adults and children deal critically with the programs. Prime Time School Television[13] is a similar organization that provides regular guides to prime time television but also publishes more extensive curriculum units, such as *Television, Police and the Law*.[14] These units focus on popular programs as a means of examining issues and encouraging discussion of such topics as law enforcement, civil rights, and the values inherent in popular television series. WNET-Thirteen, the New York public television station, has produced *Critical Television Viewing: A Language Skills Work-a-Text*[15] designed to help young people analyze the characters, plots, conflicts, and themes of television programs. A major effort in controlling television's influence over children is the Yale University Family Television Research and Consultation Center,[16] which has been working more than a year to develop materials to help elementary school children understand television. These curriculum materials are now scheduled for release in time for use in the fall of 1980. *A Public Trust*,[17] the Report of the Carnegie Commission, discussed children's programming on public television but seemed somewhat narrow in its vision of what such programming might be. This report deals with *Sesame Street* in a way that appears to set it up as the model for broadcasting for children. There is no doubt that *Sesame Street* was an exciting and influential breakthrough in children's television, but *The Electric Company*, which followed, never achieved the same success. Children's Television Workshop, producers of both *Sesame Street* and *The Electric Company*, recently released a new daily science series entitled *3–2–1 Contact*.[18] It remains to be seen if this program will have the impact of the first series; but, even if it does, it seems shortsighted to think that all children's programming should be drawn from the same pattern. We have only begun to tap the possibilities of television broadcasting for children, and we should be demanding more and better alternatives in this medium rather than resting on the laurels of one successful series.

No discussion of children and television would be complete without some mention of the treatment of violence and the effects of this violence on children. Even a casual viewer soon observes that the networks are filled with action and adventure shows in which the "good guys" as well as the "bad guys" use violent means to solve problems. The use of violence is understandable when one considers the various forms of conflict that serve as basic structural elements of story and the nature of the television medium. It is very difficult to create an exciting visual dramatization of one's internal conflict or the conflict between the individual and society, and it can be very expensive to shoot a convincing conflict between person and nature. Therefore it is the person versus person conflict that most commonly, and most violently, appears on the home screen.

There have been many studies and official reports related to this topic in the last twenty-five years,* but the question of television and violence remains and has been brought into sharper focus by a recent Florida court case. In this instance, a young man used as his defense in a murder trial the fact that he was unduly influenced by watching *Kojak* and could no longer distinguish clearly between television and reality as he reenacted what he had seen on the screen. There have been similar incidents of media-stimulated violence, but these are unusual; and, while disturbing, they probably have more to do with the psychology of the individuals than with the power of the media. It may also be important to remind ourselves here that the "body count" on the nightly news programs is much higher than that of any other half hour on television.

To many of us who care about both children and television, even more troubling than the relatively few overt acts of violence attributable to television's influence is the possibility that young viewers are becoming desensitized to acts of violence and think of them as very normal human behaviors.

---

*Chief among these have been the Hearings before the Senate Subcommittee to Investigate Juvenile Delinquency, 1955, 1961, 1964. The National Commission on the Causes and Prevention of Violence analyzed programs during 1967 and 1968.

Is it possible that too many of us, like Chance in *Being There*,[19] are constructing our sense of reality from the images on the television screen? There is some evidence that many people prefer to watch an event on television rather than see it live. Classroom experiments in which children could choose to watch a dramatic situation either live or on a television screen demonstrated that more than half selected the television image. Some sports arenas have also experimented with simultaneous large screen television projection of an ongoing game to allow spectators to look back and forth between the television version and live action. Of course, television, like all art forms, composes and shapes events to make them more "believable" than reality, and the camera can make visible much that is not seen by the human eye. It can slow down or speed up action, stop time and look at critical incidents over and over again from every possible angle. Television coverage takes viewers closer to an event than otherwise possible but, at the same time, allows that aesthetic distancing that enables us to accept violence and other forms of unacceptable behavior more comfortably than we could in actuality.

We need to know much more about how all media shape our values and our sense of the world, but we cannot eliminate the positive contributions of modern mass media in an effort to rid society of possible negative influences any more than we would burn all books to get rid of those that do not meet our standards. G.K. Chesterton wrote a sound response to those concerned with the influence of film violence on children in 1923 that merits rereading today. After cataloging some purported results of film violence, e.g., a child knifes his father after seeing a knifing incident in a film, Chesterton remarks that even if such events actually occur, it would be more sensible to know particular details about the child rather than about the film. In any case, he asks what the practical moral is.

> Is it that the young should never see a story with a knife in it? Are they to be brought up in complete ignorance of

The Merchant of Venice because Shylock flourishes a knife for a highly disagreeable purpose? Are they never to hear of Macbeth, lest it should slowly dawn upon their trembling intelligence that it is a dagger that they see before them? It would be more practical to propose that a child should never see a real carving-knife, and still more practical that he should never see a real father.[20]

Footnotes

1. Marshall McLuhan, *Understanding Media: The Extensions of Man* (New York: McGraw-Hill, 1964), p. 9.

2. Lawrence A. Cremin, *The Genius of American Education* (New York: Random House, 1965), p. 23.

3. Marie Winn, *Plug-In Drug* (New York: Viking Pr., 1977).

4. Action for Children's Television, 46 Austin Street, Newtonville, Massachusetts 02160 (617-527-7870).

5. Jeffrey Schrank, *Understanding Mass Media* (Skokie, Ill.: National Textbook Co., 1975), pp. 45–58.

6. Rudolf Arnheim, *Visual Thinking* (London: Faber & Faber, Ltd., 1969); Gyorgy Kepes, ed., *Education and Vision* (New York: George Braziller, 1965); Marshall McLuhan, *Understanding Media: The Extensions of Man* (New York: McGraw-Hill, 1964).

7. John L. Debes, "The Loom of Visual Literacy," *Audio-Visual Instruction* 14 (October 1969): 27.

8. Peter Wollen, *Signs and Meaning in Cinema* (Bloomington, Ind.: Indiana University Pr., 1969); Umberto Eco, *A Theory of Semiotics* (Bloomington, Ind.: Indiana University Pr., 1976).

9. Morton Schindel, "Dear Betty...," in *Excellence in School Media Programs*, ed. Thomas J. Galvin, Margaret Mary Kimmel, and Brenda H. White (Chicago, Ill.: American Library Association, 1980), pp. 187–98.

10. *Wolfen*, an Alan King Production, was filmed in New York City during 1979–80.

11. Andrew Wright, *Designing for Visual Aids* (London: Studio Vista, 1970), pp. 67–68.

12. Teachers Guides to Television, 699 Madison Avenue, New York, New York 10021 (212-249-2249).

13. Prime Time School Television, Suite 810, 120 South La Salle Street, Chicago, Illinois 60603 (312-368-1088).

14. Prime Time School Television, *Television, Police, and the Law* (Niles, Ill.: Argus Communications, 1977).

15. WNET-THIRTEEN, *Critical Television Viewing: A Language Skills Work-A-Text* (Cambridge: The Basic Skills Co., 1980).

16. Dick Friedman, "Like Parent, Like Child," *Panorama* 1, 1 (February 1980): 108.

17. *A Public Trust: The Report of the Carnegie Commission on the Future of Public Broadcasting* (New York: Bantam Books, 1979).

18. David Black, "They've Got It Down to a Science," *Panorama* 1, 2 (March 1980): 82–84.

19. Jerzy Kosinski, *Being There* (New York: Harcourt, Brace, Jovanovich, 1971).

20. Gilbert Keith Chesterton, *Fancies Versus Fads* (New York: Dodd, Mead, 1923), p. 61.

Children's Media Cited in Chapter Nine

American Time Capsule. Pyramid Films, 1968. 3 minutes, color.

Andy and the Lion. Weston Woods, 1956. 10 minutes, color.

Autobiography of Miss Jane Pittman. Tomorrow Productions Entertainments, n.d. (1974?). 110 minutes, color.

Bad Dog. Noyes Productions, 1973. 7 minutes, color.

Begone Dull Care. National Film Board of Canada, 1949. 9 minutes, color.

The Birds. Directed by Sir Alfred Hitchcock. Universal Pictures, 1963.

Boiled Egg. Directed and animated by Max Andrieux and Bernard Brevant, 1963. 5 minutes, color.

Bridges-Go-Round. Halcyon Films, 1962. 3½ minutes, color.

Children Adrift. (Les Enfants Des Courants d'Air.) Directed by Henri Diamont-Berger. Contemporary Films, 1958. 26 minutes, black/white.

A Child's Eyes: November 22, 1963. Contemporary Films, 1965. 10 minutes, color.

City of Gold. National Film Board of Canada, 1957. 23 minutes, black/white.

Claude. Directed by Dan McLaughlin and the UCLA Animation Group. Pyramid Films, 1965. 3 minutes, color.

Clay; The Origin of the Species. Elliott Noyes, Jr. Contemporary Films, 1964. 8 minutes, black/white.

Dance Squared. National Film Board of Canada, n.d. 4 minutes, color.

David and Lisa. Continental Films, 1962. 94 minutes, black/white.

Day After Day. National Film Board of Canada, 1962. 30 minutes, black/white.

The Doughnuts. (From Homer Price.) Weston Woods, 1964. 26 minutes, color.

Dream of the Wild Horses. Contemporary Films, 1960. 9 minutes, color.

Electric Company. Children's Television Workshop. Public Broadcasting System. First aired in October, 1971.

Eugenie. Directed by Susan Sussman. Phoenix Films, 1977. 16 minutes, color.

The Eye of the Beholder. Stuart Reynold Productions, 1955. 25 minutes, black/white.

Face. Brandon Films, n.d. (1979?). 3 minutes, color.

The Fisherman and His Wife. Minimal Productions, 1970. 20 minutes, color.

Flavio. Elektra Films, 1964. 12 minutes, black/white.

Freaky Friday. Walt Disney Productions, 1976. 95 minutes, color.

The Golem. Weston Woods, 1979. Filmstrip, 51 frames, color.

Hangman. Melrose Productions, 1964. 12 minutes, color.

Hansel and Gretel, An Appalachian Version. Tom Davenport Films, 1975. 17 minutes, color.

The Holy Ghost People. Contemporary Films, 1968. 53 minutes, black/white.

I Wonder Why. Robert M. Rosenthal Productions, 1964. 6 minutes, black/white.

The Incredible Hulk. Produced by Universal Studios, Columbia Broadcasting System. First Aired on March 10, 1978.

In the Beginning. U.S. Department of Agriculture, 1937. 17 minutes, black/white.

Jabberwocky. Made at Kratky Films, Prague, 1973, Weston Woods, Sim Productions. 14 minutes, color.

Just Say Hic. Stephen Bosustow, 1969. 9 minutes, color.

Kojak. Produced by Universal Studios. Columbia Broadcasting System. First aired on September 24, 1973. Released to syndication in September 1979.

Laverne and Shirley. Miller, Milkis, Boyett Productions. American Broadcasting Corporation. First aired January 27, 1976.

Le Merle. Norman McLaren for National Film Board of Canada, 1958. 5 minutes, color.

Little House on the Prairie. NBC Productions, National Broadcasting Corporation. First aired on September 11, 1974.

The Loon's Necklace. Crawley Films, Ottawa, 1949. 10 minutes, color.

Lopsideland. Encyclopaedia Britannica Educational Corporation, 1969. 5 minutes, color.

Make Way for Ducklings. Weston Woods, 1955. 11 minutes, monochromatic.

Mary Poppins. Directed by Robert Stevenson. Walt Disney and Bill Walsh, Producers. Walt Disney Productions, 1964.

The Mole Films. Created by Zdenek Miler for Phoenix Films. *The Mole and the Flying Carpet,* 1979; *The Mole and the Telephone,* 1979. 6 minutes, color and 7 minutes, color.

Mork and Mindy. Produced by Miller–Milkas Productions and Henderson Production Company in association with Paramount, American Broadcasting Corporation. First aired September 14, 1978.

The Muppet Movie. Directed by James Frawley. Jim Henson, Producer. Associated Film Distributors, 1979.

My Own Yard to Play In. Directed by Ed Harrison, 1959. 6 minutes, black/white.

Nanook of the North. Robert Flaherty for Revillion Freres, 1922. c.70 minutes, black/white.

An Occurrence at Owl Creek Bridge. Directed by Marcel and Paul de Roubaix. Contemporary-McGraw-Hill Films, 1962. 27 minutes, black/white.

The Old Mill. Walt Disney Productions, 1971. 9 minutes, color.

Overture/Nitany. Directed by Janos Vadasz for Mafilms, 1965. 9 minutes, color.

The Owl and the Lemming. National Film Board of Canada, 1971. 6 minutes, color.

Patrick. Weston Woods, 1977. 7 minutes, color.

The Perils of Priscilla. Churchill Films. 10 minutes, color.

Pierre. Weston Woods, 1978. 6 minutes, color.

Pigs. Directed by Carroll Ballard, Churchill Films, 1967. 11 minutes, color.

The Red Balloon. Directed by Albert Lamorisse, Brandon Films, 1956. 34 minutes, color.

Road Runner Cartoons. Included in *The Bugs Bunny/Road Runner Hour.* Warner Brothers Productions, Columbia Broadcasting System. First aired September 14, 1968.

Rocky. Directed by John G. Avildsen, United Artists, 1976.

Sea Fever. Charles Cahill and Associates, 1966. 6 minutes, color.

Sesame Street. Children's Television Workshop. Public Broadcasting System. First aired on November 10, 1969.

Sounder. Directed by Martin Ritt. Robert Radnitz, Producer. 20th Century Fox Studios, 1972.

Spring Color. Thorne Films, 1968. 5 minutes, color.

Star Trek. Norway Productions in association with Desilu and NBC Television Network. National Broadcasting Corporation. First aired September 8, 1966.

Star Wars. Directed by George Lucas. Gary Kurtz, Producer. 20th Century Fox Studios, 1977.

A Story, A Story. Weston Woods, 1973. 10 minutes, color.

The Story of a Book. Churchill Films, 1962. 11 minutes, color.

The String Bean. Contemporary Films, 1964. 17 minutes, color and black/white.

Superman. Directed by Richard Donner. Pierre Spengler, Producer. Distributed by Warner Brothers, 1978.

Thank You M'am. Phoenix Films, 1976. 12 minutes, color.

This Is New York. Weston Woods, 1962. 12 minutes, color.

3–2–1 Contact. Children's Television Workshop. Public Broadcasting System. First aired on January 14, 1980.

Tops. Produced and Distributed by Charles and Ray Eames, 1969. 7 minutes, color.

Toys. National Film Board of Canada, 1966. 7 minutes, color.

The Tramp. Essanay Film Manufacturing, 1915. 28 minutes, black/white.

Unicorn in the Garden. Bill Hurtz for United Productions of America (UPA), 1953. Color.

The Waltons. Produced by Lorimar. Columbia Broadcasting System. First aired September 14, 1972.

The Wave. Film Associates, 1968. 9 minutes, color.

What Is Poetry? Film Associates of California, 1963. 10 minutes, color.

Where the Lilies Bloom. United Artists, 1974. 97 minutes, color.

White Mane. Rembrandt Film Library, 1953. 39 minutes, black/white.

The Wizard of Oz. Directed by Victor Fleming. Mervin LeRoy, Producer. MGM, 1939.

Chapter Ten
Centering on the
Literary Connection

Story brings a special richness to a child's life. It taps the child's sense of wonder and releases her to reach out to others, to look at the world through another pair of eyes, and to tune her ears to the beauty and the excitement of the language. Through story she discovers something of herself in someone else's work, sees unity rather than distinctions in the world, and thus begins the connection with others beyond the immediate environment—the connection that makes one truly human.

We live in a world of many meanings, but each child must take up her own meaning in that world. As she establishes a personal position among the collective meanings of the world and imposes her own original perspective upon that world, both she and the world are made anew. Of course, humans are intersubjective beings whose personal meanings are shaped through interactions, both actual and imaginative, with the meanings of others. Story provides a form in which the single child can make her own authentic meanings but simultaneously hear other meanings, both as a member of the world community with her own part to play and as a critic of the whole. Responses to story make up a multifaceted design containing many ideas, each related to the others but in a relationship that is not fixed. Each reader establishes her own position within the possibilities of that design, plots her own course of action, makes her own meaning, and asserts herself in her own dignity as a member of the human community. When adults try to use literature to help children toward some predetermined destination, their responses remind us that story has more to do with personal destiny than with destination.

Those of us who care about children and literature are always looking beyond the here and now to affirm in some way possibilities for the future. We know that most of life is lived in the imagination and want to help educate and strengthen those imaginative visions that may well be that future. In a time in which television and travel are commonplace, children have broadened their acquaintances with the world, but they often see only its surface. Story takes them both out far and in deep and helps them to be pioneers in depth perceived as well as distance measured. In order to help children develop their educated imaginations, we must respect the capabilities of each child both to comprehend and to compose meaning and to share it with others in whatever form and whatever medium is chosen.

We should try to keep ourselves as close to that wellspring of language and of life as are the children with whom we share story, and at the same time we should continue to increase our knowledge and understanding of adult literature and criticism. Those who work with children and literature straddle two worlds. They invest part of their lives in the world of children and their literature and then return to the adult critical community to renew their own connections with adult literature. It is a mistake to think that one can work successfully with children's literature without keeping abreast of developments in adult literature and criticism. Children's literature is indeed a part of all literature and can only be seen insightfully in light of a variety of other works. Some of those who cry that English professors and critics do not take children's literature seriously do not themselves seem to take the rest of literature seriously. If we isolate ourselves by our own lack of knowledge of the larger field, we cannot expect to be accepted into the literary community, nor will others be convinced of the power of the literature with which we work.

In order to help keep the connections between child and story and between children's and adult literature fresh and strong, adults must build a deductive framework by means of which children may bring their inductive knowing about literature into contact with established fields of literary knowledge. The brief introduction to theories and works of criticism found in Chapter Three may serve as a starting point for those who would increase their knowledge of this field. The ideas and materials cited there, however, are just a beginning. Our knowledge should be so firmly grounded that we can recognize sound critical ideas in the simple language of children's statements about story and help them to see when the contents of their minds correspond to a context of the field.*

Adults concerned with children's literature should also work toward, perhaps demand, more and better criticism of children's books. There are a number of journals that provide brief reviews of recent publications but too few that contain detailed critical analyses of particular works.

It may be useful here to distinguish between reviewing and criticism, particularly as they relate to children's books.

---

*An introductory list of adult works of literary criticism for those interested in children's books is suggested in Peter Hunt's "Critical Method for Children's Literature: A Booklist," *Signal* 17 (May 1975): 12–21.

Richard L. Darling, in his study of children's book reviewing in this country immediately after the Civil War, says that "most writers agree that the review is part of journalism, rather than a part of literature, or of literary criticism proper."[1] As such, reviewing concentrates on brief analyses of contemporary works and may assume little or no previous knowledge of children's literature in general, of the particular author, or of similar books for young readers. Criticism, on the other hand, does assume such knowledge and frequently gives more in-depth analyses, placing particular works in the larger context not only of children's literature but of all literature. John Rowe Townsend calls reviewing a "special and limited form of criticism, a rapid testing rather than a leisurely consideration."[2] Even within the limitations of book reviewing, children's literature differs significantly from literature for adults. Ethel Heins reminds us that the adult book "reviewer is writing for the potential reader of the book. But no matter how bookish a child may be, he rarely, if ever, reads reviews of children's books—which are, of course, written for adults."[3] Too often the reviewer's awareness of this audience leads to a very utilitarian or pragmatic approach to children's books; reviewers and readers of reviews seem to be more concerned with a book's moral or instructional virtues than with its literary value.

Those who select books for children's collections frequently do so on the basis of very brief reviews, often little more than announcements of new publications, without ever reading the books themselves. Thus reviews—sometimes unsigned ones—in the major reviewing media exert a tremendous influence over what is ultimately available to children. A single negative review in one of these journals may virtually eliminate a work from consideration, especially in a time when financial constraints inhibit the purchase of "questionable" items. And since children ordinarily have little direct access to materials not already preselected by adults, there is almost no possibility of a popular response overriding critical opinion, as often happens in the adult world of the arts. Of course, the only way to really evaluate a review is to read the reviewed item yourself and test out your own judgment against that of the reviewer; even for adult selectors, however, this is often impossible. For these reasons, it is absolutely essential that adults concerned with children's literature insist upon the highest standards in reviewing, including information about reviewers and their particular biases regarding young people and their reading. What is required is that " . . . the reviewer and critic . . . should have a personal, longstanding, and catholic acquaintance with all literature, past and present, adult and children's . . . the ability to deal in words with the elusive intangibles that make for greatness in art of any kind, and the ability to re-create the image of the work with which they are concerned."[4]

This question of reviewing is especially important in a time when too many specialists in children's literature are willing to accept content-laden reviews in place of serious criticism. In fact, there seems to be a trend not only to accept but to study these reviews instead of the works themselves. We become so fascinated by what others have said about a story that we neglect seeing what the story itself says. In part this situation arises because we are always standing between the work and its primary audience and, if selecting literature for large numbers of children, need to go beyond our own personal judgments to provide for all readers. Unfortunately, however, we sometimes go so far beyond that we lose sight of our own critical sense of story and are unable to help children develop theirs.

This insistence on the need for quality reviewing and more comprehensive criticism of children's literature is not intended to add fuel to the fire that rages between purist and pragmatist in the evaluation and discussion of children's books. Children's literature is of sufficient size and significance to accommodate a variety of critical approaches and honest disagreements among those who truly value the field.★ Even those who acknowledge only intrinsic criticism of adult literature are often more willing to accept some forms of extrinsic criticism of works for children because of the special ways in which adults mediate a child's experiences with literature. What is disturbing, however, is the emphasis on the social, psychological, or educational impact of story regardless of its literary import. It should be obvious that no work of literature can have any secondary effect on readers unless it first involves them in and convinces them of the believability of its imagined world. The positive presentation of a particular idea, character, or portion of society is not sufficient cause for the recommendation of a title, nor would it necessarily improve the image of these positions or people in the minds of readers. An insipid little story is unlikely to arouse sympathy for its characters no matter how unprejudiced their presentations.

There are, on the other hand, aesthetically sound literary works that, I believe, should be retained as part of our literary heritage but that I would not normally choose to share with children because of some element within them that could be offensive. *Little Black Sambo* is perhaps one of the best examples of a book of this sort. As story it is marvelously engaging, but the unfortunate selection of the character's name combined with the stereotypical illustrations of early editions makes this book unacceptable to many people in our society. This is true in spite of the knowledge that the story is set in India and that exaggerated, stereotypical pictures are appropriate for this type of modern folktale. Nonetheless, the fact that it may be interpreted as a negative view of blacks is reason enough not to draw it to the attention of children

---

★Some of the most lively and informative contemporary criticism of children's books is found in *Signal's* "Book Post" column, an exchange of letters about recent works by Lance Salway and Nancy Chambers.

without discussing this concern with them.

Of course, a sympathetic adult cannot accompany such books each time they are taken from the library shelves, but we can try to pay closer attention to their circulation in order to be available to deal with potential problem situations. Life teaches us that we cannot root out prejudice by ignoring it. We might therefore begin by helping children confront such prejudice in literature so that they may be more prepared to eliminate it in their lives. We also need to respect children enough to trust that, with a little guidance, they will be able to make distinctions between realistic and fanciful presentations of meaning, recognizing that the creatures of any folk literature are more caricature than fully developed character.

I would hope that the day will soon arrive when literature for children includes enough positive presentations of all peoples that *Little Black Sambo, The Five Chinese Brothers*, and other such stories can be accepted along with the "wise fool" and the "trickster" tales of all cultures. The power of story is its potential to reach out over time and distance to make connections that tie human beings together in a recognition of their common humanity. These stories have exhibited this power, and it is because of their appeal as literary works that we need to be aware of any considerations that could put that human connection in jeopardy.

Too great an emphasis on extrinsic studies of children's books may also lead to or encourage certain practices that, in themselves, are destructive of the authentic experiencing of literary works and thus cause disconnections rather than connections between children and story. These disconnections may result even when the work itself is aesthetically sound and generally enjoyed by children. One of these destructive practices is the subversion of the literary experience to the decoding process in reading. Children certainly need to learn to decode, and they need to have materials to read that make the decoding worth the effort. Combining these concerns, some advocates of individualized reading have children practicing their "W" sounds, for instance, on *Where the Wild Things Are*. This exercise breaks the connection between child and story by destroying the unity of the work and drawing the child's attention away from its essential meaning.

Turning Max's imaginative trip into a reading text reduces it to almost the same level as the old Dick and Jane readers. Some basal reading series now even use the texts of trade books for young children as their basic content for instruction. Such use further destroys the integrity and the unity of the aesthetic composition by separating the written word from the illustration, book design, and overall format of the work. In general, the basal readers have gotten better and better over the years and are an excellent, but not the only, means to introduce reading skills and provide material on which to practice those skills. The difficulty has always been in attempting to delude children that these practice materials are the kinds of stories that make the difficult task of learning to read worthwhile, which for the most part they are not. Children can practice their reading skills on the basal readers, but they also should be hearing good literature read aloud and practicing their literary abilities in discussions of a variety of fine books selected for them. If a child chooses to try to decode *Peter Rabbit* or *Where the Wild Things Are*, that is a very different matter than a teacher assigning them as a reading lesson. The child's interest may carry him through , and if he is not able to decode "camomile tea," it does not really matter because he can read enough to re-create the story. The truth is that most of us do not decode every word in our reading of material that is difficult for or foreign to us, which is precisely what almost all reading is to the beginner. There are also many words that we can decode that we may not be able to define precisely. We all know what Little Miss Muffet sat on, but how many of us could define precisely or draw an accurate picture of a tuffet?

Children who have already mastered basic reading skills sometimes disconnect from the power of story when overanxious parents or teachers push them to read adult books before they have had an opportunity to experience fully the richness of their own literature. The market for books to help parents teach their babies to read is indicative of the roots of this problem. Babies do read gestures and facial expressions quite early and are continually in the process of learning to make meanings from a variety of symbol systems. Nonetheless, years of research in education and child development were behind the decision in this country to have children begin the first grade, and thus reading instruction, at age six. Some nursery schools, kindergartens, and day care facilities that were first established as play or socialization groups or as babysitting services for parents are now teaching reading to younger and younger children. It has gotten to the point that many parents of four-year-olds are embarrassed if their children are not already reading when they enter nursery school. This kind of pushing children to go beyond what might reasonably be expected of them is evident right through the schooling years. Parents point with pride at their fourth graders who have gone from *Charlotte's Web* to Shakespeare or at eighth graders reading Kafka and Camus. Some child readers may move quickly into adult books on their own, but even these youngsters should be encouraged not to miss the wealth of good children's literature available to them. There is a danger in adults pushing their literature at children before they are ready for it, either overtly or by the subtle pressure exerted by the discussion of and the beaming pride taken in those who are reading adult books. Some of these children may be excellent decoders who can "read" all the words in a difficult book but are unable to enter fully into the total re-creative experiencing of story that is the essence of reading.

Another practice that sometimes causes children to disconnect from story is the insistence that they dissect the work in order to extract its informational or curriculum-related content. One can, of course, learn a great deal of factual information from literature, but focusing on that kind of content may be destructive of story. Many of us read fictional works in order to gain a better sense of a time or place we are learning about factually, but the aesthetic knowing retains prominence over factual knowledge. Often the demand for factual recall is a way of assuring an adult that a child has actually read a book; it is about as effective in stimulating interest in and appreciation of story as the writing of book reports is. When exciting things are happening in the interaction between children and story, there is no need for any artificial means of measurement or for prizes given to those who read the most books. The reward should be *in* the reading, not *for* the reading. Probably the greatest value in any of these systems of measurements and rewards is the ingenuity stimulated in youngsters trying to "beat the system." During my years in public schools, both the poor readers and those who cared too much about stories to reduce six of them a year to the little boxes on the cumulative record card took it as a challenge never to read anything they reported on. I, for one, got away with it. A young friend of mine recently won enough coupons for a hamburger, shake, and fries at a McDonald's by rushing through fifty very easy and very uninteresting books in a summer reading program. His reading tree on the library wall was full of titled leaves and his stomach full of instant food, but he was effectively diverted from finding and reading anything of real substance. There are many ways for children to share the excitement and the joy of their literature with others, and they should be encouraged to find the best means and medium for doing so. This decision must be made in response to the unique interaction of that child and that book, and the privacy of that interaction must also be respected when a public response is not appropriate.

Bibliotherapy is, at its best, a means of helping one make connections between books and his own life. As it is most frequently practiced, however, it is a basic cause of disconnection between child and story. In the sense that literature takes a reader outside of himself and enables him to think about what it feels like to be in another time, place, and situation, or even what a character feels like in a situation similar to his own, all story is therapeutic. But it is doubtful that story lends itself well to the attempts of adults to match problem books to problem children or at least to children with problems. The resurgence of interest in bibliotherapy is so great now that one could fill shelf after shelf with book-sized bibliographies that read like catalogs of all the world's ills. It may be useful at times to have this kind of analysis of children's literature, but these bibliographies would make a content analysis of all the major soap operas read like a light romance. In compiling these topical bibliographies, a story is often reduced to its lowest common denominator, so that a perfectly pleasant story about a little girl who happens to be overweight is thought of only as a book about a weight problem. Most people who read these bibliographies know that there is a great deal more than a "topic" or a "problem" in any story worth reading, but continual contact with this type of analysis may change, in subtle ways, our perceptions of children's books.

Even more dangerous is the tendency among teachers and librarians to place children into problem categories to match the labels applied to the books. The cartoon picturing a librarian who, when asked to suggest a book for a ten-year-old boy, replied "What's his problem?" is too close to the truth to have much humor in it. Those who begin to think of children and books in this way may also begin to think of themselves as therapists and start dabbling in psychology rather than dealing with literature. Reading a few articles on bibliotherapy, usually by those with no more training than our own, and studying lists of books about problem situations does not qualify us to practice medicine. It is amazing, and terribly disturbing, to see one who would not consider splinting a broken finger plot what amounts to major surgery on the mind and the emotions of a child. This is not to deny that readers are at times helped in coping with their own problems by reading about those problems in fiction. They must, however, seek out those stories themselves or have the stories given to them by another in whose caring and trust they are quite confident. Only one very close and very caring can know when the moment is right.

One of the most serious causes of the disconnection between children and story is the absence of opportunities for authentic encounters with story forms. These encounters should begin in the home with parents who demonstrate the importance of reading and literature in their own lives, who take the time to read aloud and discuss story, and who respect and encourage a child's own creative imagination. Even the process of being selective about a child's television viewing and sharing the reasoning behind that process with the child is important in the development of a critical appreciation of story forms. Helping a child select books to borrow from a public library or to purchase for his own personal library is also important in this development.

Of course, this kind of aid assumes parents who are knowledgeable as well as concerned about good literature for children. Too often parents who wish to purchase books for children go to a bookstore where they are confronted with little more than Nancy Drew, the Hardy Boys, and editions of the traditional classics that range from the "heavy," dull, and unappealing to the glossy forty-page versions in words of no more than two syllables. Shops that sell children's paperbacks often have much better selections because, for the most part, the children's books published in this format have already been proven successful with children. Except for those few bookshops that specialize in children's books, there is usually no salesperson available who either knows or cares about this literature and, unfortunately, little in the popular press exists to assist parents in the selection process.

Occasionally there are books that receive a great deal of attention in the media and are widely available in department and book stores. These may be volumes related to a contemporary event, print versions of motion picture or television productions, or works with some unique appeal to adults as well as children. Kit Williams's *Masquerade* has been on both the adult and children's best seller list in Britain and is challenging readers of all ages to decipher the clues in its illustrations and text that lead to an actual buried treasure, a pendant of gold and precious jewels in the shape of Jack Hare, the protagonist of the story. *Time* magazine reports that this book "has replaced Scrabble as a family preoccupation" in England. Even if the basic concern is not a literary one, such books bring adults and children together with a book and may encourage parents to share other works with their children.

Those who have themselves had rich literary experiences as children of course will share some of their own favorites with their child and will also have knowledge and more confidence in selecting new titles, if they are available to them. The importance of children's rooms and children's specialists in public libraries cannot be underestimated in this process. Those who would curtail or eliminate these facilities and services might remember that these resources are often the only ones available to those who need information and encouragement in stimulating the next generation of readers and library users. Of course, school media centers are also important, but the process of becoming a reader begins long before either decoding or schooling begins.

Teachers, librarians and booksellers might also be more imaginative in their attempts to reach out to adults and convince them of the value and the joy to be found in children's books. Many public libraries are now offering toddler programs in which parents and children as young as eighteen months share stories and simple activities. Such programs not only introduce children and parents to good literature but also give adults an opportunity to observe the techniques that professionals use in working with youngsters. For those parents who do not come into the library, information about children's literature might be sent out to wherever young parents gather, in civic clubs or shopping centers. Once children reach school age, parent–teacher association meetings and school visitations could be used, from time to time, to encourage parents to read to and discuss literature with their children. Schools might even attempt to reach young adults before they become parents by including children's literature in genre studies in high school English classes and by expanding home economics or child care classes to include the selection and sharing of children's books.

Young children not fortunate enough to have parents who introduce them to fine children's literature are nonetheless coming to know story through the medium of television. Television seems a very poor substitute to those who are familiar with the richness of children's books, but it is at least a first step in the experiencing of imaginative creations. It is also a starting point for those who later interact with these children in day care centers, public library outreach programs or preschool experiences. We may need to analyze favorite television programs to determine their appeal to young children and use this analysis in the selection of books to be shared with them. We must remember also that the reading experience is very different from that of watching television and requires more determination and concentration on the part of the child. One who has never been read to will have to learn to sit quietly and follow the action of story before she can comprehend or appreciate its content. The process may be a difficult one, but the expression of joy or awe on the face of even one child who has discovered the wonders within the pages of a book is well worth the effort.

Adults may unwittingly cause a disconnection between children and story by trying to "protect" them from works that are perceived to be strange, frightening, or unpleasant. *Rabbit Island* and *na-ni*, discussed in Chapter Six, are examples of books that many adults have said are good books but not for children, or at least not for the age suggested by their formats, because of the topics with which they deal. Some adults also feel the need to "protect" youngsters from a number of the books published by Harlin Quist, Inc., either because they seem to be more for adults who interact with children than for children themselves or because they are difficult for many of us to comprehend.

Ed Leander's *What's the Big Idea?* presents an infant's and child's eye view of parents and other adults who are a part of the young child's world. In rhyming text and bold, full-page illustrations, these pages startle adults into a realization of what a baby's bottle or a spoonful of food must look like as it approaches an infant's face, or of a child's bravado as he copes with the shadowy forms of the night. One of the most frightening images in this book is drawn from the perspective of a young child in a playpen who sees a huge head and oversized hands hanging over the bars that encage him; he thinks "Those wiggling, squiggling tentacles/Will pick me up and clutch me./Oh! Why does every passer-by/Feel so compelled to touch me?"[5] Albert Cullum's *The Geranium on the Window Sill Just Died But Teacher You Went Right On* and *You Think Just Because You're Big You're Right* disclose what youngsters supposedly think and feel about teachers, parents, and other adults who exercise control over their lives. These books were recommended for and primarily read by teachers rather than children. When a third volume, *Blackboard, Blackboard on the Wall, Who Is the Fairest One of All?*, similar in content and in format to the others but told from the teacher's point of view, was published, it included a publisher's note that said "Be sure the children see *Blackboard, Blackboard* . . . . It is for them, so they can find out who Teacher is."[6]

The four Harlin Quist, Inc., books mentioned above contain individual series of incidents that could each stand alone. Cullum's *Murphy, Molly, Max and Me*, discussed in Chapter Four for its unusual use of angle or point of view in illustration, is closer to the traditional picture story book although its message is basically the same. *Animal Man*, by

Alain Hervé, is quite different in its approach but also seems to be directed more to adults than to children. It is told from the point of view of a whale who, in rather sophisticated and poetic language, warns "killer man" that "you need not exist merely to kill all that is fragile and joyous and alive" or the time may come when, as this book closes, "man no longer exists . . . ."[7]

Patrick Courtain's *Shh!* is one of the Harlin Quist, Inc., publications that adults have tended to dismiss because they do not quite know what to make of it. It begins: "For some unknown reason, Gladys, an apple rotten to the core, wanted to communicate with Jules and Francis, shoes, born of a Javanese father and a Hungarian mother, each usually occupied by a foot, each foot usually covered by a stocking. But, instead, Gladys communicated with Janice, a cow, daughter of a steak, future steak."[8] The many misdirected communications on the pages that follow certainly do not communicate clearly to this adult, but I have seen children laugh uproariously at this text with its glossy, surrealistic illustrations. Incidently, *Shhh!* ends with a moral: "Don't believe everything you read. Or see. Or hear."[9] Henri Galeron presents readers with a similar form of surrealistic pictures in which imaginary animals have heads with pots, pumps, human feet, forks and spoons, cups, bottles, and revolvers as snouts in John Goldwaite's *Roll Call: The Story of Noah's Ark & The World's First Losers.* This book is, however, a more traditional form of nonsense alphabet, similar to the work of Edward Lear, and is more humorous than frightening, even to adults. In fact, *Roll Call* might serve as an appropriate transition from the kind of children's books we have known in the past to works such as *Shhh!* that often leave us more confused than satisfied. Whatever one thinks of the books published by Harlin Quist, Inc., it cannot be denied that the company is one of the most innovative publishers of children's books today. Even when I can neither understand nor truly appreciate them, I often recognize a childlike playfulness with language and ideas in many of these books that keeps me coming back to them.

My own experiences in sharing these books with children reminds me that we cannot, or should not, always "protect" children from that which we do not understand or appreciate. Sometimes this "protection" takes the form of censorship, but even more often adults' uncertainties about children's responses to anything new or unusual leads to a kind of conservatism in selection that effectively limits a child's access to new forms of expression. This attitude may be triggered by illustration as well as by text. Of course, in times of increasing costs and shrinking resources, those who select materials for children want these materials to be appreciated by the widest possible audience, but one's own sense of what is or is not appropriate for children can itself be limiting. Because as adults we stand between children and their literature, we should be especially careful not to hold too tight to the status quo; we should deliberately provide opportunities for children to test and try works about which we ourselves may be uncertain. We must trust that children who have had many enjoyable experiences with fine literature will be able to cope with these books and eventually separate the wheat from the chaff. It may also be true that youngsters who have grown up with the mass media may be more willing to accept and more able to understand newer forms of both visual and verbal art than many adults are, and they should be given the opportunity to encounter these forms. Through the responses of children, we may expand our own abilities to comprehend and to appreciate that in which we previously saw little of value.

Another, albeit more indirect, way in which adults who truly care about children and their literature cause a disconnection between the two is by approaches to scholarship that do not draw others into a concern for the field. Adults who study and write about children's literature sometimes do a disservice to this literature by approaching it too broadly and superficially or, on the other hand, by focusing too narrowly on aspects of specific works that can be interpreted as esoterica. There has been too much repetition of the same ideas and approaches in the field when what is really needed is more in-depth treatment of some of those ideas and approaches. There is no doubt that May Hill Arbuthnot made a very valuable contribution to children's literature, but too many others have followed with works that seem to be only slight revisions of her *Children and Books** rather than with thoughtful responses to and more thorough treatments of some of its content. Many recent works, however, have looked at children's literature from different perspectives, and books such as *The Uses of Enchantment*[10] and *Fairy Tales and After*[11] have certainly reached wider audiences than most studies of children's literature. The following brief sampling of the variety of works currently available about children and their literature reveals a number of directions in which the field is now moving. Some of these are very exciting approaches to an area of study that has become more and more fashionable in recent years. Others seem to have capitalized on this popularity without contributing anything new or significant to our understanding of the literature.

In surveying all that is available about children's literature, one might categorize the items in a number of ways. Certainly the best known of all the books about children's literature are the general, all-purpose texts for teachers and librarians working with children. *Children and Books*[12] and *Children's Literature in the Elementary School*[13] have gone through several editions and are still the most influential, although the competition is increasing with new works entering the marketplace each year. Among the works published since 1975 that are competing for textbook sales are *Literature for Thursday's Child*,[14] *Word Music and Word Magic: Children's Literature Meth-*

Children and Books was first published by Scott, Foresman in 1947. It is now in its fifth edition, with Zena Sutherland listed as the primary author.

ods,[15] and *Introduction to Children's Literature*.[16] Historical overviews or chronologies, such as those by Cornelia Meigs,[17] Bettina Hürlimann[18] and John Rowe Townsend,[19] examine the context in which current children's literature developed through analyses of what went before. Some of the most insightful criticism of children's literature is found in the various collections of essays and reviews previously published in other sources. *Only Connect*[20] and *Children and Literature: Views and Reviews*[21] are among the best and most widely known of these, with new publications such as *The Cool Web*,[22] *Crosscurrents of Criticism*,[23] and *A Peculiar Gift*[24] contributing significantly to this body of work.

Other major categories of books about children's literature include those that serve primarily as selection aids or as guides to the use of books with children, those concerned with bibliographic control either of the field in general or in the form of detailed descriptive bibliographies of particular collections, personal and critical commentaries by authors and editors, comparative studies of the literature of different nations, and works focusing on particular theories of literary criticism or literary genres. There are also a number of anthologies that reprint well-known or favorite children's works to serve as a handy collection for those who want a single source from which to read to children or as an introduction to and sampling of what is available in this field. In most instances these rely heavily on the traditional literature and other works that have become "classics" rather than on the varieties of what is currently available for children. (For this reason and because I would hope that all readers would come to know modern literature in its original format, I have eliminated these anthologies from this discussion.)

One useful and frequently revised compilation of resources is *Aids to Media Selection for Students and Teachers*,[25] which can be used along with the better known *Children's Catalog*,[26] *Best Books for Children*,[27] and *The Elementary School Library Collection*[28] to guide adults in the selection of books for children. Books such as *Using Literature with Young Children*[29] and *Literature with Children*[30] offer general suggestions for sharing literature with children, while the Dell publications *When Children Read*,[31] *Releasing Children to Literature*,[32] and *Bringing Children and Books Together*[33] are guides to the exploration and use of specific books. Virginia Haviland's *Children's Literature: A Guide to Reference Sources* with its first and second supplements[34] is the most comprehensive means of bibliographic control of the entire field of children's literature currently available.

Although the Library of Congress is the greatest resource for scholars of children's literature in this country, many other libraries both in this country and in other English-speaking nations have excellent collections and have published detailed descriptive bibliographies of their holdings. Some of the best known and most useful of these works are Toronto Public Library's two volumes of *The Osborne Collection of Early Children's Books*[35] and *Early Children's Books and Their Illustrations*[36] from the Pierpont Morgan Library. A recent addition is *The May Massee Collection, 1923–1963: A Checklist*,[37] which includes the books published by one of the most influential of children's book editors. Safford and Smith's *Children's Literature: A Guide to Research Collections in Libraries of Columbia University and Union Theological Seminary*[38] does not list specific items within these libraries but may be useful as a model of a guide to means of access to large and complex collections.

Many children's authors have written about their work and about children's literature in general. Two fine contemporary writers, Mollie Hunter[39] and Jane Yolen,[40] give many insights into the field today, while earlier works such as Claudia Lewis's *Writing for Young Children*[41] and Elizabeth Yates's *Someday You'll Write*,[42] intended for young people, still provide both enjoyment and information for readers. *The Thorny Paradise: Writers on Writing for Children*[43] is, as its title indicates, a collection of essays by some of the best-known British and American authors for children. Editors such as Jean Karl[44] and Jean Poindexter Colby[45] have also contributed significantly to knowledge about children's books, their creation, and production.

Comparative studies of children's literature help us to put the works of this country into a broader context and see them with a new perspective. Mary Ann Nelson's *A Comparative Anthology of Children's Literature*[46] is a good introduction to this approach, stressing alternative forms of the traditional tales we all know. Hürlimann's *Picture-Book World: Modern Picture Books for Children from Twenty-Two Countries*[47] and *Graphis* magazine's *International Survey of Children's Book Illustration*[48] provide a clear and closer look at books for young children from many countries. *Bookbird*[49] and *Phaedrus*[50] magazines continue to provide the best information about both new developments and new resources internationally.

Mary Lou White's *Children's Literature: Criticism and Response*[51] is an excellent beginning for those who want to get some idea of how general approaches to literary criticism have been applied to children's literature. The 1970s has seen the publication of many works on particular literary genres in this field. A sampling of these include *Beyond Words: Mystical Fancy in Children's Literature*,[52] *Animal Land: The Creatures of Children's Fiction*,[53] *Once Upon a Time: On the Nature of Fairy Tales*,[54] *Child and Tale: The Origins of Interest*,[55] *The Renaissance of Wonder in Children's Literature*,[56] and *The Hills of Faraway: A Guide to Fantasy*.[57] Each of these is a study of a genre that has a long and distinguished tradition in the literature for children.

One might also categorize the works about children's literature according to the various approaches to criticism discussed in Chapter Three. Mimetic approaches are numerous and influential in the field of children's literature today. The majority of this criticism may be divided into two basic categories. The first category includes works such as Anne Scott MacLeod's *A Moral Tale*,[58] R. Gordon Kelly's *Mother*

Was a Lady,[59] and Mary Cadogan and Patricia Craig's *You're a Brick, Angela*,[60] which examine the literature for children in a particular period of history in order to make statements about society of that time, particularly about the social history of childhood. The other category focuses on current issues or problems in society and treats children's literature primarily as a cause of, a reflection upon, or a solution to those problems. Masha Rudman's *Children's Literature: An Issues Approach*,[61] Myra and David Sadker's *Now Upon a Time: A Contemporary View of Children's Literature*,[62] and the publications of the Council on Interracial Books for Children[63] are among the most controversial of such works, with several English publishers also contributing to this form of study.[64]

Throughout its history, children's literature has most frequently been discussed from the vantage point of pragmatic criticism. The earliest English and American books for children were respected more for their educational, moral, or social instruction than for any literary merit, and the field has never entirely escaped its association with the schoolroom and the church. Although recent studies of children's literature have moved somewhat away from viewing these books as ideals of good taste and decorum, or as means of instruction in reading and other traditional school subjects, schooling has assumed new responsibilities in the total education of that child. Programs in values clarification and the attendant analysis of materials to support these programs[65] or the attempts to assign children's books to the various stages of moral development outlined by Lawrence Kohlberg[66] are rather well known examples of this trend. More influential as pragmatic criticism, however, have been works such as Bettelheim's, mentioned previously, that are concerned with the effects of literary experiences on the psychological development of the child. The earlier British publication *I Could a Tale Unfold*[67] is another example of this type of pragmatic analysis.

Another form of literary criticism focusing on the reader,

but not as pragmatic as those mentioned previously, seems to be gaining strength both in this country and abroad. These studies, probably beginning with the NCTE research monographs in the 1960s,[68] are concerned with reader responses to literary works. Along with this, critics are examining these works to attempt to identify the reader implied by the author in his composition. Aidan Chambers's award-winning article entitled "The Implied Reader"[69] based on the work of Wolfgang Iser[70] has brought this idea to the forefront among those concerned with children and their literature. The Summer 1979 issue of *Children's Literature in Education*[71] also has two articles concerned with this type of criticism and undoubtedly there will be many additional studies of this sort in the next few years.

Impressionistic criticism, not highly regarded by the literary community in general, has been prominent in the history of children's literature and may be thought of as tangential to pragmatic criticism. Authors such as Mary Ellen Chase,[72] Annis Duff,[73] and Ruth Hill Viguers[74] have written of their own companionship with books in ways that inspire parents and teachers to try to replicate such experiences so that their children may also grow up to be sensitive and cultured readers of the next generation. One might also include Sale's *Fairy Tales and After* within the realm of impressionistic criticism although he goes beyond the "I like what I like because I like it" school to touch upon a variety of forms of literary analysis.

Expressive criticism of children's literature, like that for adults, seeks to identify how an author has expressed either the outer world in which he lived or the inner world of his own psyche in his work. Obviously the two of these may be combined in a single study but they also exist independently. In fact, most expressive criticism seems to me to fall into one of three fairly distinct categories. First, there are the straight biographies that maintain the focus on what can actually be known of an author's life and allow readers to draw their own conclusions as to the relationships to published works. Doris Langley Moore's biography of E. Nesbit[75] and Barbara Stoney's of Enid Blyton[76] are two examples of this type. Second, there are critical biographies, or those that deal with both life and works and, either implicitly or explicitly, reveal the relationships between the two. Probably the series of Bodley Head Monographs published in London are among the best of this type of expressive criticism.[77] Third are the psycho-literary studies that view literary works as revelations of the emotional or psychological states of their authors. Granted, once one knows much of the lives of such writers as Lewis Carroll,[78] Hans Christian Andersen,[79] and Horatio Alger,[80] it is very difficult to consider their published stories totally independent of their own personal and emotional struggles. The danger is, however, that critics assume too much and attempt to psychoanalyze over time and space those they have known only through their work and the preserved details of their public lives.

Objective or formal criticism of children's literature may range from that of the close analysis of particular texts, such as the annotated versions of *Mother Goose*[81] or *Alice in Wonderland*,[82] to works such as Glenna Davis Sloan's *The Child as Critic*[83] that place children's books within the context of the work of a major literary theorist. *The Unreluctant Years*[84] published in 1953 relied heavily on Matthew Arnold's "touchstones" approach to literature and was one of the first truly literary studies of children's books. Obviously any work that views children's literature as representative of a particular literary theory could be classified according to that type or school of criticism rather than as falling within the objective or formal approach.

Between these two extremes of objective criticism are genre studies such as Higgins's work on mystical fancy,[85] Greenlaw's[86] and Antczak's[87] studies of science fiction, and the book by Waggoner on fanciful literature in general.[88] Also in this middle ground is Rebecca Lukens's *A Critical*

Handbook of Children's Literature[89] and other works that focus on literary elements common to all imaginative literature. William Anderson and Patrick Groff's *A New Look at Children's Literature*[90] includes both some treatment of literary elements and analysis of various genres in children's literature.

Finally, there are several books that look at the variety of critical approaches applied to children's literature. White's *Children's Literature: Criticism and Response*[91] classifies a number of articles about children's books according to psychological, sociological, archetypal, and structural theories of criticism. And just to remind ourselves that one must not become too entrenched in any particular approach to or school of criticism, we ought to know and go back from time to time to such works as "The Three Little Pigs: From Six Directions,"[92] *The Pooh Perplex*,[93] and *Aspects of Alice*.[94] These works look at a single story from many different perspectives and demonstrate, often very humorously, that there is no "right way" to read or interpret a story.

There is much work yet to be done in the field of children's literature. We need more information about the ways children respond to literature, but we also need greater understanding of the uniquenesses of the literature itself. We need an understanding of the historic roots of children's literature, but we do not, at this time, need studies that are so esoteric that few people read them and those who do find little that relates to the totality of the field. We need solid studies of biography, informational materials, historical fiction, and other types of children's literature as well as analyses of such things as humor and symbolism for children. There is a great deal yet to be discovered about a topic such as the illustration of story, which is almost unique to children's literature. There is also a need for drawing relationships between children's literature and adult literature, perhaps through the analysis of formulitic approaches to popular story forms as one example. Finally, but not exhaustively, those interested in children's literature should look more seriously at the popular nonprint literature that is the regular fare of today's children and the relationship of these media productions to both the literature and the life of the child. Although an understanding of literature and criticism remains primary, one can also gain insight into the connections between literature, as a form of meaning-making in the world, and other aspects of life by a knowledge of related areas of study. This is especially true for those of us who, in some way, interact with others to become part of or to shape children's encounters with literary works. It is useful, for instance, to examine relationships among the works of archetypal critic Northrop Frye, philosopher Susanne Langer, anthropologist Joseph Campbell, psychologist Carl Jung, and educator John Dewey. The writings of each of these theorists help to clarify and bring perspective to the works of the others and to our work with children and literature. This constellation of scholars has been particularly influential in my thinking about story as a primary means of connection between children and the world.

There are, however, others who have opened up new vistas through which I have gained insight into literary works or into means of sharing those works with children. Iser's writings on the implied reader seem to be very useful for those of us who work with children, but the kind of analysis that relates Frye's critical theories very specifically to children and their literature is just beginning to be done with his work. Of course, there are many other theorists, such as Roland Barthes and Gaston Bachelard, whose work almost cries out for this kind of analysis. *The Structure of Magic: A Book about Language and Therapy*[95] is another work from a quite different discipline that, along with studies of learning styles from educators,[96] may increase our insight into the ways we communicate and share literary meanings with children. All of the books included in the Bibliography have, in some way, shaped my thoughts or my feelings about children's literature (as have many films, plays, novels, and television programs).

Working with children and their literature reminds us to cultivate that childlike openness to meaning that explores the ideas of others without trying to force those ideas into positions that support our own but instead tries to see the world in a new way through a genuine respect for the work of others. We need to see children and their literature as James saw fiction, through his house with many windows, going from window to window but always maintaining a focus on what lies beyond and yet within. When my adult perspective causes me to lose sight of this particular kind of vision, I go back to a book that, for me, captures the essence of this way of thinking about literature and about life. Mary Caroline Richards introduces "Recovery of the Child in Manhood," the long poem that is the last chapter of *Centering in Pottery, Poetry and the Person*, with these words:

> I will end this book with my poem of awakening and regeneration. Its composition was a revelation to me of connections I had deeply felt but had not understood. Connections between sea and land and the mind of man. Between childhood and middle age. Between myth and person. Between space and time: how time is curved, how space is made by what fills it. Between alchemy and daily bread. You will remember that Wallace Stevens said that poetry is a process of the personality of the poet. We may commit ourselves to each other's poems as to a fellowship.[97]

In this statement and in my observation of children, I find the reminders my adult self sometimes needs of the power of literature to connect the person of the reader with other persons in a fellowship of concern for meaning, and of the power of composition in sorting out one's own sense of meaning in the world. In its composition or its re-creation, story becomes not just a tale told but meaning shaped and shared, a way of coming to know what we are while reaching out for what we might become. For the child it is a way of playing "grown-up" with words rather than with high heels or daddy's hat. The child is like a magnet, attracting fragments of meaning to him and combining disparate elements in a profoundly personal way. In reading as well as composing story, he does not attempt to know the truth but makes a new truth, if an imaginative one, by re-creating the world from its own parts. More than most adults, he realizes that existing views of the world have not exhausted its possibilities, that our perceptions of the world are not the limits of its being. Life is not a puzzle to be solved but a mystery to be felt and appreciated with awe. In that awe is the intuition of the unity and the dignity of all things and a sense of the transcendent. Story transcends the world of everyday to help readers wonder at, appreciate, and value ideas, people, and places beyond their normal range of experience while at the same time preserving the mystery of all that can never be known.

Changes in society and in the nature of the literature available to young people may, in some ways, be strengthening the connections among all the world's children. The post-World-War-II accent on youth, the concept of the global village, and the growing realization that survival is more dependent on world conditions than on national ones have combined with greater freedom of both content and form in children's materials to contribute to the move toward a truly international literature for children. Translations increasingly permit us to share both the children's books themselves and information about children and their media across language barriers and national boundaries. International conferences, publications, and organizations such as The International Board on Books for Young People (IBBY) are all means of making connections among those with common interests and concerns.

At the same time, children's literature is moving into a closer connection with adult literature. With a Nobel-Prize-winning author writing for and about children, adult critics examining children's books, and those concerned with children's literature discussing adult critical theories, the lines between the two literatures are beginning to dissolve. As we move from a broadcasting to a networking system of communication in which we "talk back" to the voices out there on our own CBs, show our own video productions on public access television channels, and see people lined up on street corners waiting to interact with a bank computer, we have the potential to increase the range and the power of our connections with the world community in more personal ways.

Although each of us must continue to walk alone and authenticate our own meanings and sense of truth in the world we know, there is always that tension between the uniqueness of the person and the commonalities of the human condition. This tension is evident in everyday life but revealed most fully in story. Story has always been a very powerful way of venturing beyond the scenes we know to connect with people, places, ideas, and events beyond our normal range. Today, when the need is at least as great as it has ever been, we have better means to share and to reach out to others than ever before; and those of us who truly care about children and their literature must take advantage of all the media and materials available to us. If we are to be accountable to children, we must provide them with a variety of literary experiences that are both aesthetically sound and personally meaningful. We must provide appropriate materials and significant social interactions that will first allow for the experiencing of the imagery, emotions, and ideas of story but that then go beyond the immediacy of the moment to a mindfulness of common meanings and a human community. In all of these ways adults must work to preserve and extend that literary connection between child and story that shares with each new generation of children the best that has gone before and, at the same time, gives them images and ideas with which to shape a better future.

Footnotes

1. Richard L. Darling, *The Rise of Children's Book Reviewing in America, 1865–1881* (New York: R.R. Bowker Co., 1968).

2. John Rowe Townsend, *A Sense of Story* (Philadelphia: J.B. Lippincott Co., 1971).

3. Ethel Heins, "The Criticism and Reviewing of Children's Books," in *Proceedings of the Fifth Annual Conference of the Children's Literature Association. Harvard University, March, 1978,* ed. Margaret P. Esmonde and Priscilla A. Ord (Villanova, Penn.: Villanova University, 1979), p. 50.

4. Elizabeth Nesbitt, "The Critic and Children's Literature," *The Library Quarterly* 37, 1 (January 1967): 119–126.

5. Ed Leander, *What's the Big Idea?* (New York: Harlin Quist, Inc., 1975), pp. 4–5.

6. Albert Cullum, *Blackboard, Blackboard on the Wall, Who Is the Fairest One of All?* (New York: Harlin Quist, Inc., 1978), p. 7.

7. Alain Hervé, *Animal Man* (New York: Harlin Quist, Inc., 1976), p. 20.

8. Patrick Courtain, *Shhh!* (New York: Harlin Quist, Inc., 1976), p. 1.

9. Ibid., p. 21.

10. Bruno Bettelheim, *The Uses of Enchantment: The Meaning and Importance of Fairy Tales* (New York: Alfred A. Knopf, 1976).

11. Roger Sale, *Fairy Tales and After: From Snow White to E.B. White* (Cambridge, Mass.: Harvard University Pr., 1978).

12. Zena Sutherland and May Hill Arbuthnot, *Children and Books* 5th Edition (Glenview, Ill.: Scott, Foresman, 1977).

13. Charlotte Huck, *Children's Literature in the Elementary School,* 3rd Edition (New York: Holt, Rinehart and Winston, 1979).

14. Sam Leaton Sebesta and William J. Iverson, *Literature for Thursday's Child* (Chicago, Ill.: Science Research Associates, 1975).

15. James A. Smith and Dorothy M. Park, *Word Music and Word Magic: Children's Literature Methods* (Boston: Allyn and Bacon, 1977).

16. Joan I. Glazer and Gurney Williams III, *Introduction to Children's Literature* (New York: McGraw-Hill, 1979).

17. Cornelia Meigs and others, eds., *A Critical History of Children's Literature,* rev. edition (New York: Macmillan, 1969).

18. Bettina Hürlimann, *Three Centuries of Children's Books in Europe* (Cleveland, Ohio: World, 1968).

19. John Rowe Townsend, *Written for Children: An Outline of English Language Children's Literature*, rev. edition (Philadelphia: J.B. Lippincott Co., 1974). See also the work of Frank Eyre, *British Children's Books in the Twentieth Century* (New York: E.P. Dutton, 1973).

20. Sheila Egoff and others, eds., *Only Connect: Readings on Children's Literature*, 2nd ed. (Toronto: Oxford University Pr., 1980).

21. Virginia Haviland, ed., *Children and Literature: Views and Reviews* (Glenview, Ill.: Scott, Foresman, 1973).

22. Margaret Meek and others, *The Cool Web* (New York: Atheneum Publishers, 1978).

23. Paul Heins, ed., *Crosscurrents of Criticism: Horn Book Essays 1968–1977* (Boston: The Horn Book, Inc., 1977).

24. Lance Salway, ed., *A Peculiar Gift: Nineteenth Century Writings on Books for Children* (Harmondsworth, Middlesex, England: Kestral Books, 1976).

25. Beatrice T. Simmons and Yvonne B. Carter, comps., *Aids to Media Selection for Students and Teachers* (Washington, D.C.: U.S. Department of Health, Education, and Welfare, Office of Education, 1979).

26. *Children's Catalog*, 13th edition (Bronx, N.Y.: H.W. Wilson Co., 1976).

27. John T. Gillespie and Christine Gilbert, eds., *Best Books for Children: Preschool through the Middle Grades* (New York: R.R. Bowker Co., 1978).

28. Phyllis Van Orden, ed., *The Elementary School Library Collection*, 11th edition (New Brunswick, N.J.: Bro-Dart Foundation, 1977).

29. Leland B. Jacobs, ed., *Using Literature with Young Children* (New York: Teachers College Pr., 1965).

30. Monroe D. Cohen, ed., *Literature with Children* (Washington, D.C.: Association for Childhood Education International, 1972).

31. Charles F. Reasoner, *When Children Read* (New York: Dell, 1975).

32. Charles F. Reasoner, *Releasing Children to Literature* (New York: Dell, 1976).

33. Charles F. Reasoner, *Bringing Children and Books Together* (New York: Dell, 1979).

34. Virginia Haviland, *Children's Literature: A Guide to Reference Sources* (Washington, D.C.: Library of Congress, 1966); *Children's Literature: A Guide to Reference Sources, First Supplement* (Washington, D.C.: Library of Congress, 1972); *Children's Literature: A Guide to Reference Sources, Second Supplement* (Washington, D.C.: Library of Congress, 1977).

35. Toronto. Public Library. Osborne Collection, *The Osborne Collection of Early Children's Books, 1566–1910*, Vol. I, a catalogue prepared at Boys and Girls House by Judith St. John (Toronto: Toronto Public Library, 1958); *The Osborne Collection of Early Children's Books, 1476–1910*, Vol. II, a catalogue prepared at Boys and Girls House by Judith St. John (Toronto: Toronto Public Library, 1975).

36. *Early Children's Books and Their Illustrations.* Gerald Gottlieb, ed. (New York: The Pierpont Morgan Library, 1975).

37. *The May Massee Collection, 1923–1963: A Checklist.* George V. Hodowec, ed. (Emporia, Kan.: William Allen White Library, Emporia State University, 1979).

38. Barbara Ripp Safford and Sharyl G. Smith, comp., *Children's Literature: A Guide to Research Collections in Libraries of Columbia University and Union Theological Seminary* (New York: School of Library Service, Columbia University, 1979).

39. Mollie Hunter, *Talent Is Not Enough: Mollie Hunter on Writing for Children* (New York: Harper & Row, 1975).

40. Jane Yolen, *Writing Books for Children* (Boston: The Writer, Inc., 1976).

41. Claudia Lewis, *Writing for Young Children* (New York: Simon & Schuster, 1954).

42. Elizabeth Yates, *Someday You'll Write* (New York: E.P. Dutton, 1962).

43. Edward Blishen, ed., *The Thorny Paradise: Writers on Writing for Children* (Harmondsworth, Middlesex, England: Kestral Books, 1975).

44. Jean Karl, *From Childhood to Childhood: Children's Books and Their Creators* (New York: The John Day Co., 1970).

45. Jean Poindexter Colby, *Writing, Illustrating and Editing Children's Books* (New York: Hastings House, 1967).

46. Mary Ann Nelson, *A Comparative Anthology of Children's Literature* (New York: Holt, Rinehart and Winston, 1972).

47. Bettina Hürlimann, *Picture-Book World: Modern Picture Books for Children from Twenty-Four Countries* (Cleveland, Ohio: World, 1969).

48. *International Survey of Children's Book Illustration: Graphis*, No. 140 (Zurich, Switzerland: The Graphis Pr., 1975).

49. *Bookbird.* International Board on Books for Young People and International Institute for Children's Literature and Reading Research. (The International Institute, Fuhrmannsgass 18a, A-180 Vienna, Austria or Package Library of Foreign Children's Books, Inc., 119 Fifth Avenue, New York, New York 10003.)

304 • Child and Story: The Literary Connection

50. *Phaedrus*. James Fraser, ed. (K.G. Saur Publishing, 45 N. Broad Street, Ridgewood, New Jersey 07450.)

51. Mary Lou White, *Children's Literature: Criticism and Response* (Columbus, Ohio: Charles E. Merrill Co., 1967).

52. James E. Higgins, *Beyond Words: Mystical Fancy in Children's Literature* (New York: Teachers College Pr., 1970).

53. Margaret Blount, *Animal Land: The Creatures of Children's Fiction* (New York: William Morrow and Co., 1975).

54. Max Luthi, *Once Upon a Time: On the Nature of Fairy Tales* (Bloomington, Ind.: Indiana University Pr., 1976).

55. F. André Favat, *Child and Tale: The Origins of Interest* (Urbana, Ill.: National Council of Teachers of English, 1977).

56. Marion Lochhead, *The Renaissance of Wonder in Children's Literature* (Edinburgh: Canongate Publishing Ltd., 1977).

57. Diana Waggoner, *The Hills of Faraway: A Guide to Fantasy* (New York: Atheneum Publishers, 1978).

58. Anne Scott MacLeod, *A Moral Tale: Children's Fiction and American Culture, 1820–1860* (Hamden, Conn.: The Shoe String Pr., 1975).

59. R. Gordon Kelly, *Mother Was a Lady: Self and Society in Selected American Children's Periodicals, 1865–1890* (Westport, Conn.: Greenwood Pr., 1974).

60. Mary Cadogan and Patricia Craig, *You're a Brick Angela! A New Look at Girl's Fiction from 1839–1975* (London: Victor Gollancz Ltd., 1976).

61. Masha Kabakow Rudman, *Children's Literature: An Issues Approach* (Lexington, Mass.: D.C. Heath, 1976).

62. Myra Pollack Sadker and David Miller Sadker, *Now Upon a Time: A Contemporary View of Children's Literature* (New York: Harper & Row, 1977).

63. Council on Interracial Books for Children, Racism and Sexism Resource Center for Educators, *Human Value in Children's Books* (New York: Council on Interracial Books for Children, n.d.); *Human and Anti-Human Values in Children's Books: A Content Rating Instrument for Educators and Concerned Parents: Guidelines for the Future* (New York: Council on Interracial Books for Children, 1978). See also CBIC's journal, *Interracial Books for Children* (CBIC, Inc. 1841 Broadway, New York, New York 10023).

64. Bob Dixon, *Catching Them Young 1: Sex, Race and Class in Children's Fiction* (London: Pluto Press Ltd., 1977); *Catching Them Young 2: Political Ideas in Children's Fiction* (London: Pluto Press Ltd., 1977); Children's Rights Workshop, *Racist and Sexist Images in Children's*

Books, Papers on Children's Literature No. 1 (London: Writers and Readers Publishing Cooperative, n.d.); *Sexism in Children's Books: Facts Figures and Guidelines*, Papers on Children's Literature No. 2 (London: Writers and Readers Publishing Cooperative, 1976).

65. Ruth K. Carlson, "Baker's Dozen of Personal Values in Children's Literature," in *World Congress on Children's Reading* (Vienna: International Reading Association, 1976); Cheryl Gosa, "Moral Development in Current Fiction for Children and Young Adults," *Language Arts* 54 (May 1977): 529–536; Laura Arksey, "Books, Children and Moral Values: A Subliminal Approach," *Top of the News* 24 (Summer 1978): 375–386; Peter Scharf, "Moral Development and Literature for Adolescents," *Top of the News* 33 (Winter 1977): 131–136; and James Cross Gilbin, "Esthetic or Functional, Saccharine or Shocking? An Editor Looks at Values in Children's Books," *Children's Literature in Education* 8, 3 (Autumn 1977): 120–126.

66. Lawrence Kohlberg, *Moral Education: Five Lectures* (Cambridge, Mass.: Harvard University Pr., 1970); "Moral Education in the School," *School Review* 14, 1 (1966): 1–30; John C. Gibbs "Kohlberg's Stages of Moral Judgment: A Constructive Critique," *Harvard Educational Review* 47, 1 (February 1977): 43–61.

67. P.M. Pickard, *I Could a Tale Unfold* (London: Tavistock Publications, 1961).

68. Alan C. Purves and Richard Beach, *Research in Response to Literature, Reading Interests, and the Teaching of Literature* (Urbana, Ill.: National Council of Teachers of English, 1972); Alan C. Purves with Victoria Rippere, *Elements of Writing About a Literary Work: A Study of Response to Literature* (Urbana, Ill.: National Council of Teachers of English, 1968).

69. Aidan Chambers, "The Reader in the Book: Notes from Work in Progress," *Signal* 23 (May 1977): 64–87. Also published in *Proceedings of the Fifth Annual Conference of the Children's Literature Association, Harvard University, March, 1978*, ed. Margaret P. Esmonde and Priscilla A. Ord (Villanova, Penn.: Villanova University, 1979), pp. 1–18.

70. Wolfgang Iser, *The Implied Reader* (Baltimore: The Johns Hopkins University Pr., 1974) and *The Act of Reading: A Theory of Aesthetic Response* (Baltimore: The Johns Hopkins University Pr., 1978).

71. Michael Benton, "Children's Responses to Stories," *Children's Literature in Education* 10, 2 (Summer 1979): 68–85; Reinbert Tabbert, "The Impact of Children's Books: Cases and Concepts" (Part I), *Children's Literature in Education* 10, 2 (Summer 1979): 92–102; "The Impact of Children's Books: Cases and Concepts" (Part II), *Children's Literature in Education* 10, 3 (Autumn 1979): 144–150.

72. Mary Ellen Chase, *Recipe for a Magic Childhood* (New York: Macmillan, 1967).

73. Annis Duff, *Bequest of Wings* (New York: Viking Pr., 1944); *Longer Flight* (New York: Viking Pr., 1955).

74. Ruth Hill Viguers, *Margin for Surprise* (Boston: Little Brown, 1964).

75. Doris Langley Moore, *E. Nesbit: A Biography* (Philadelphia: Chilton Books, 1966).

76. Barbara Stoney, *Enid Blyton: A Biography* (London: Hodder and Stoughton, 1974).

77. Jasper Rose, *Lucy Boston* (London: The Bodley Head, 1965); Cornelia Meigs, *Louisa M. Alcott and the American Family Story* (London: The Bodley Head, 1970); and Roger Lancelyn Green, *Lewis Carroll*; Anthea Bell, *E. Nesbit*; Elizabeth Nesbitt, *Howard Pyle* (London: The Bodley Head, 1968).

78. Jean Gattegno, *Lewis Carroll: Fragments of a Looking Glass* (New York: Thomas Y. Crowell Co., 1976).

79. Elias Bredsdorff, *Hans Christian Andersen: The Story of His Life and Work, 1805–75* (London: Phaidon Pr., 1975).

80. Ralph D. Gardner, *Horatio Alger: or, The American Hero Era* (Mendota, Ill.: Wayside Pr., 1964); Edwin P. Hoyt, *Horatio's Boys: The Life and Works of Horatio Alger, Jr.* (Radnor, Penn.: Chilton Books, 1974).

81. William S. Baring-Gould and Ceil Baring-Gould, *The Annotated Mother Goose* (New York: Bramhall House, 1962).

82. Charles L. Dodgson, *The Annotated Alice: Alice's Adventures in Wonderland & Through the Looking Glass, by Lewis Carroll (pseud.)*, intr. and notes Martin Gardner (New York: C.N. Potter, 1960).

83. Glenna Davis Sloan, *The Child as Critic* (New York: Teachers College Pr., 1975).

84. Lillian Smith, *The Unreluctant Years* (Chicago, Ill.: American Library Association, 1953).

85. James E. Higgins, *Beyond Words: Mystical Fancy in Children's Literature* (New York: Teachers College Pr., 1970).

86. Marilyn Jena Greenlaw, "A Study of the Impact of Technology on Human Values as Reflected in Modern Science Fiction for Children," Ph.D. dissertation, Michigan State University, 1970.

87. Janice Antczak, "The Mythos of a New Romance: A Critical Analysis of Science Fiction for Children as Informed by the Literary Theory of Northrop Frye," D.L.S. dissertation, Columbia University, 1979 (New York: Neal-Schuman, in prep.)

88. Diana Waggoner, *The Hills of Faraway: A Guide to Fantasy* (New York: Atheneum Publishers, 1978).

89. Rebecca Lukens, *A Critical Handbook of Children's Literature* (Glenview, Ill.: Scott, Forsman, 1976).

90. William Anderson and Patrick Groff, *A New Look at Children's Literature* (Belmont, Calif.: Wadsworth, 1972).

91. Mary Lou White, *Children's Literature: Criticism and Response* (Columbus, Ohio: Charles E. Merrill Co., 1967).

92. Robert D. Robinson, "The Three Little Pigs: From Six Directions," in *Aspects of Reading*, ed. Eldonna L. Evertts (Champaign, Ill.: National Council of Teachers of English, 1970).

93. Frederick C. Crews, *The Pooh Perplex* (New York: E.P. Dutton, 1965).

94. Robert Phillips, ed. *Aspects of Alice* (London: Victor Gollancz, 1972).

95. Richard Bandler and John Grinder, *The Structure of Magic*, Vols. I and II (Palo Alto, Calif.: Science and Behavior Books, 1975).

96. Rita Dunn and Kenneth Dunn, *Teaching Students through Their Individual Learning Styles: A Practical Approach* (Reston, Va.: Reston Publishing Co., 1978); in addition, see the January 1979 *Educational Leadership*, the journal of the Association for Supervision and Curriculum Development, for a special issue on "Learning Styles."

97. Mary Caroline Richards, *Centering in Pottery, Poetry and the Person* (Middletown, Conn.: Wesleyan University Pr., 1964), p. 148.

Children's Books Cited in Chapter Ten

Bannerman, Helen. *The Story of Little Black Sambo*. Philadelphia: J.B. Lippincott Co., n.d.

Bishop, Claire H. *The Five Chinese Brothers*, illus. Kurt Wiese. New York: Coward-McCann, 1938.

Couratin, Patrick. *Shhh!* New York: Harlin Quist, Inc., 1974.

Cullum, Albert. *The Geranium on the Window Sill Just Died But Teacher You Went Right On*. New York: Harlin Quist, Inc., 1971.

———. *You Think Just Because You're Big You're Right*. New York: Harlin Quist, Inc., 1976.

———. *Murphy, Molly, Max and Me*. New York: Harlin Quist, Inc., 1976.

———. *Blackboard, Blackboard on the Wall, Who Is the Fairest One of All*. New York: Harlin Quist, Inc., 1978.

Deveaux, Alexis. *na-ni*. New York: Harper & Row, 1973.

Goldwaite, John. *Roll Call: The Story of Noah's Ark & The World's First Losers*, pictures Henri Galeron. New York: Harlin Quist, Inc., 1978.

Hervé, Alain. *Animal Man*, pictures Jacques Rozier and Monique Gaudriault. New York: Harlin Quist, Inc., 1976.

Leander, Ed. *What's the Big Idea?* New York: Harlin Quist, Inc., 1975.

Potter, Beatrix. *The Tale of Peter Rabbit*. New York: Frederick Warne, 1902.

Sendak, Maurice. *Where the Wild Things Are*. New York: Harper & Row, 1963.

Steiner, Jörg. *Rabbit Island*, pictures Jörg Müller and trans. Ann Conrad Lammers. New York: Harcourt, Brace, Jovanovich, 1978.

White, E.B. *Charlotte's Web*. New York: Harper & Row, 1952.

Williams, Kit. *Masquerade*. London: Jonathan Cape, 1979.

Bibliography

The bibliography that follows represents a personal odyssey in my thinking about children and their literature. It is a sampling of some of the types of materials that I believe to be necessary reading for those with the personal and intellectual commitment to strengthening the connection between child and story. Although the majority of these titles deal with general literature and criticism or with some aspect of children's print or nonprint media, a few works in philosophy, psychology, child development, and child history are included. This is by no means an exhaustive list. In most instances, I have chosen to list only one of multiple works of an author or one book representative of a type of work about children's literature. There are no periodical articles included although these certainly contribute significantly to the growth of any professional.

Abrams, M.H. *The Mirror and the Lamp: Romantic Theory and the Critical Tradition*. New York: Oxford University Pr., 1953.

American Council for the Arts in Education. Arts Education and Americans Panel. *Coming to Our Senses*. New York: McGraw-Hill, 1977.

Antczak, Janice. "The Mythos of a New Romance: A Critical Analysis of Science Fiction for Children as Informed by the Literary Theory of Northrop Frye." D.L.S. dissertation, Columbia University, 1979. New York: Neal-Schuman, in prep.

Anderson, William, and Groff, Patrick. *A New Look at Children's Literature*. Belmont, Calif.: Wadsworth Publishers, 1972.

Aries, Phillipe. *Centuries of Childhood*, trans. Robert Baldick. New York: Vintage Books, 1962.

Aristotle. *Poetics*, trans. S.H. Butcher and intro. Francis Fergusson. New York: Hill & Wang, 1961.

Arnheim, Rudolf. *Art and Visual Perception: A Psychology of the Creative Eye*. Berkeley, Calif.: University of California Pr., 1969.

——. *Visual Thinking*. London: Faber & Faber, Ltd., 1969.

Avery, Gillian. *Childhood's Pattern: A Study of the Heroes and Heroines of Children's Fiction 1770-1950*. London: Hodder and Stoughton, 1975.

Bachelard, Gaston. *The Poetics of Space*, trans. Maria Jolas. Boston: Beacon Pr., 1969.

——. *The Poetics of Reverie: Childhood Language and the Cosmos*, trans. Daniel Russell. Boston: Beacon Pr., 1969.

——. *The Psychoanalysis of Fire*, trans. Alan C. Ross. Boston: Beacon Pr., 1964.

Bader, Barbara. *American Picturebooks from Noah's Ark to the Beast Within*. New York: Macmillan, 1976.

Bandler, Richard, and Grinder, John. *The Structure of Magic*. Vol. I and II. Palo Alto, Calif.: Science and Behavior Books, 1975.

Barthes, Roland. *Elements of Semiology*, trans. Annette Lavers and Colin Smith. New York: Hill & Wang, 1967.

——. *Image, Music, Text*, trans. Stephen Heath. New York: Hill & Wang, 1977.

——. *Mythologies*, trans. Annette Lavers. New York: Hill & Wang, 1972.

Barzun, Jacques. *The Use and Abuse of Art*, (Bollingen Series 35, 22) Princeton, N.J.: Princeton University Pr., 1975.

Berger, Arthur Asa. *The TV-Guided American*. New York: Walker & Co., 1976.

Bergsten, Staffan. *Mary Poppins and Myth.* Stockholm, Sweden: Almqvist and Wiksell International, 1978.

Bettelheim, Bruno. *The Uses of Enchantment: The Meaning of Fairy Tales.* New York: Alfred A. Knopf, 1975.

Bleich, David. *Readings and Feelings: An Introduction to Subjective Criticism.* Urbana, Ill.: National Council of Teachers of English, 1975.

Blount, Margaret. *Animal Land: The Creatures of Children's Fiction.* New York: William Morrow and Co., 1975.

Bodkin, Maude. *Archetypal Patterns of Poetry.* Oxford: Oxford University Pr., 1943.

Boulton, Marjorie. *The Anatomy of the Novel.* London: Routledge & Kegan Paul, 1975.

Brace, Gerald Warner. *The Stuff of Fiction.* New York: W.W. Norton & Co., 1969.

Brett, R.L. *Fancy and Imagination.* London: Methuen & Co., Ltd., 1969.

Cadagan, Mary, and Craig, Patricia. *You're a Brick, Angela! A New Look at Girl's Fiction from 1839–1975.* London: Gollancz, 1976.

———. *Women & Children First.* London: Gollancz, 1978.

Cameron, Eleanor. *The Green and Burning Tree: On the Writing and Enjoyment of Children's Books.* Boston: Little, Brown, 1969.

Campbell, Joseph. *The Hero with a Thousand Faces.* 2nd edition. Bollingen Series 17. Princeton, N.J.: Princeton University Pr., 1968.

Casebier, Allan. *Film Appreciation.* New York: Harcourt, Brace, Jovanovich, 1976.

Cassirer, Ernst. *An Essay on Man: An Introduction to a Philosophy of Human Culture.* New Haven, Conn.: Yale University Pr., 1944.

Cawelti, John G. *Adventure, Mystery and Romance.* Chicago, Ill.: University of Chicago Pr., 1976.

Chambers, Aidan. *Introducing Books to Children.* London: Heinemann Educational Books, 1973.

———. *The Reluctant Reader.* New York: Pergamon Pr., 1969.

Chase, Richard. *Quest for Myth.* Baton Rouge, La.: Louisiana State University, 1949.

Cianciolo, Patricia. *Illustrations in Children's Books.* 2nd edition. Dubuque, Iowa: William C. Brown Co., 1976.

———. *Picture Books for Children.* Chicago, Ill.: American Library Association, 1973.

Cohen, Monroe, ed. *Literature with Children.* Washington, D.C.: Association of Childhood Education International, 1972.

Crane, Walter. *Of the Decorative Illustration of Books Old and New*. London: Bell & Hyman, 1979. (First published in 1896.)

Crouch, Marcus. *The Nesbit Tradition: The Children's Novel in England, 1945–1970*. Totowa, N.J.: Rowman & Littlefield, 1972.

———. *Treasure Seekers and Borrowers: Children's Books in England, 1900–1960*. London: The Library Association, 1962.

Daiches, David. *A Study of Literature for Readers and Critics*. New York: W.W. Norton & Co., 1964.

Darling, Richard L. *The Rise of Children's Book Reviewing in America, 1865–1881*. New York: R.R. Bowker Co., 1968.

Davison, W. Phillips; Boylan, James; and Yu, Frederick T.C. *Mass Media: Systems and Effects*. New York: Praeger, 1976.

Dedek, Louis. *The First Person in Literature*. Toronto, Canada: Canadian Broadcasting Co., 1967.

DeMause, Lloyd, ed. *The History of Childhood*. New York: Psychohistory Pr., 1974.

Denham, Robert D., ed. *Northrop Frye on Culture and Literature: A Collection of Review Essays*. Chicago, Ill.: University of Chicago Pr., 1978.

———. *Northrop Frye and Critical Method*. University Park, Penn.: The Pennsylvannia State University Pr., 1978.

Dewey, John. *Construction and Criticism*. The First Davies Memorial Lecture Delivered February 25, 1930 for the Institute of Arts and Sciences. New York: Columbia University Pr., 1930.

Diamant, Lincoln. *The Anatomy of a Television Commercial*. New York: Hastings House, 1970.

Dipple, Elizabeth. *Plot*. London: Methuen & Co., Ltd., 1970.

Eco, Umberto. *A Theory of Semiotics*. Bloomington, Ind.: Indiana University Pr., 1976.

Egoff, Sheila and others, eds. *Only Connect: Readings On Children's Literature*. 2nd ed. Toronto, Canada: Oxford University Pr., 1980.

———. *The Republic of Childhood: A Critical Study of Canadian Children's Literature*. 2nd edition. London: Oxford University Pr., 1975.

Eliot, T.S. *To Criticize the Critic: And Other Writings*. New York: Farrar, Straus & Giroux, 1965.

Ellis, Anne W. *The Family Story in the 1960's*. London: Clive Bingley, 1970.

Excellence in School Media Programs: Essays Honoring Elizabeth T. Fast, ed. Thomas J. Galvin, Margaret Mary Kimmel, and Brenda H. White. Chicago, Ill.: American Library Association, 1980.

Fantastic Illustration and Design in Britain, 1850–1930, a catalogue for exhibition, March 29–May 13, 1979 at the Museum of Art, Rhode Island School of Design; June 5–September 2, 1979 at Cooper-Hewitt Museum by Diana L. Johnson. March, 1979.

Favat, André F. *Child and Tale: The Origins of Interest.* Research Report: National Council of Teachers of English, No. 19. Urbana, Ill.: National Council of Teachers of English, 1977.

Fenwick, Sarah Innis, ed. *A Critical Approach to Children's Literature.* Chicago, Ill.: University of Chicago Pr., 1967.

Fisher, Margery. *Intent Upon Reading.* New York: Watts, 1962.

——. *Matters of Fact.* New York: Thomas J. Crowell, 1972.

Forster, E.M. *Aspects of the Novel.* New York: Harcourt, Brace, Jovanovich, 1955.

Foster, Harold. *The New Literacy: The Language of Film and Television.* Urbana, Ill.: National Council of Teachers of English, 1979.

Fraser, James H., ed. *Society & Children's Literature.* Boston, Mass.: David R. Godine, 1978.

Frye, Northrop. *Anatomy of Criticism: Four Essays.* Princeton, N.J.: Princeton University Pr., 1957.

——. *The Educated Imagination.* Bloomington, Ind.: Indiana University Pr., 1964.

——. *Fables of Identity: Studies in Poetic Mythology.* New York: Harcourt, Brace, Jovanovich, 1963.

——. *On Teaching Literature.* New York: Harcourt, Brace, Jovanovich, 1972.

——. *The Secular Scripture: A Study of the Structure of Romance.* Cambridge, Mass.: Harvard University Pr., 1976.

——. *Spiritus Mundi: Essays on Literature, Myth, and Society.* Bloomington, Ind.: Indiana University Pr., 1976.

Gibson, Walker. *Tough, Sweet & Stuffy: An Essay on Modern American Prose Styles.* Bloomington, Ind.: Indiana University Pr., 1966.

Goldstein, Laurence, and Kaufman, Jay. *Into Film.* New York: Dutton, 1976.

Goodman, Paul. *The Structure of Language.* Chicago, Ill.: University of Chicago Pr., 1954.

Gottlieb, Robin. *Publishing Children's Books in America, 1910–1976: An Annotated Bibliography.* New York: The Children's Book Council, 1978.

Haining, Peter. *Movable Books.* London: New English Library Ltd., 1979.

Harvey, W.J. *Character and the Novel*. Ithaca, N.Y.: Cornell University Pr., 1965.

Haviland, Virginia, ed. *Children and Literature: Views and Reviews*. West Caldwell, N.J.: Lothrop, Lee & Shepard, 1973.

——. *Children's Literature: A Guide to Reference Sources*. Washington, D.C.: Library of Congress, 1966.

——. *Children's Literature: A Guide to Reference Sources. First Supplement*. Washington, D.C.: Library of Congress, 1972.

——. *Children's Literature: A Guide to Reference Sources. Second Supplement*. Washington, D.C.: Library of Congress, 1977.

Hawkes, Terence. *Structuralism and Semiotics*. Berkeley, Calif.: University of California Pr., 1977.

Hazard, Paul. *Books, Children and Men*. 4th edition. Boston: Horn Book, Inc., 1960.

Heins, Paul, ed. *Crosscurrents of Criticism: Horn Book Essays 1968–1977*. Boston: Horn Book, Inc., 1977.

Higgins, James E. *Beyond Words: Mystical Fancy in Children's Literature*. New York: Teachers College Pr., 1970.

Hill, Janet. *Children Are People*. London: Hamish Hamilton Children's Books, Ltd., 1973.

Hoggart, Richard. *The Uses of Literacy*. New York: Oxford University Pr., 1970.

Holland, Norman N. *The Dynamics of Literary Response*. New York: W.W. Norton & Co., 1975.

Hubert, Karen M. *Teaching and Writing Popular Fiction: Horror, Adventure, Mystery and Romance in the American Classroom*. New York: Virgil Books, 1976.

Hunter, Mollie. *Talent Is Not Enough: Mollie Hunter on Writing for Children*. New York: Harper & Row, 1975.

Hürlimann, Bettina. *Picture-Book World*. New York: Oxford University Pr., 1968.

——. *Three Centuries of Children's Books in Europe*. Cleveland, Ohio: World Publishing Co., 1968.

Huss, Roy and Silverstein, Norman. *The Film Experience*. New York: Dell, 1968.

Huus, Helen, ed. *Children, Books, and Reading*, Perspectives in Reading 3. Newark, Del.: International Reading Association, 1964.

——. *Evaluating Books for Children and Young People*. Perspectives in Reading 10. Newark, Del.: International Reading Association, 1968.

Hyman, Stanley Edgar. *The Armed Vision: A Study in the Methods of Modern Literary Criticism.* 2nd edition. New York: Alfred A. Knopf, 1955.

International Survey of Children's Literature: Graphis. 140 (Zurich, Switzerland: The Graphis Pr., 1975).

Iser, Wolfgang. *The Act of Reading: A Theory of Aesthetic Response.* Baltimore, Md.: The Johns Hopkins University Pr., 1978.

————. *The Implied Reader: Patterns of Communication in Prose Fiction from Bunyan to Beckett.* Baltimore, Md.: The Johns Hopkins University Pr., 1974.

Jacobs, Leland B., ed. *Using Literature with Young Children.* New York: Teachers College Pr., 1965.

Jan, Isabelle. *On Children's Literature,* trans. Catherine Storr. London: Allen Lane, 1973.

Jung, Carl. *Man and His Symbols.* New York: Doubleday, 1964.

Karl, Jean. *From Childhood to Childhood: Children's Books and Their Creators.* New York: John Day Co., 1963.

Kelly, R. Gordon. *Mother Was a Lady; Self and Society in Selected American Children's Periodicals, 1865–1890.* Westport, Conn.: Greenwood Pr., 1974.

Kermonde, Frank. *The Sense of an Ending: Studies in the Theory of Fiction.* London: Oxford University Pr., 1967.

Kingston, Carolyn T. *The Tragic Mode in Children's Literature.* New York: Teachers College Pr., 1974.

Klingberg, Göte. *The Fantastic Tale for Children: A Genre Study from the Viewpoints of Literary and Educational Research.* Gothenberg, Sweden: Department of Educational Research, Gothenberg School of Education, 1970.

Krieger, Murray. *Theory of Criticism: A Tradition and Its System.* Baltimore, Md.: The Johns Hopkins University Pr., 1976.

Kuhns, Richard. *Structures of Experience: Essays on the Affinity between Philosphy and Literature.* New York: Harper & Row, 1970.

Kuhns, William and Stanley, Robert. *Exploring the Film.* Dayton, Ohio: George A. Pflaum, 1968.

Langer, Susanne K. *Philosophy in a New Key: A Study in the Symbolism of Realism, Rite, and Art.* Cambridge, Mass.: Harvard University Pr., 1942.

Lepman, Julia. *A Bridge of Children's Books.* Leicester, England: Brockhampton Pr., 1969.

Lewis, C.S. *An Experiment in Criticism.* Cambridge, England: Cambridge University Pr., 1969.

Leyda, Jay. *Films Beget Films*. New York: Hill and Wang, 1964.

Lukács, Georg. *Soul and Form*, trans. Anna Bostock. Cambridge, Mass.: MIT Pr., 1974.

Lukens, Rebecca. *A Critical Handbook of Children's Literature*. Glenview, Ill.: Scott, Forseman, 1976.

MacCann, Donnarae, and Richard, Olga. *The Child's First Books: A Critical Study of Pictures and Text*. New York: H.W. Wilson Co., 1973.

MaCann, Richard Dyer, ed. *Film: A Montage of Theories*. New York: Dutton, 1966.

Mandel, Eli. *Criticism: The Silent-Speaking Words*. Toronto, Canada: Canadian Broadcasting Corporation, 1966.

Mast, Gerald, and Cohen, Marshall, eds. *Film Theory and Criticism*. New York: Oxford University Pr., 1974.

McLuhan, Marshall; Hutchon, Kathryn; and McLuhan, Eric. *City as Classroom: Understanding Language and Media*. Agincourt, Ontario, Canada: The Book Society of Canada, Ltd., 1977.

Meigs, Cornelia, and others, eds. *A Critical History of Children's Literature*. rev. edition. New York: Macmillan, 1969.

Monaco, James. *Media Culture*. New York: Dell, 1978.

Monson, Dianne L., and Peltola, Bette J., comps. *Research in Children's Literature: An Annotated Bibliography*. Newark, Del.: International Reading Association, 1976.

Munari, Bruno. *Design as Art*, trans. Patrick Creagh. Middlesex, England: Penguin Books, 1966.

Nassar, Eugene Paul. *The Rape of Cinderella: Essays in Literary Continuity*. Bloomington, Ind.: Indiana University Pr., 1970.

Nisbet, Robert. *Sociology as an Art Form*. London: Oxford University Pr., 1976.

Nye, Russel. *The Unembarrassed Muse*. New York: Dial Pr., 1970.

Oakeshott, Michael. *The Voice of Poetry in the Conversation of Mankind*. London: Bowes and Bowes, 1959.

O'Connor, John E., and Jackson, Michael E., eds. *American History/American Film*. New York: Frederick Ungar Publishing Co., 1979.

Oldsey, Bernard, and Lewis, Jr., Arthur. *Visions and Revisions in Modern American Literary Criticism*. New York: Dutton, 1962.

Ovenden, Graham, ed. *The Illustrators of Alice in Wonderland and Through the Looking Glass*. London: Academy Editions, 1972.

Parker, Elizabeth Ann. *Teaching the Reading of Fiction.* New York: Teachers College Pr., 1969.

Peyre, Henri. *The Failure of Criticism.* Ithaca, N.Y.: Cornell University Pr., 1967.

Pickard, P.M. *I Could a Tale Unfold: Violence, Horror, and Sensationalism in Stories for Children.* London: Tavistock Pr./Humanities Pr., 1961.

Pitz, Henry C. *Illustrating Children's Books.* New York: Watson-Guptill, 1963.

Poirier, Richard. *The Performing Self.* New York: Oxford University Pr., 1971.

Poltarnees, Welleran. *All Mirrors Are Magic Mirrors.* La Jolla, Calif.: The Green Tiger Pr., 1972.

Praeger, Arthur. *Rascals at Large or the Clue of Old Nostalgia.* New York: Doubleday, 1971.

Propp, Vladimir. *Morphology of the Folktale,* trans. Laurence Scott. Austin, Tex.: University of Texas Pr., 1968.

Rice, Susan, and Mukerji, Rose, eds. *Children Are Centers for Understanding Media.* Washington, D.C.: Association for Childhood International, 1974.

Richards, Mary Caroline. *Centering: In Pottery, Poetry, and the Person.* Middletown, Conn.: Wesleyan University Pr., 1964.

Rosenblatt, Louise M. *Literature as Exploration.* 3rd edition. New York: Noble & Noble Publishers, 1976.

Rouse, John. *The Completed Gesture: Myth, Character and Education.* New Jersey: Skyline Books, 1978.

Ruthven, K.K. *Myth.* London: Methuen & Co., 1976.

Salway, Lance, ed. *A Peculiar Gift: Nineteenth Century Writings on Books for Children.* London: Kestral Books, 1976.

Sartre, Jean-Paul. *Literature and Existentialism,* trans. Bernard Frechtmen. New York: The Citadel Pr., 1965.

Scholes, Robert, and Kellogg, Robert. *The Nature of Narrative.* London: Oxford University Pr., 1966.

Schorsch, Anita. *Images of Childhood: An Illustrated Social History.* New York: Mayflower Books, 1979.

Schrank, Jeffrey. *Understanding Mass Media.* Skokie, Ill.: National Textbook Co., 1975.

Sebesta, Sam L. *Ivory, Apes, and Peacocks: The Literature Point of View.* Newark, Del.: International Reading Association, 1968.

Sebesta, Sam, and Iverson, William J. *Literature for Thursday's Child.* Chicago, Ill.: Science Research Association, 1975.

Singer, Isaac Bashevis. *Nobel Lecture.* London: Jonathan Cape, 1979.

Singer, Jerome L. *The Inner World of Daydreaming.* New York: Harper & Row, 1975.

Sloan, Glenna Davis. *The Child As Critic.* New York: Teachers College Pr., 1975.

Smith, Frank. *Understanding Reading: A Psycholinguistic Analysis of Reading and Learning to Read.* New York: Holt, 1971.

Smith, James Steel. *A Critical Approach to Children's Literature.* New York: McGraw-Hill Co., 1967.

Smith, Lillian. *The Unreluctant Years.* Chicago, Ill.: American Library Association, 1953.

Smith, Robert Rutherford. *Beyond the Wasteland.* Falls Church, Va.: Speech Communication Association, 1976.

Sontag, Susan. *Against Interpretation.* New York: Farrar, Straus & Giroux, 1966.

Steiner, George. *Language and Silence: Essays on Language, Literature, and the Inhuman.* New York: Atheneum Publishers, 1967.

Stewig, John Warren, and Sebesta, Sam L. *Using Literature in the Elementary Classroom.* Urbana, Ill.: National Council of Teachers of English, 1978.

Southall, Ivan. *A Journey of Discovery: On Writing for Children.* New York: Macmillan, 1975.

Sutherland, Zena and Arbuthnot, May Hill. *Children and Books.* 5th edition. Glenview, Ill.: Scott, Foresman Co., 1977.

Tanyzer, Harold, and Karl, Jean, eds. *Reading, Children's Books and Our Pluralistic Society.* Newark, Del.: International Reading Association, 1972.

Television, The Book, and the Classroom, ed. John Cole. Washington, D.C.: Library of Congress, 1978.

Tolkien, J.R.R. *Tree and Leaf.* New York: Houghton-Mifflin, 1965.

Townsend, John Rowe. *A Sense of Story.* Philadelphia, Penn.: J.B. Lippincott, 1971.

———. *Written for Children: An Outline of English Language Children's Literature.* rev. edition. Philadelphia, Penn.: J.B. Lippincott, 1974.

Tucker, Nicolas, ed. *Suitable for Children?* Edinburgh: Sussex University Pr., 1976.

Turow, Joseph. *Getting Books to Children: An Exploration of Publisher-Market Relations.* Chicago, Ill.: American Library Association, 1978.

Vandergrift, Kay E. *The Teaching Role of the School Media Specialist.* Chicago, Ill.: American Library Association, 1979.

Vickery, John B. *Myth and Literature: Contemporary Theory and Practice.* Lincoln, Neb.: University of Nebraska Pr., 1966.

Walsh, William. *The Use of Imagination: Educational Thought and the Literary Mind.* New York: Barnes and Noble, 1966.

Wellek, René, and Warren, Austin. *Theory of Literature.* 3rd edition. New York: Harcourt, Brace, Jovanovich, 1977.

Whalley, Joyce Irene. *Cobwebs to Catch Flies: Illustrated Books for the Nursery and Schoolroom, 1700–1900.* Berkeley, Calif.: University of California Pr., 1975.

Wheelwright, Philip. *Metaphor and Reality.* Bloomington, Ind.: Indiana University Pr., 1962.

White, Mary Lou. *Children's Literature: Criticism and Response.* Columbus, Ohio: Charles E. Merrill Co., 1976.

Wollen, Peter. *Signs and Meaning in Cinema.* Bloomington, Ind.: Indiana University Pr., 1969.

Index